WOMEN AND EMPOWERMENT

WOMEN'S STUDIES AT YORK SERIES

General Editors: Haleh Afshar and Mary Maynard

Haleh Afshar (*editor*)
WOMEN AND EMPOWERMENT: Illustrations from the Third World

WOMEN IN THE MIDDLE EAST: Perceptions, Realities and Struggles
for Liberation

Haleh Afshar and Carolyne Dennis (*editors*)
WOMEN AND ADJUSTMENT POLICIES IN THE THIRD WORLD

Judy Giles
WOMEN, IDENTITY AND PRIVATE LIFE IN BRITAIN, 1900–50

Joanna de Groot and Mary Maynard (*editors*)
WOMEN'S STUDIES IN THE 1990s: Doing Things Differently?

Haideh Moghissi
POPULISM AND FEMINISM IN IRAN: Women's Struggle in a Male-
Defined Revolutionary Movement

Women and Empowerment

Illustrations from the Third World

Edited by

Haleh Afshar
Reader in Politics
University of York

First published in Great Britain 1998 by
MACMILLAN PRESS LTD
Houndmills, Basingstoke, Hampshire RG21 6XS and London
Companies and representatives throughout the world

A catalogue record for this book is available from the British Library.

ISBN 0–333–71973–5 hardcover
ISBN 0–333–71974–3 paperback

First published in the United States of America 1998 by
ST. MARTIN'S PRESS, INC.,
Scholarly and Reference Division,
175 Fifth Avenue, New York, N.Y. 10010

ISBN 0–312–17646–5

Library of Congress Cataloging-in-Publication Data
Women and empowerment : illustrations from the Third World / edited by
Haleh Afshar.
p.   cm. — (Women's studies at York series)
Includes bibliographical references and index.
ISBN 0–312–17646–5
1. Women—Developing countries—Social conditions—Case studies.
2. Women—Government policy—Developing countries—Case studies.
3. Women in development—Developing countries—Case studies.
I. Afshar, Haleh, 1944–   II. Series.
HQ1870.9.E56 1997
305.42'09172'4—DC21   97–14130
                                                         CIP

Selection, editorial matter and Introduction © Haleh Afshar 1998
Chapters 1–11 © Macmillan Press Ltd 1998

This book is printed on paper suitable for recycling and made from fully managed and sustained forest sources.

10   9   8   7   6   5   4   3   2
07   06   05   04   03   02   01

Printed & bound by Antony Rowe Ltd, Eastbourne

Contents

Acknowledgements

I would like to thank the Development Studies Association for funding and supporting the Women and Development Study group and the Political Studies Association for funding and supporting the Women's Group. I would also like to thank members of these groups for participating in the meetings held at York, where earlier drafts of these papers were discussed. Thanks are similarly due to the University of York's Centre for Women's Studies and its members for hosting the PSA's and DSA's women's groups annual meeting and offering kind hospitality to many of the participants.

In particular I would like to thank the contributors to this volume who have given much of their time generously to this book; they have come to meetings to present their papers, to discuss the drafts of the chapters and to comment and contribute to one another's work. For me it has been a most enriching experience and I thank them all for putting up so cheerfully with the exacting editorial demands showered on them. I am particularly enchanted with all the contributors to this volume for heroically meeting the deadline and patiently waiting during the lull that followed; their pervasive good humour and supportive and sisterly responses were invaluable. In particular I would like to thank Tim Farmiloe for his continuous support and encouragement; his faith in our series is the shining light at the end of the long tunnel of writing and editing.

Last but not least, I would like to thank Molly and Ali for giving me the time and even giving up their beds to accommodate contributors, and Maurice Dodson for holding the fort.

Haleh Afshar

Notes on the Contributors

Haleh Afshar teaches Politics and Women's Studies at the University of York and Islamic Law at the Faculté Internationale de Droit Comparé at Strasbourg. She was born and raised in Iran where she worked as a journalist and a civil servant before the revolution. She is the joint convenor of the Development Studies Association's Women and Development Study Group and has edited several books produced by this group: The most recent include *Women in the Middle East*, (1994); and, jointly edited with Mary Maynard, *The Dynamics of Race and Gender* (1994). Haleh Afshar is also the convenor of the Political Studies Association's Women's groups. Jointly with Mary Maynard she is the series editor of the York Women's Studies Series, published by Macmillan and Routledge's Women and Politics series. The most recent volume published in the Routledge series is *Women and Politics in the Third World*, (1996), edited by Haleh Afshar. She remains active in feminist Iranian politics and has written extensively on the subject.

Stephanie Barrientos is a Senior Lecturer in Economic Development at the University of Hertfordshire. She has researched and published on the effect of neo-liberalism on women in Chile and temporary female employment in the fruit export sector. She is currently involved in research on the global fruit supply-chain between Chile and Europe, and an examination of the links between women as fruit workers in Chile with supermarket workers and consumers in the UK.

Delia Davin teaches Chinese Studies in the Department of East Asian Studies at the University of Leeds. She lived in China for several years and is still a frequent visitor to that country. She has written extensively on women, gender issues and population policy in China.

Elsa Dawson is a Strategic Planning and Evaluation Adviser for Oxfam UK and Ireland. As such, she shares responsibility with the rest of her team for the development of planning and evaluation systems and procedures in Oxfam's overseas programme. She previously held posts with World University Service as Latin America Programme Officer, and with the Save the Children Fund, for whom she carried out research aimed at identifying the most effective role NGOs can play in contributing to the development process. The research was based on eight years' experience as Field Director for the Fund in Peru, where she managed a programme of community-based projects carried out by Peruvian NGOs with funding from SCF. The research was carried out as a Visiting Fellow at the Institute of Development Studies and resulted in a number of published articles on attempts by Peruvian NGOs to contribute to policy reform from the basis of grassroots work in health and education. She holds an MA in Development Studies from East Anglia University, for which she wrote a dissertation on the achievements and limitations of the Sandinista government for Nicaraguan women. A member of the Development Studies Association Council, she hopes through her work to build better links between academics and practitioners in development, and thereby contribute to improved thinking and understanding aimed at increasing the effectiveness of aid agency programmes.

Leila Djabari was born and raised in a liberal aristocratic family from Aleppo. She studied political economy and went on to read law. She is now a leading lawyer and activitst in Syria. Since 1977 she had been an indefatigable defender of women and their rights, and has been supporting their cause both at home and in the international arena. She is a member of the Municipal Council in Damascus and a member of the Women's Committee of the Lawyers Syndicate in Syria. She is also a legal adviser to the General Union of Women in Syria. Leila Dajabari is currently writing a book on law and personal status.

Lutfun Nahar Khan Osmani is a graduate student at the Department of Economics, Queen's University, Belfast. She is writing her doctoral thesis on 'Empowerment of Women though Credit: A Case Study of Grameen Bank in Bangladesh'. She has co-authored a report on 'Women and Economic Policy: A Gendered Perspective' for the Equal Opportunities Commission of Northern Ireland.

Jocelyn Kynch is a part-time lecturer at the Centre for Development Studies, University of Wales, Swansea. Her research includes an analysis of British Indian data for the period 1880–1940, in collaboration with Maureen Sibbons, and an examination of the impact of poverty and transition on tuberculosis in Wales and Russia. She teaches agrarian change and rural development and has undertaken consultancies for ESCOR, UN/WIDER and ODA. Previous work as a contract researcher at the university of Oxford covered famines, gender, nutrition, agricultural changes, epidemiology and criminology, although her formal qualifications are BA (Hons) in PPE and MSc in Agricultural Economics.

Fiona Macaulay is currently completing a DPhil in Politics at St Antony's College, Oxford. She has worked and conducted research in Nicaragua, Chile and Brazil. Her research interests include gender policy, local government and political parties in Latin America, and she has contributed articles and papers to a number of journals and colloquia. She also has a long-standing involvement with women's issues and international solidarity and human rights groups in the UK, and is a non-executive director of the NGO Third World First.

Donna Pankhurst is a lecturer in the Department of Peace Studies, University of Bradford. She has published on several African countries, including 'Towards Reconciliation of the Land Issue in Namibia: Identifying the Possible, Assessing the Probable' *Development and Change* 26, 3(1995): 551–85.

Jennie Pearce is a lecturer in The Department of Peace Studies, University of Bradford. She has published widely on Latin America including *Colombia: Inside the Labyrinth* (1990).

Jo Rowlands is an Evaluation Officer in the Evaluation and Programme Development Dept, VSO, London. Previously, she worked as a management consultant and trainer with NGOs and Co-operatives in Britain and Latin America; and was a lecturer at the University of Durham before moving to her present post.

Purna Sen worked in adult, community and further education for several years and then moved into training on equality issues. She has also worked with refugees in inner London. She returned to study as a mature student and parent student and has focused on gender issues. Her research in Calcutta is towards a Phd.

Maureen Sibbons is a lecturer in Health Studies and Gender and Development at the Centre for Development Studies, University of Wales, Swansea. Her research includes the analysis of the relationship of poverty, mortality and morbidity in several locations, including Kerala, Zambia, Zimbabwe and Ghana; in collaboration with Jocelyn Kynch, an analysis of British India data from 1870 to 1940; and an exploration of gender issues of access to healthcare in Sub-Saharan Africa.

Introduction: Women and Empowerment – Some Illustrative Studies
Haleh Afshar

As development studies moves towards a more integrally gendered approach, issues of empowerment and advocacy come to the foreground. Academic women and practitioners are now aware of the need for them to act as facilitators to articulate the perceived needs of the poorest women as formulated by them themselves. The discipline is shifting away from grand paradigms and panaceas to the specificities and differentiated needs of differing groups in different places. Yet the questions of politics, power, violence against women and strategic use of scarce resources remain paramount.

In this context, what must be defined are the questions: what is empowerment, and who empowers whom? How do academics and practitioners recognise and deal with the tensions that invariably exist between the conflicting demands and ideas at the top and the bottom of the empowerment hierarchies, between people and the state and its formal and informal agencies? How are the problems of access to and use of resources at the urban/rural level, and at the economic, political and social levels, dealt with by facilitators as well as recipients? How can general feminist policies be moulded to meet needs in particular circumstances?

It is no longer possible to assume that intervention by facilitators will always or necessarily be positive. As the case studies in this volume show, changing structures may or may not be advantageous to women. All too often commercial strategies and socially acceptable activities may be in conflict. As in the case of the reconstructed labour market relations in China, Chile or Bangladesh, or the new gendered relation of the theocratic structures in Iran, economic or political processes may re-create new forms of patriarchal control and subordination.

The new configurations of women's needs and socioeconomic structures and their fluidity and permeability have meant that scholars of development studies must be explicit about the relevance of different ideologies and historical contexts. The debate on empowerment must

1

be widened to balance different cases, and contextualised to illustrate specificities. The term itself must be critically evaluated, and its definition in terms of the ability of the individual to maximise her utility must be challenged. The focus on the individual and her particular circumstances may easily undermine communal activities and goals. Empowered women are not necessarily those women who wish to or can separate their personal and familial needs.

Thus the authors in this volume ask, 'What is empowerment?' Is it power over resources? Is it the ability to create 'effective demand?' Is it about the ability to make choices? Is it about access to resources and how they are controlled, politically or economically, by NGOs, by political parties, by the state? Do political parties facilitate, or do they channel energies away from empowerment? To what extent is empowerment explicit or implicit? Is it important to evaluate the degree to which, in different circumstances, the state has been seen as a provider of resources?

The answers to these questions may be different in different places and at different times. There certainly is a different emphasis on different priorities when it comes to understanding what empowerment means to the women in the different case studies analysed in this volume. Some structural and social conditions, such as labour laws and restrictions on trade unions, or ideological definition of women as dependants, prevent women making demands and overshadow their ability to express their subjective assessments. Furthermore, women work to different agendas, sometimes simultaneously. They make alliances across the divides as a way of accessing power. In such circumstances some forms of empowerment may hide power relations and obscure differences. Where do we draw the line across such alliances? Policy analysis must incorporate diversity. There are no single answers. Different circumstances demand different strategies, and configurations differ in different situations.

Once a working definition of empowerment has been formulated, the question is how to facilitate empowerment without imposing agendas? Women must have confidence in what they do, and must have access to resources. They must perceive that they can make choices.

This volume brings together academics and practitioners to delineate a clearer understanding of what empowerment is and how it might be measured in terms of the lived experiences of women. The contributors to this volume address the difficult question of empowerment as it has been articulated by the women they have worked with in different places addressing similar questions.

On the grander scale, where women are concerned, the issues of war and peace and violence never leave the stage. Both at the macro- and micro-level violence distorts and disjoints the lives of many women; if empowerment is ever to have a meaning it must enable those women who are most affected by violence to find ways of articulating the pain and accommodate the slow processes of healing. Feminists have always had a role to play in this process and, as the case studies in this volume show, they will continue to do so.

Politics at the national state level too frequently inflicts violence on women and dictates different negotiating tactics. The chapter on Chile and Brazil compares and contrasts the political paths which have facilitated women's greater participation in the formal democratic processes and assesses the limitation of the formal structures. The chapters on the Middle East focus on different ways that women in Iran and Syria have negotiated the power of the state – in Syria by using the existing legal structures, in Iran by reverting to the stated creed.

At the level of economic participation once more there is an interesting comparison to be made between the Latin American experience, where the 'feminisation' of the labour market has gone a long way in the now internationally integrated agricultural processes and China and Bangladesh, where the process is just beginning. As the case studies on Chile, China and Bangladesh demonstrate, access to resources has both costs and benefits for women; economic participation, though empowering in some sense, must be negotiated through familial bargaining and levering of power by degrees. These chapters make a valuable contrast to the historical study of mortality during epidemics where, conceivably because of the lesser mobility of women, their morbidity was lower than that of men. A glance at history textures our understanding of the increasing participation of women in the economic sphere.

Defining empowerment as a process, and something which cannot be done to/for women, but which has to be their own, raises serious questions for development agencies. Is there a role for 'enablers' or for any kind of interventions in the empowerment process? What is the relationship between micro-level processes and the macro-picture? Does empowerment in one sphere of activity lead to empowerment in others? Can empowerment ever be a measurable outcome? Chapter 1 presents the theoretical perspectives and offers some specific answers. These issues are analysed in Chapter 2 and the volume ends by an analysis of the measurement of success and the new approaches by aid donors to evaluating their contributions to the process of empowering

of women. Once more we return to the questions of academic definitions and their impact on the practical contribution of donor agencies.

POWER AND EMPOWERMENT

Chapter 1 analyses the term empowerment and places it within its
recent historical context. Jo Rowlands focuses on the meaning and
understanding of power and empowerment. She argues that the dominant understanding within social sciences has been of power as 'power
over', whereas the feminist understanding of empowerment should be a
dynamic one, which conceptualises power as a process rather than a
particular set of results. Then 'power to', 'power with' and 'power from
within' would come to construct differing sets of meanings for empowerment. Rowlands quotes Harstsock in contrasting the definition of
power in terms of 'obedience' with the 'energy' definition of power – a
power which generates activity and raises morale (Hartsock 1985: 223).
In this context empowerment becomes a process that cannot be done
to or for women, but has to emerge from them. This conception of
empowerment as a dynamic, enabling process in turn has implications
for political action and for development agencies. The question, then,
is what kind of intervention in the empowerment process is enabling
and what is not?

The questions raised in this chapter are dealt with by the case studies
that follow. Looking at the part played by non-governmental agencies
in Honduras and Mexico, Rowlands' case studies of grassroot and
non-governmental organisations develop a concept of empowerment
which draws on an understanding of power in its various manifestations. Her case studies show the processes at work as women change
the way their lives are and redesign their relationship both with each
other and with men. Rowlands concludes that empowerment must not
be seen as an instrumentalist notion, but rather as an active tool which,
if used thoughtfully, can be used to achieve change-with-justice. Such a
definition requires taking on a multidimensional view that accounts for
the specificities of a situation without losing sight of the generalities of
the experiences of women.

WAR AND VIOLENCE

Violence is an arena where such a focused and multidimensional
definition of empowerment could help to delineate gendered differ-

ences in needs and goals. The two chapters that follow note the macro-
and micro-levels of experiences of women and violence. These two
contrasting chapters demonstrate clearly the impact that intellectuals
and activists can have on a central arena of women's lives. As Donna
Pankhurst and Jenny Pearce demonstrate in the domain of conflict
analysis, women as actors have generally been subsumed within masculine terminology and their interests have been rendered invisible. By
contrast, Purna Sen's chapter demonstrates that on the issue of violence
against women at the micro-level, the active participation of feminists
has helped to carve out textured patterns of activities and strategies.

In their chapter on engendering conflict, Donna Pankhurst and
Jenny Pearce argue that a gendered analysis of conflict would facilitate
a better understanding of peace and delineate clearer paths towards
ending conflict. They criticise the paucity of mainstream conflict analysis, which is more concerned with locating the origins of conflict in
identity rather than structure. Pankhurst and Pearce note that
although the approach is gender-blind, conflict settlements rest on
essentially gendered deals. But such 'peace deals' do not allow violence
at the micro-level to be included in the negotiation process. They tend
to draw a veil over the reality that though armed conflict may have
been subsumed, ex-combatants are often responsible for domestic and
other forms of violence. Failure to resolve the structural issues which
led to the conflict generate frustrations in the form of increased crim-
inality, which frequently affects women and their freedom to occupy
public spaces in safety. Agreements around resource distribution in the
peace settlement, particularly with reference to issues such as land, also
frequently exclude women. Women are usually the majority of the
internally displaced and refugee population after periods of conflict,
but resettlement generally fails to address their differential needs. A
focus on gender raises questions about structure and identity in the
analysis of conflict and allows it to move away from an unproductive
dichotomising of identity and structure towards a more complex and
coherent understanding of the problems to find more appropriate
paths towards peace.

The analysis of the complex interrelationships of social, economic,
legal and ideological processes which envelop violence and oppress
women is considered in relation to violence within the home by
Purna Sen. Focusing on the Indian experience, Sen has compiled
detailed histories of male violence in a study that cuts across class,
caste and age. The chapter seeks to explore the ways in which women
respond to violence and where they find support. Sen asked questions

about the people to whom they had spoken about the violence and
what those people had said or done to help. Although some aspects of
their histories and domestic violence were known to others, many
women said that the interview was the first time they had spoken
about some aspects of sexual violence. Many women also commented
that they felt much 'lighter' for having spoken out. They felt that
speaking out served to validate their experiences and end their isolation. The stories of women who had moved from violent to violence-
free lives provide important indications of what can be done to enable
women to resist such violence.

POLITICS

The Constitution of India declares equality for all citizens. Many laws
and policies translate this statement of intent into measures which
address gendered disadvantage. Yet the problem of violence does not
lend itself to easy solutions. To succeed, women must be active both at
the level of discovering strategies and implementing them and at the
level of national politics. They must continue to fight to maintain the
language of equality and translate it into practicable measures. To do
so women must secure access to the processes of policy-making at the
local, national and international levels. A gendered approach to conflict resolution would help at the international level; at the national
and local levels specific historical circumstances permit specific interventions. Fiona Macaulay's study of Brazil and Chile examines the
relative permeability of political parties to gender demands and to
women's participation as political agents. Often political parties disempower women relative to men and impose particular visions of gender
relations through their programmes and public policy once in office.
However, opportunity spaces are available, especially at local level, for
the greater empowerment of women. Decentralisation of power and
government has this potential, but only if the municipality is regarded
as a site of political contestation and negotiation, not as a locus for
more efficient management of welfare/developmentalist agendas. Public administration has been a poor instrument for implementing gender
policies. This is not just because it reflects gender relations in society,
but also because, as a part of social relations, public administration is
itself an engendering process. Therefore it is crucial for feminists to
ensure that emerging local governments and decentralised administrations are facilitators, and empower rather than manage, women.

The processes of political empowerment are framed by the patriarchal context of national political relationships which are frequently exacerbated by ideologies, which overtly or covertly dismiss, disregard or undermine concepts of gender equality. In the three chapters that follow, the experiences of Syrian and Iranian women and their struggles for empowerment are highlighted. The chapters by Jabiri and Afshar look at the ways in which women lawyers in Syria and Iran have sought to eradicate the abuse of human rights to the detriment of women in their respective countries. Quoting an Iranian leading lawyer, Mehrangiz Kar, Afshar reiterates the points made by Jabari to denounce the two states' policies of denying women rights to their own incomes and curtailing their rights to protect and raise their children. The legal definition of the status of women as 'dependants', both on personal and economic grounds, in Iran and Syria have resulted in placing severe limitations on their constitutional rights to freedom and equality. Jabiri draws attention to the blatant inconsistencies that exist between Syrian women's constitutional and personal rights. Their constitutional rights are based on the formulation of political freedom, which recognises and respects women as political actors, but the personal laws classify women as mothers, daughters or wives and define their role in the context of their unequal familial obligations. Thus their political rights are relegated to their formal rights under the catchall cover of an ascribed 'Arab' and 'Islamic' identity.

A similar point is made by Afshar in her chapter on Iranian women's 'disempowerment'. Once more under the guise of religiosity, Iranian women have been deprived of hard fought for and shortly held constitutional equal rights. The advent of Islamification created a national identity of a 'Muslim woman' who was required to abandon all her civil rights in order to assume her maternal and domestic duties. But, as both these chapters demonstrate, such 'disempowerment' cannot easily or permanently be imposed.

THE LABOUR MARKET

The dismantling of the gender barriers in religious circles had long since been preceded by the deconstruction and reconstruction of the gendered labour market, which poses problems for both theoreticians and practitioners. In her analysis of women agricultural workers in Chile, Stephanie Barrientos examines they way in which temporary women workers have been incorporated into global fruit production through the transformation of the traditional rural sector into modern, high-technology fruit farming, based on a largely urbanised, waged labour force.

This chapter outlines the way in which agribusiness has transformed the traditional rural gender division of labour. Agribusiness has enhanced the potential empowerment of women temporary workers drawn into paid employment, increasing their independence as wage earners during the season, and bringing them together in a social group with common needs and experiences. For this reason, many women embrace working in the fruit industry. At the same time, these women face a number of problems relating not only to their pay and conditions at work, but also to long periods of enforced unemployment outside the season. Poverty is combined with the double burden of working long hours when in fruit work and fulfilling domestic responsibilities.

Barrientos argues that with the transition to democracy in Chile, neither the state nor traditional trade unions have been able to address the problems faced by women temporary workers seriously, and they remain a fragmented marginalised force. In a global market, the question is raised as to whether new forms of community organisation, which transgress the boundaries between the productive and reproductive roles of women temporary workers, can further enhance their empowerment and act as an alternative challenge to the pervasive dominance of agribusiness. The example of Chile is thus used to raise the issue of women's empowerment within the context of a modern global agro-export sector.

Whereas in Chile, with the industrialisation of agriculture, it is no longer easy to distinguish between the rural and urban contexts, in China with the recent relaxation of barriers to migration, rural–urban migration is markedly changing the age and sex structure of the villages. Delia Davin's study looks at the impact that the current wave of out-migration by the young is having on family networks and structures. Davin looks at both the experiences of those women who move out and those who are left behind to tend the land. Remittances, broken family ties, greater mobility and intermarriage with the new host communities have created new experiences, problems and solutions for the recently mobile rural women in China. Davin examines some of the tensions and contradictions that these new freedoms and responsibilities bring both in terms of empowerment and disempowerment to migrant and non-migrant women.

The tensions between economic participation, mobility and familial relations is also addressed by Lutfun Khan Osmani, who analyses the experiences of poor rural women in Bangladesh who have just found an economic foothold and been able to enter the economic domain, with the help of credit from the Grameen Bank. Osmani contends that access to credit has gone some way towards empowering these women by making their perceived contribution to the family far clearer, thereby strengthening their familial bargaining position. But the women's own perception of their self-interest has not necessarily improved much. If empowerment is measured in terms of intra-household allocation of resources, then they may not have been empowered very much. The prevailing cultural conditions prevent women from making full economic use of the available credit; by and large it is the husband who uses the credit and the wife who stands surety for its repayment.

Khan Osmani contends that empowerment may not necessarily be achievable within a single generation and access to resources would not immediately wipe out centuries of cultural conditioning.

CATALYSTS AND INTERVENTIONS

Thus what emerges from these studies is that empowerment as a process must be textured and historically- and geographically-specific if it is to improve the lives of particular groups of women in particular times and places. As Kynch and Sibbons demonstrate, specificities denote different solutions. They look at how examples of potential empowerment in discourses between implementers of British Indian policy, Indian men and women actually resulted in *dis*empowerment: they argue that a key factor in women's empowerment was presence in the public space. Women's knowledge about health was not recognised, and constraints on their access to famine relief employment dislocated them from the public arena. Kynch and Sibbons argue that in the process of reducing mortality from epidemic and famine, external agents such as British Indian officials unwittingly entrenched women's vulnerability in the absence of a working male, combined with the low valuation of little girls. They argue that the failure to recognise how gender roles, and not sex, pattern mortality, and consequently how gender roles could affect future survival chances, has led to inadvertent but robust and enduring low levels of well-being for Indian women.

To counter such unintended results, non-governmental agencies are increasingly seeking to evaluate their strategies and measure their gender impact. In the concluding chapter Elsa Dawson discusses aid agencies such as Oxfam and its Dutch sister agency, Novib. These agencies have been working towards the empowerment of poor people, especially women, and are seeking to act as *catalysts* in the empowerment process. The question increasingly being asked, however, is whether the programmes funded by such agencies aimed at local capacity building and empowerment, are actually producing tangible benefits for the poor women concerned. The challenge facing the agencies is to develop systems and procedures to show to what extent the investment made in their programmes has produced an impact in the form of such concrete benefits.

As a result of this concern, Novib and Oxfam are engaged in a research programme to identify methods and systems for the assessment of impact. Elsa Dawson's chapter evaluates those impact assessment methods currently in use in development programmes to see how far they can be used to evaluate whether their programmes can be empowering in terms such as those defined by Jo Rowlands in the introductory chapter of this volume.

ACKNOWLEDGEMENT

I am most grateful to all the contributors to this volume for their extensive help in formulating the arguments and discussing the outline of the book. I am particularly grateful to Stephanie Barrientos for her meticulous comments on an earlier version of this Introduction. All mistakes and misunderstandings, however, are entirely due to me.

REFERENCE

Harstock, N. (1985) *Money, Sex and Power: Towards a Feminist Historical Materialism.* Boston: Northeastern University Press.

1 A Word of the Times, but What Does it Mean? Empowerment in the Discourse and Practice of Development[1]

Jo Rowlands

Empowerment has become rather a buzz word for the 1990s. As well as now being used by Western politicians, it was a word frequently heard at the UN Conference on Women in Beijing in 1995 and at the World Population Conference in Cairo in 1994. Current use of the word remains ill-defined, however, in the development context: its users tend to assume that the appropriate meaning will be understood without being explained. It is used by people representing a wide range of political and philosophical perspectives, from the World Bank to feminists. In a book considering empowerment, then, it is crucial to start by paying attention to the meaning(s) of empowerment as an idea. This chapter explores the way that the term has come to be used in the development discourse,[2] and proposes a 'meaning' for the term that will help in the consideration of the chapters that follow, as well as assisting in the development of appropriate policy and practice aimed at women's empowerment.

Much use of the term has laid emphasis on economic and political empowerment, and on a conception of empowerment well-rooted in the 'dominant culture' of Western capitalism. It is significant that empowerment as a concept has arisen alongside the strengthening of focus on individualism, consumerism and personal achievement as cultural and economic goals. The notion of empowerment thus contributes to the construction and validation of changing emphases of the global economic and political system and, indeed, of legitimising particular policies and practical approaches to development efforts which involve women. Given this, how do we construct a definition of empowerment that can serve a useful purpose in analysing and debating issues of the empowerment of women? Since the word is built around the notion of power, a brief detour into the highly contested area of the nature of power is necessary here.

Power has been the focus of much debate within the social sciences. The dominant understanding has been of power as 'power over' (Dahl 1961; Polsby 1963; Wolfinger 1971; Bachrach and Baratz 1970), where one person, or grouping of people, is able to control in some way the actions or options of another. This can be overt, such as through the use of physical coercion, or hidden, as when psychological processes are influenced in such a way as to restrict the range of options perceived, or to lead someone to perceive the desired option as being their own desire. The use of 'power over' can be very subtle. Various writers have described the way in which a group of people who are systematically denied power and influence in the dominant society will internalise the messages it receives about its supposed roles and capacities, and will come to believe the messages to be true (for example, Pheterson 1990; Jackins 1983). This 'internalised oppression' is adopted as a survival mechanism, but becomes so well ingrained that the effects are mistaken for reality. Thus, for example, a woman who is subjected to violent abuse when she expresses her own opinions may start to withhold her opinions and eventually come to believe that she has no opinions of her own. When control becomes internalised in this way, overt use of power over is no longer necessary.[3] Many groups of people have controlled their own behaviour and sense of self in this way.

The development discourse, and the set of practices associated with it, have been very much in this mould. A particular view of 'development-as-Westernisation' has come to dominate to such a degree that is has become virtually impossible for any different possibility even to be imagined. Empowerment, used as described above within the development discourse and within the 'Women In Development' (WID) perspective on women which has predominated within thinking on women and development since 1970, is constructed on that 'power over' view of power. The view is that women should somehow be 'brought into development' and become 'empowered' to participate within the economic and political structures of society. They should be given the chance to occupy positions of 'power', in terms of political and economic decision-making. This view of empowerment is consistent with the dictionary definition of the term,[4] which focuses on delegation, i.e. on power as something which can be bestowed by one person upon another. The difficulty with this view of 'empowerment' is that if it can be bestowed, it can just as easily be withdrawn: in other words, it does not involve a structural change in power relations. It is therefore illusory. Women's 'empowerment' is, in this sense, an instrumentalist approach to achieving the economic growth of the developmentalist discourse, where the placing of emphasis on women becomes a means to a particular end.

Most models of power are apparently 'neutral', that is, they make no mention of how power is actually distributed in society. There is no consideration of the power dynamics of gender or indeed of race or class,[5] where it is predominantly one group (men, white people, propertied people/elites) which has power over another group (women, people of colour, working-class people). Such 'neutrality' precludes analysis, therefore, not only of, say, gender power dynamics, but also of how one set of such dynamics can interact with others to produce complex power relationships. Power, in this 'power over' model, is in finite supply; if some people have more, others have less. If power is 'power over', then it is easy to see why it is that the notion of women becoming empowered could be seen as inherently threatening: the assumption will be that there will be some kind of reversal of relationships, and people currently in positions of power will face not only losing that power but also the possibility of having power wielded over them in turn. Men's fear of losing control is an obstacle to women's empowerment, but is it necessarily an outcome of women's empowerment that men should lose power or, crucially, that a loss of power should be something to be afraid of? With a 'power over' view of power, it is hard to imagine otherwise.

There are, however, other ways of understanding and conceptualising power, which focus not just on a particular set of results but on *process*. Power can take other forms, variously described as 'power to', 'power with' and 'power from within', all of which allow the construction of a very different meaning (or set of meanings) for 'empowerment'. Drawing on the writings of various women writers,[6] Hartsock contrasts the obedience definition of power with what she calls an 'energy' definition of power. This is power which does not involve the domination of 'power over', but is a power which is generative, for example, 'the power some people have of stimulating activity in others and raising their morale' (Hartsock 1985: 223). One aspect of this 'power to' is the kind of leadership that comes from the wish to see a group achieve what it is capable of, where there is not necessarily any conflict of interests and the group is setting its own agenda. It is a form of power which can persuade or open up new possibilities.

Foucault uses a different model of power. For Foucault, power is not a finite entity that can be located; power is relational, not a substance, and is something which exists only in its exercise. Power is constituted in a network of social relationships among subjects who are free to act to at least a minimal extent; without power those relationships cannot exist (Gordon 1980; Foucault 1982; Dreyfus and Rabinow 1982). He sees power as a 'mode of action upon actions' (Foucault 1982: 222). His is a notion of power as productive, as intimately bound up with knowledge. Foucault's model of power includes an understanding of resistance as a form of power (a form of action upon an action); he suggests that where there is power there is resistance. His focus is mainly on micro-politics: the local exercise of power at particular points, and the resistance to it. Power relations, in this model, are multiple and are rooted in systems of social networks.

A feminist model of power would draw on the thinking of Foucault, but would incorporate a gender analysis of power relations that includes an understanding of how 'internalised oppression' places internal barriers to women's exercise of power, thereby contributing to the maintenance of inequality between men and women.[7] It would also draw on an analysis of how the gendered phenomenon of male violence against women conditions women's experience. For Radtke and Stam (1994: 8), power is the 'capacity to have an impact or produce an effect',[8] so that 'Power is both the source of oppression in its abuse and the source of emancipation in its use' (ibid.: 1). It is therefore useful to differentiate between different types of exercise of power: 'power over' as controlling power, which may be responded to with compliance, resistance,[9] which weakens processes of victimisation (Faith 1994), or manipulation and 'power to' as generative or productive power (sometimes incorporating or manifesting as forms of resistance and/or manipulation), which creates new possibilities and actions without domination. Some analysts also identify 'power with', which 'involves a sense of the whole being greater than the sum of the individuals, especially when a group tackles problems together' (quoted in Williams *et al.* 1995: 234). One person standing up against an unjust law is unlikely to achieve much on their own; many people working together, however, are more likely to provoke a change. There is also 'power from within', 'the spiritual strength and uniqueness that resides in each one of us and makes us truly human. Its basis is self-acceptance and self-respect which extend, in turn, to respect for and acceptance of others as equals' (ibid.). This power can be what enables the individual to hold to a position or activity in the face of over-whelming opposition, or to take a serious risk.

Empowerment, then, is not restricted to the achievement of the 'power over' form of power, but can also involve the development of power to, with and from within. These kinds of power are not finite; indeed, one might argue that the more they are exercised the more power can grow. One group of people developing and exercising power of this kind does not necessarily reduce the power of others – although it may. There are many cases in the history of Non-violent Direct Action, for example, where 'power over' has been thwarted or diverted by the principled action of small numbers of people.

So we now have a picture of women's empowerment which encompasses women moving into positions of 'power over', but which also embraces their movement into 'power to, with and from within' – generative power rather than controlling power. Where does this fit with the development discourse and theories of women's development?

In the late 1970s and 1980s a new 'Gender and Development' analysis emerged which tackled not just the nature of women's various roles (as reflected in WID), but the interactions of those roles with those of men. Gender and Development (GAD) is an approach concerned not simply with women's roles, therefore, but with the dynamics and structures of gender relations. Women are not housewives, for example, in a vacuum: they are housewives in a context where men and other women expect them to be housewives, as does society at large. Gender relations are seen as central to social processes and social organisation (though not as their only important feature) and therefore to development, which is defined as 'a complex process involving the social, economic, political and cultural betterment of individuals and of society itself' (Young 1988a: 6). GAD theorists have highlighted the value systems which lead to a sexual division of labour, varyingly constituted, and lay emphasis on the socially constructed nature of gender and gender relations. An understanding of the processes by which gender relations are negotiated and renegotiated, and the resultant social formations, can assist greatly in understanding the nature of households, of the constitution of the labour force, of the 'informal economy' and other basic constructs of development analysis. Gender analysis which takes account of the variety of 'women' (and men), and the diversity of their circumstances, necessitates a move away from the simple dichotomies of public/private, formal/informal, urban/rural and production/reproduction. It also requires the inclusion of all aspects of women's lives within the ambit of 'relevant issues' – their physical situation, intra-household relations, health, sexuality, education, means of livelihood, and so on, since gender inequalities touch all aspects of women's lives. In particular, a GAD approach makes visible the power relations that exist between men and women in most societies, the situation of subordination that most women face. Gender analysis also enables a critique of the many supposedly neutral institutions (Kabeer 1994) and the many manifestations of male bias in the development process (Elson 1995).

Gender analysis has led to a more detailed questioning of aspects of development which affect women. Why is the incidence of women as heads of household apparently increasing? Why is the division of responsibility for domestic and reproductive activity apportioned in a way that makes women's burden so heavy? Why is very little work being done with men towards changing the nature of men's participation so that women are more able to become involved? It also enables a consideration not only of women's economic or project participation, but also their other activities and responsibilities and of issues that affect their general well-being, such as violence, widowhood and abandonment. These gender issues affect women's lives just as surely as limited access to credit or training opportunities. A gender analysis also highlights the needs of women who are not household heads, who are otherwise rendered invisible within male-headed households.

The notion of the 'empowerment' of women has been increasingly a part of this gender and development discourse over the past ten years or so, although here too it has been ill-defined. In her categorisation of the spectrum of development interventions with women, Moser (1989) identified the 'empowerment approach' as one approach available to gender planners. Where the 'welfare', 'equity', 'efficiency' and 'anti-poverty' approaches might be seen as connected to a WID analysis, the 'empowerment approach' can be seen as arising from a gender and development perspective, perhaps combined with an approach to development that values 'bottom-up' or 'actor-oriented' strategies. The focus on empowerment has been strengthened by the theoretical advance which enabled a distinction to be drawn between women's practical and strategic gender interests (Molyneux 1985; Moser 1989). Woman's condition, the material situation of her life (Young 1988b), mean that she has practical needs, resulting from her gendered position in society. That gendered position means that she also has strategic needs, needs that challenge the gender hierarchies and other mechanisms of subordination.[10] Although I concur with Wieringa (1994) in not seeing practical and strategic interests and needs as being as clearly separable as most of the use of the distinction in the literature implies, the formulation of the distinction has made it possible to think deliberately and strategically about what is required to tackle gender and development issues in a pragmatic way in the context of existing programmes and projects, without losing sight of the fundamental changes required to truly tackle gender inequalities.[11] Eliminating male bias and moving women out of the condition of near-universal subordination they still currently occupy will require cultural, economic and political changes; it will not be achieved by tinkering with the structures of employment or national accounting. Differentiating between the 'practical' and the 'strategic' has also made it easier to see clearly in theoretical terms that in order to tackle 'strategic' issues, the power dynamics of gender have to be addressed. The terminology of empowerment in this context has, however, not grown out of some theoretical debate, but primarily out of the practical experiences of women working for change at the grassroots level in many parts of the world. Unlike the WID analysis, significant contributions to the thinking behind the 'empowerment approach' have come from 'third world' women (for example, Sen and Grown 1988; Batliwala 1993). Debates on the empowerment of women have been strong in South Asia and the Philippines among development practitioners and grassroots activists in their search for effective ways of supporting and enabling women to make changes (Batliwala 1993).

Empowerment, as used within a gender and development context, is clearly not only concerned with women's ability to exercise 'power over' only; it also analyses their access to other forms of power. Since GAD is concerned with power relations, it is also concerned with how power interacts with other power, both in relations between men and women, and between different women.

THE HONDURAN CASE

The discussion of empowerment so far in this chapter has derived from a theoretical analysis of power and has relied heavily on academic accounts. It is with the practical and 'real-life' implications, however, that I am most concerned. I am interested in whether the idea of empowerment, and changes in practice which do or might derive from it, can contribute to significant and positive change for women. What does it mean, in particular, for poor and very poor women? What does it mean for individual women? For the organisations of which they may form a part? Of what does or might it consist? What does it mean for women's relationships with men? What are the implications for any individual or organisation wanting in some way to support processes of empowerment? Such questions cannot be answered without considering specific circumstances. In 1992–3 these and other questions took me to Honduras, where I spent ten months exploring issues of women's empowerment. An account of one of the organisations I worked with will enable me to illustrate some of the issues. I have chosen this organisation not because it is in any way 'perfect' as far as women's empowerment is concerned, but because it does show in some interesting ways some of the challenges that have to be faced, as well as some creative approaches to tackling areas of difficulty. I give here a very sketchy account of the organisation and its achievements, in order then to discuss a model of empowerment, derived in part from this case study (Rowlands 1995b, 1997).

Programa Educativo de la Mujer (PAEM)

PAEM, the *Programa Educativo de la Mujer* (Women's Educational Programme) was set up in the parish of Macuelizo in the department of Santa Barbara in 1986. It grew out of a loosely constructed network of women's groups in local communities, which in turn came out of a mission organised by the local parish priest. He asked a local woman, María Esther Ruiz, to work with women during the event. She, unusually for *campesina* (peasant) women in Honduras, had completed primary education, and had worked as a promoter with CARITAS, the Catholic welfare organisation, and in other organising work. The opportunity to try a different way of working with women was one she leapt at. To begin with she worked with ten informal groups, slowly encouraging them to identify their needs and wants and to learn about their situation as poor women in Honduras. Gradually new groups formed. At its largest, PAEM consisted of 110 groups spread across four departments. Small amounts of funding from Oxfam UK/I enabled them to pay four co-ordinators to work with the groups.

One problem that became apparent was that María Esther was spreading herself too thinly. Discussions with Oxfam about how her input could be most effective, as well as about the sustainability of the work, led to a proposal that PAEM produce its own educational materials as a way of making the work with the groups more reproducible. The result was '*Conociéndome a mi misma*' ('Getting to know myself'), a 'popular education' booklet for use by members of the groups in meetings, and the '*Guía de la animadora*' ('Guide for animators'), a booklet providing guidance to group animators in how to use the other booklet with the groups, and providing some supplementary materials such as relevant biblical passages and explanations of issues raised. Both booklets were put together out of the experience of the women in the groups, in a way that involved them in determining the content and producing the results (for example, in acting for the photographs). The booklets, which took about three years to produce, were distributed to the various groups, and are still in regular use there, as well as being used by other organisations. Each group is autonomous, and consists of up to 15 women. There was an early decision to keep the groups small, and to have more than one group in a community rather than a single one which gets larger and larger. This means that there can be space within the activity of the group for each woman to contribute and participate. The groups generally meet on a weekly basis, setting their own programmes; meetings start with a recitation of a 'women's prayer'. Sometimes they study a section of '*Conociéndome a mi misma*', discussing and reflecting on some aspect of their lives as poor rural women. Each group works to its own agenda: some of them take on small projects such as growing vegetables or making *tamales* (steamed maize wrapped in banana leaves) for sale. They raise small amounts of money, which enable them to cover any costs the group may incur. Each group chooses two women to act as animators[12] of the group. These women attend meetings with other animators to prepare the themes that will be worked on in the groups and to discuss any issues that arise.

The notion of having promoters who come in to animate a group from outside was abandoned, and the task of animating the group is now filled from within the group, and is no longer a permanent task of one person. The groups get together in zonal meetings (there are four zones in Macuelizo) with perhaps 6–10 other groups; there is a theme and each group brings an activity to share.

A *consejo* (central council) of about 20 women also meets regularly to discuss any issues that arise, analyse and plan activities, and generally play a co-ordinating role. Decisions in this group are taken by a process of consensus, with the decision evolving gradually out of discussion and exploration rather than being taken by the more customary vote.

As well as the regular group, zone and council meetings, and an annual assembly, a series of bigger workshops has enabled PAEM to look at some themes with benefit of support from outside. In the mid-1980s, awareness of gender issues within Honduran NGOs was more or less non-existent, and the NGOs that now exist with specific gender analysis and focus had not yet formed. PAEM found help from a Mexican NGO, *Grupo de Educación Popular para Mujeres* (GEM; Popular Education Group for Women), holding workshops on gender and sexuality, gender and democracy and other themes.

It has not all been plain sailing: PAEM has had its share of internal difficulties, most notably over the change from external promoters to internal animators. There has also been a significant area of difficulty resulting from external pressures. With a change of parish priest in 1991, PAEM lost a strong supporter and shield. The new priest was not supportive of the organisation, and a conflict developed between him and his close supporters and the women's organisation. The conflict centred on whether or not PAEM was part of the church. The women felt strongly that they were; the priest and his supporters felt that if they were, they should not be organising autonomously. This emotive issue raged (and may well still rage) hard and long, and opinions were very divided. It was a hard time for PAEM as an organisation, and the number of groups in Macuelizo halved.

Through interviews and observation, I was able to build up a picture of the impact of involvement in PAEM on women's lives, and of the ways in which their lives had changed since they became involved. On a personal level, nearly all the women spoke of feeling more confident and of being able to participate actively in the group and to interact with others, including with strangers and people in authority. Two short examples illustrate this:

> When I started I was embarrassed even with the other women. We met, talked a bit; you begin to talk in meetings, have more confidence. Then later, the domestic work in the home, the way you behave.... You change a lot with your husband and children. You learn things there that you didn't know. It helps a lot...
>
> (Margarita,[13] aged 36)

> I have [confidence] with whoever... now I will not be shy, but before I would stay like that to one side of the door. 'Come in', 'oh no'; or 'come and eat', 'no, I'm not hungry'. I was so shy. Today, no. If there's food you have to eat. So that's how things have been. I've woken up, my mind, and I know things.
>
> (Esperanza, aged 47)

In some cases women never used to leave their homes unaccompanied; through involvement in PAEM, they have the opportunity to travel outside their immediate communities. The animators and *consejo* members learned to organise others, lead, negotiate and in other ways act to cause plans which they and the other women had made to come to fruition, through sharing experiences, discussing difficulties and searching for solutions together, as Teresa (aged 50) told me:

> We knew what was happening to us and that we had to find our own solutions. People from outside couldn't do that for us... perhaps they would only know what we had told them about things, but the people who knew about our problems were us.
>
> ...you leave your timidity, whatever it is, because you join with other people, get to know others, perhaps talking and finding out that they have the same problems as you have had; other people have them too. So because of that you no longer feel alone when something happens, no, there are many of us with the same problems.

Some women have made significant changes in their relationships with their husbands, as Esperanza (aged 47) recounts:

> Well, the changes I've seen, really... my husband has been very annoyed and he stayed at home angry if I went out to meetings and when I came back he said 'better if you were to go once and for all'. I never would have said that I would have this capacity to go; I always put up with him and then he... he saw that... recently he's said 'back then I shouted at you but you stayed in the organisation, well, stay in it anyway'. Now he doesn't shout at me but at first he would threaten to punish me.

But this kind of change was quite limited. Many women had seen little change in these relationships; others, as Elsa (aged 22) described, found they could go so far but no further:

> He doesn't stop me going to the group. But he doesn't let me be *animadora*. But I'd like to do it – to enjoy oneself and... and learn, but he won't let me.
>
> [And you haven't thought about doing it even if he says no?]
>
> (Laughter) Afterwards there would be problems.

Talk of empowerment, as we have seen, can be rather empty rhetoric; in the case of PAEM, however, the changes achieved by the women have been tangible, with the potential for transforming the lives of the women and their communities. At the time I completed my interviewing in 1993, the PAEM women in Macuelizo were in the midst of negotiations to take over and run a disused grain warehouse in one of the communities. They had won approval for this from the state agricultural marketing agency, and had been promised significant funding by a UK aid agency. This was an ambitious project which the women would never have contemplated a few years earlier.[14]

CONSTRUCTING A MODEL OF EMPOWERMENT

It became clear to me through working with PAEM that 'empowerment' was a complex phenomenon, which took different forms in different 'spaces' of women's lives. The process of empowerment for individual women was a personal and unique experience, even though one woman may go through some similar experiences to those of other individuals. This 'personal' empowerment involved very distinct processes from those which made up empowerment in a group or collective sense. In turn, the process of empowerment for women in terms of their closest personal relationships, in particular with husbands and immediate family members, could be differentiated from the personal and collective experiences. I have found these distinctions between personal and collective empowerment, and empowerment in close relationships, a necessary and helpful one in thinking further about processes of empowerment and how to approach a conceptualisation which might serve a practical purpose in organisational and planning terms.

The 'personal empowerment' experienced by PAEM women took many forms, ranging from literally becoming able to leave the house/yard unaccompanied, to moving into positions of active leadership in the organisation and in the wider community. In considering each women's experience, it was possible to identify the changes she went through because of her involvement in the organisation, and to tease out what were the various elements of her situation, the context, the culture, the organisation and so on that either contributed positively to the change, or that operated in some way to impede the change. Likewise with 'collective empowerment': the groups also changed in many ways over time, and it was possible to identify aspects of the way in which they were organised, the activities they undertook, the relationships within them and between them, relationships with the wider community and with formal institutions, which either enhanced or inhibited the empowerment process.

'Empowerment in close relationships' was harder to distinguish. Listening to women talking about their relationships with husbands, boyfriends and fathers – and also with mothers and mothers-in-law – it was evident that this is the area of change that comes hardest: it is the place where the individual woman is 'up against it on her own', and where positive and negative aspects of her life tend to be most closely intertwined. Some women had achieved remarkable changes in their relationships with their husbands; others reported no change, or cited instances of conflict and discouragement. Even so, it is still possible to consider the elements of the situation which encourage or inhibit change in this difficult area of women's lives.

Empowerment can be seen to happen, then, because changes over time give women more access to power, in one or more of its forms. In this example, there are many instances of women increasing their ability to act, to perceive themselves as capable, to hold opinions, to use time effectively, to control resources, to interact with others, to initiate activities, to respond to events, and so on. These instances of increased power to, power with, power from within and, on occasion, power over are significant. They do not in themselves, however, demonstrate empowerment processes: they demonstrate the product of empowerment processes – the evidence that empowerment has been taking place. In order for such changes to happen, there appears to be a core set of necessary elements. From my research in Honduras, I identify these as follows:

Personal empowerment	Collective empowerment
• Self-confidence	• Group identity
• Self-esteem	• Collective sense of agency
• Sense of agency	• Group dignity
• Sense of 'self' in a wider context	• Self-organisation and management
• Dignity	

Any individual or group will have a history, prior experience, and may therefore already have some of any of these elements, but their increase in some way is the crucial piece; this increase appears to need to be in all of these elements, not just in one or two. For example, to have more confidence and self-esteem do not in themselves produce more power: without a greater sense of being able to act in the world, or without a concept of a world beyond the confines of the immediate circumstances, they are meaningless.

Dignity as an element of the core of empowerment deserves some explanation, since I include it because of the particular meaning it has in Spanish. It is a word many interviewees used, with a meaning not only of dignity as English uses it, but of self-respect, self-worth, honour and the expectation of receiving, *and of having the right to receive*, respect from others.[15]

The core of the empowerment process in the area of close relationships is slightly different. I would say this is because in order to achieve empowerment in this area of one's life, some personal empowerment is necessary: it could be seen as an area of change arising from personal empowerment processes. The core I identified for this aspect was:

Empowerment in Close Relationships

- Ability to negotiate
- Ability to communicate
- Ability to get support
- Ability to defend self/rights
- Sense of 'self' in the relationship
- Dignity

With the core processes of empowerment identified, and an understanding that it is possible to identify what can encourage and/or inhibit them, it now becomes possible to analyse any given situation and deliberately set about organising things in such a way as to support empowerment processes. This can be done either by increasing the strength or likelihood of the 'encouraging' elements, or by reducing, avoiding or counteracting the 'inhibiting' elements.

It is important to be aware that we are not looking at a linear process here: as time passes, the changes achieved can in turn feed into the strengthening of the core elements, so that the image of a loop or a spiral is perhaps more appropriate than a line. Neither is 'forward' movement inevitable, as was the case for the PAEM groups which did not survive the conflict described above, and for whom the pressure from within the parish to conform to a different model of organisation was too strong. An 'inhibiting' element in the environment will not always be counteracted successfully for everyone. It is also completely possible that one person's 'empowerment' process may be another person's 'disempowerment', either because they share some situation where their two sets of needs are incompatible, or because similar processes acting in different contexts or within different power relationships have diverse impacts. The PAEM example shows that particular events or circumstances which impede empowerment for some can encourage it for others: for some PAEM women, particularly but not exclusively those already taking some leadership role, the same conflict provided the impetus for very rapid development of the core elements of empowerment. For the individual woman (or group) therefore, an empowerment process will take a form which arises out of her particular cultural, ethnic, historical, economic, geographic, political and social location; out of her place in the life-cycle, her specific life-experience and out of the interaction of all the above with the gender relations that prevail around her.

REFLECTIONS ON THE ROLE OF THE OUTSIDER/ DEVELOPMENT AGENCY

The implications of more exact thinking about empowerment for 'outsiders' working with women are significant.[16] When empowerment is defined more precisely, both in terms of the issue of what constitutes power, and of the specifics of the process, the notion of an 'empowerment approach' to development for women becomes more useful as a tool for analysis and planning, whether in relations to the 'closest in' scale of personal empowerment, the 'furthest out' scale of international relations, or intermediate points. With a definition of 'empowerment', it becomes possible to think more precisely about the process(es) within a given context (whether from the position of 'insider' or 'outsider'). A set of questions could be devised which could be used to identify areas for action that would enhance the empowerment process in a particular place. For example: In what aspects of our/their lives is there self-confidence? Where is it lacking? Why? What are the elements of the situation which, through their presence or absence, encourage or inhibit self-confidence? Where do we/they have a sense of being able to act, to cause things to happen? Where not? Why? How do we/they perceive our/themselves? Do we/they have a sense of being worthy of the respect of others or our/them selves? Do we/they relate to a wider context? What? Where is it limited? Why? Then, in terms of planning and designing programmes, projects or activities: How could we/they set about tackling the issues identified by the earlier questions? What activities are needed? What existing or new structures will be needed? What support or encouragement would make a difference? From whom? What might get in the way? How could that be mitigated?

What might encourage the process? How could that be strengthened? What 'changes' might we/they look for? What methodology can be used that would be consistent with the process? How do we incorporate an appropriate notion of time, or is this rendered irrelevant? What are our power relationships with the group (for outsiders) and what forms of power do we have available to draw on in this work?

The role of the change agent in programmes intended to promote empowerment with women is potentially a pivotal one. Change agents are usually (though not always) 'outsiders'; they are often extension workers, 'experts' in some form. The attitudes they bring to their work, and the form their work takes, can have an immense impact, positively or negatively, on the people they work with. With empowerment in mind, there are a number of attitudes and skills which can be derived from the foregoing discussion as essential for the change agent to have. The attitudes are those necessary for working with women on developing self-confidence, self-esteem and a sense of themselves as able to act in a wider sphere. They include complete respect for each individual and for the group; humility and a willingness (or even, perhaps, eagerness) for learning to be mutual; commitment to the empowerment process. The skills of the change agent need to be consistent with the open-ended nature of the process: facilitation skills, active listening skills, non-directive questioning skills. The role of the change agent is essentially one of catalyst – except that unlike a chemical catalyst, the change agent is unlikely to emerge unchanged at the other end. All human beings are the product of their particular life-history and culture; it is vital for change agents to have self-awareness in terms of their own biases, priorities and areas of similarity/difference in relation to the women with whom they are working.

In view of the above, the training of change agents becomes an important issue. The skills and attitudes outlined above are not quickly acquired and require much practice and constant monitoring. I shall not attempt to go into detail here of how this might be achieved (e. g. Araki 1991, Williams *et al.* 1995), except to say that I suspect that such training needs to be ongoing and to contain many opportunities for self-reflection and self-evaluation. That may imply formal training, or may be an informal process. For example, in the PAEM case study, María Esther filled the role of change agent with the organisation; her training had been a mixture of some formal training and a lot of on-the-job informal training, with constant analysis of the process, and appropriate support to combat isolation.

Organisations which want to support processes of empowerment in grassroots groups or within local or national non-government development organisations (NGDOs) (which I am here referring to as 'supporting organisations') cannot do so by imposition, since that would defeat the purpose. This could lead to a dilemma. What, for example, if in a particular case, women perceive that by becoming consumers – say, by buying televisions and other material symbols of achievement – they will become empowered? If the supporting organisation agrees to back the women in their goals, it risks colluding with a limited vision of what is possible, and leaving the women with little change in terms of their ability to actively influence their situations. If, however, it does not support the women's goals, seeing them as not contributing to empowerment processes, it runs the risk of imposing its own agenda and therefore disempowering the women. The challenge, then, is to encourage women to set their own goals whilst also encouraging them to question their assumptions (and those of others) about what is possible: to leave the women in charge whilst at the same time challenging the 'internalised oppression' that pushes them to accept less than what they are capable of. The methodology used becomes a crucial issue.

The role of the supporting organisation is therefore a delicate one if the purpose of empowerment is to be achieved. It cannot, by definition, be a directing role. In some ways it is a role of solidarity – except that solidarity can be passive. I have found it useful to think in terms of building alliances. Allies are not only supportive and in solidarity with you, but will also put their weight behind you in places where you need it, whilst leaving you in charge. Allies are interested in your meeting your goals, because in some fundamental way that enables them to meet their goals as well.[17]

Supporting organisations as allies to groups or organisations in the empowerment process face some other important challenges. One is that of holding on to the empowerment aim whilst complying with the requirements of their own accountability processes. These do not always appear to be compatible. Depending on the source of funding, there will be reporting cycles and criteria of success or failure that provide pressures that work against many of the requirements of an empowerment approach. For example, funding tied to short-term 'projects' brings pressure for quick, clearly visible results which are quantifiable. Yet processes of empowerment can be long-term and may require an open-ended approach with unpredictable and inconclusive outcomes. Talk of 'empowerment projects' may be a contradiction in terms, since the 'project' is generally seen as a short (usually 3–5 years), specific activity with predetermined objectives and targets. With an empowerment approach women themselves need to set the agenda and manage the pace of change. For supporting organisations working within British charity law, there is another challenge: that of remaining 'non-political' in their activities in order to maintain charitable status and the tax advantages that go with that. Yet we have seen that empowerment is about nothing if it is not about power – and therefore is a fiercely political issue, albeit within a definition of 'political' that is wider than that usually employed in the British context. A challenge faced by organisations that rely on charitable giving is one of image (including self-image). The images that have encouraged charitable giving in the past have been the antithesis of empowerment images, or have been tangible images, such as new water systems or immunisation programmes. Empowerment programmes are unlikely to generate the kind of pitiful images that have been used traditionally to raise funds. This implies a major re-education of donors to respond to more positive, perhaps less tangible images – a challenge which some organisations are tackling with some effect.

An additional challenge faced by supporting organisations is that of working alongside 'project partners' who may not themselves have any particular interest in empowerment of women. Grassroots organisations, local and national NGDOs and popular organisations are products of the culture within which they are situated, and, unless they are feminist women's organisations, are unlikely to have developed an approach which prioritises the empowerment needs of women. There is a challenge, then, of 'undoing' structures which at best ignore women's empowerment and at worst, actively disempower women, yet avoiding the imposition of an outside agenda. In addition, organisations looking for funds are quick to identify trends in funding criteria, and will strategically, or even cynically, include in funding applications the wordings necessary to obtain funding approval. This was freely admitted to by several organisations I spoke with in the course of my research. 'Empowerment of women' has become one such trend.

The central issue of empowerment is one of *process*. The 'core' of empowerment as identified here can be supported in myriad ways, some of which fall happily within other development approaches and many of which can be linked with tangible changes. You can build a well in a way that supports the empowerment of women by encouraging them to do the necessary analysis and decision-making and to take control over their lives. You can teach women to read in a way which generates debate and analysis and which supports them to become more confident and more able to act. Any of these kinds of activities can be planned *with* people rather than *for* people. As Wieringa observes,

Any project concerned with women can potentially entail a transformative element. Sewing courses, literacy programmes, cooking lessons can be given in a way that allows for discussion of the gender division of labour, of women's control over their finances, of sexual violence.

(Wieringa 1994: 843)

In a sense, what the supporting organisation needs to look for is a leverage point. Taking an empowerment approach to work with women does, however, require the exploration of 'new' approaches as well as a revision of the way in which 'old' approaches are used. For example, networking, and the maintenance and strengthening of women's organisations, are not activities which have generally attracted funding. Within an empowerment approach, they take on a significance that other approaches did not recognise. There may also be an appropriate lobbying role for the supporting organisation, whilst maintaining an assumption that women can and will lobby on their own behalf if supported to do so. It is also worth pointing out, here, that the resources that supporting organisations bring to the empowerment process are not simply financial. There are many non-financial resources that can make a significant impact, such as personal support at key moments, providing contacts with relevant individuals and organisations, support for the networking process, and so on. There is a role for the supporting organisation in relation to mixed organisations, not just to women-only organisations, in applying the analytical questions suggested earlier. In this case, any 'change agents' will have to develop the capacity to focus on the empowerment of women as a gender issue and be skilled enough to keep the process moving without getting 'hijacked' by the existing power dynamics.

There are implications of an empowerment approach for the supporting organisation in terms of the evaluation of its activity. In order to 'capture' the degree of effectiveness of the approach, 'performance indicators' of empowerment need to be developed. The fact that the well was built or that the women learned to read will not communicate the process through which that was achieved. Qualitative indicators will be an essential, significant part of evaluation, although these will have to be used with great caution if yet another instrumentalisation of women is to be avoided (Feuerstein 1986).

One more implication of an empowerment approach to work with women for supporting organisations is related to their own organisational culture. It is not easy to make a commitment to processes of women's empowerment when there are so many social, political and cultural pressures working against it. It is even harder if your own organisational culture is not one that encourages women's empowerment. Several women I have talked with who work for development agencies as gender specialists have told me that their organisations systematically marginalise the work of the gender specialists whilst ostensibly having a commitment to women's development and even specifically to women's empowerment.[18] This can result in tokenism and ineffective work. Given the demands made on change agents outlined above, and the accompanying demands made on the organisation itself, the effectiveness of any work to support empowerment processes outside the organisation will be adversely affected by an organisational culture that works against the empowerment of women.

There have been criticisms of empowerment as a term which potentially obscures conflicts of interest between different categories of women, hiding power relations (Yuval-Davies 1994). This raises an important issue: empowerment to what end? The empowerment of women is also not just a women's issue, but is a gender issue which necessitates a re-examination of gender relations, and which, ultimately, will require changes of men as well as of women. It is also a development issue, since women who become empowered to act in a wider sphere take a more active role not only in economic activity, but in exerting political pressure for change in many ways. We need to move away from any notion of empowerment, and perhaps even development, as something that can be done 'to' people or 'for' people. Empowerment is important not as an instrumentalist notion or rhetorical device, but as an active tool which, if used thoughtfully, can be used to achieve change with justice.

NOTES

1. Parts of this chapter have appeared in Rowlands (1995a & b). The research was financed by a research studentship award from the Economic and Social Research Council.

2. There is a significant literature on empowerment in other contexts, including education, counselling, social work and psychology, on which I have drawn more explicitly elsewhere (Rowlands 1995, 1997).
3. This mechanism is also described by Foucault in relation to Bentham's Panopticon prison model: 'There is no need for arms, physical violence, material constraints. Just a gaze. An inspecting gaze, a gaze which each individual under its weight will end by interiorising to the point that he is his own overseer, each individual thus exercising this surveillance over, and against, himself. A superb formula: power exercised continuously and for what turns out to be minimal cost' (in Gordon 1980: 155).
4. 'The action of empowering; the state of being empowered' OED (1989: 192), where empower means 'Empower: 1). To invest legally or formally with power or authority; to authorise, license. 2). To impart or bestow to an end or for a purpose; to enable, permit'. There is also an interesting obsolete version: 'To gain or assume power *over*' (emphasis in original).
5. Or, indeed, of many other issues, including, for example, disability, sexuality, age, and so on.
6. Including Hannah Arendt, Mary Parker Follett, Dorothy Emmett, Hannah Pitkin and Berenice Carroll.
7. Foucault, in his later work, does show some awareness of this: 'I don't believe that this question of 'who exercises power?' can be resolved unless that other question 'how does it happen?' is resolved at the same time' (1988: 103). For me, however, this is not sufficient. Perhaps, had he lived longer, he would have provided a more satisfactory account!
8. I take this to include the possibility that the impact or effect produced can include the maintenance of the status quo.
9. For an exploration of forms of resistance, see Scott (1985).
10. Alsop (1993) provides a clear critique of the practical/strategic framework in the context of gender planning in north-east India, cautioning that the complexities of gender relations and social/economic factors and the limitations of 'projects' can easily lead to unintended outcomes, especially if 'outsiders' are identifying the needs/issues. She suggests that satisfying a practical need can positively support a strategic concern and that women need to be identifying the needs and issues for themselves.
11. Wieringa (1994) criticises the concept of practical/strategic gender needs or interests (and women's condition/position, on similar grounds) as theoretically flawed, since (a) they change over time, (b) they vary depending on who is defining them, (c) they encourage a homogenisation of 'women's interests' where these are diverse, (d) the distinction implies a hierarchical relation between the two which lends itself to a top-down approach, (e) it is empirically impossible to distinguish between the two. She suggests that 'the "success" of certain development efforts may be better "measured" by the way new interests surface or come to be defined along the way, than by the progress made in relation to certain interests which were defined during the planning stage' (p. 836).
12. Animator is a term used to describe someone whose role is to motivate individuals to participate in group activities and to motivate the group to continue to meet and be active.
13. The women's names have been changed.

14. In 1995 I heard that the warehousing scheme was defeated by local political dynamics, but that the women were persisting with a different large project.
15. This issue of the meanings of words in translation is very pertinent to the word 'empowerment' itself. There is no direct equivalent in Spanish; where a translation is used, it is an invented one, *'empoderamiento'*. Whilst undertaking more recent research on empowerment in Mexico (also ESRC-funded) I invited a group of Mexican women activists and development workers to brainstorm possible equivalent words. We came up with a long list of possibilities, including *autonomía, potenciarse, autogestión*. After discussion we concluded that none of the words was a satisfactory equivalent for the English concept, although several of them accurately described 'components' of empowerment. They were not particularly happy with using the fabricated translation from the English word, but they agreed that the ideas behind it were ones they wanted to be able to express.
16. The implications for 'insiders' of a clearer understanding of empowerment processes is also great, particularly in terms of organisational structures and management. This is an area which merits detailed discussion and is beyond the scope of this chapter, though I have touched on it elsewhere (Rowlands 1995b, 1997).
17. The idea of the supporting organisation as ally is, as far as I have been able to ascertain, a new one. For a debate around alliance building, see the various contributions that make up Albrecht and Brewer (1990).
18. Personal communications; they asked not to be identified.

REFERENCES

Albrecht, L. and Brewer, R.M. (eds) (1990) *Bridges of Power: Women's Multicultural Alliances*. Philadelphia, New Society Publishers.

Alsop, R. (1993) 'Whose Interests? Problems in Planning for Women's Practical Needs', *World Development* Vol. 21, No. 3, pp. 367–77.

Araki, M. (1991) 'Towards Empowerment of Women in the Third World: The Training of the Change Agent'. Unpublished MA thesis, Reading University.

Bachrach, P. and Baratz, M.S. (1970) *Power and Poverty: Theory and Practice*. New York, Oxford University Press.

Batliwala, S. (1993) *Empowerment of Women in South Asia: Concepts and Practices*. New Delhi, FAO–FFHC/AD.

Dahl, R.A. (1961) *Who Governs? Democracy and Power in an American City*. New Haven, CT & London: Yale University Press.

Devaux, M. (1994) 'Feminism and Empowerment: A Critical Reading of Foucault', *Feminist Studies* Vol. 20, No. 2, pp. 223–47.

Dreyfus, H.L. and Rabinow, P. (1982) *Michel Foucault: Beyond Structuralism and Hermaneutics*. Brighton: Harvester Press.

Elson, D. (ed.) (1995) *Male Bias in the Development Process*, 2nd edition. Manchester: Manchester University Press.

Faith, K. (1994) 'Resistance: Lessons from Foucault and Feminism', in H.L. Radtke and H.J. Stam (eds.), *Power/Gender: Social Relations in Theory and Practice*. London: Sage.

Feuerstein, M.T. (1986) *Partners in Evaluation*. London: Macmillan.

Foucault, M. (1982) 'The Subject and Power', Afterword in H.L. Dreyfus and P. Rabinow, *Michel Foucault: Beyond Structuralism*. Brighton: Harvester Press.

Foucault, M. (1988) 'Truth, Power, Self: An Interview with Michel Foucault', in L. Martin, H. Gutman and P. Hutton (eds.) (1988) *Technologies of the Self: A Seminar with Michel Foucault*. London: Tavistock.

Gordon, C. (ed.) (1980) *Power/Knowledge: Selected Interviews and Other Writings*. Brighton: Harvester Press.

Hartsock, N. (1985) *Money, Sex and Power: Towards a Feminist Historical Materialism*. Boston, MA: Northeastern University Press.

Jackins, H. (1983) *The Reclaiming of Power*. Seattle: Rational Island Publishers.

Kabeer, N. (1994) *Reversed Realities: Gender Hierarchies in Development Thought*. London: Verso.

Lukes, S, (1974): *Power: a Radical View*. London: Macmillan.

Molyneux, M. (1985) 'Mobilization without Emancipation: Women's Interests, State and Revolution in Nicaragua', *Feminist Studies* Vol. 11, No. 2, pp. 227-54.

Moser, C. (1989) 'Gender Planning in the Third World: Meeting Practical and Strategic Gender Needs', *World Development* Vol. 17, No. 11, pp.1799-825.

PAEM (1990a) *Conociéndome a mí Misma: Cuaderno de Temas* Tegucigalpa: Programa Educativo para la Mujer.

PAEM (1990b) *Guía de la Animadora*. Tegucigalpa: PAEM.

Pheterson, G. (1990) 'Alliances between Women: Overcoming Internalised Oppression and Internalised Domination', in A. Albrecht and R.M. Brewer (eds.), *Bridges of Power: Women's Multicultural Alliances*. Philadelphia: New Society Publishers.

Polsby, N.W. (1963) *Community Power and Political Theory*. New Haven, CT & London: Yale University Press.

Radtke, H.L. and Stam, H.J. (eds.) (1994) *Power/Gender: Social Relations in Theory and Practice*. London: Sage.

Rowlands, J.M. (1995a) 'Empowerment Examined', *Development in Practice*, Vol. 5, No. 2, pp. 101-7.

Rowlands, J.M. (1995b) *Empowerment Examined: An Exploration of the Concept and Practice of Women's Empowerment in Honduras*. PhD Thesis, Durham University.

Rowlands, J.M. (1997) *Questioning Empowerment: Working with Women in Honduras*. Oxford: Oxfam Publications.

Sen, G. and Grown, C. (1988) *Development, Crises and Alternative Visions: Third World Women's Perspectives*. London: Earthscan.

Wieringa, S. (1994) 'Women's Interests and Empowerment: Gender Planning Reconsidered', *Development and Change* Vol. 25, pp. 849-78.

Williams, S., with Seed, J. and Mwau, A. (1995) *The Oxfam Gender Training Manual*. Oxford: Oxfam.

Wolfinger, R.E. (1971) 'Nondecisions and the Study of Local Politics', *American Political Science Review* Vol. 65, No. 4, pp. 1063–80.

Young, K. (1988a) *Women and Economic Development: Local, Regional and National Planning Strategies.* Oxford: Berg.

Young, K. (1988b) 'Gender and Development: A Relational Approach', mimeo. Brighton, Institute of Development Studies.

Yuval-Davies, N. (1994) 'Women, Ethnicity and Empowerment', *Feminism and Psychology* Vol. 4 (1), pp. 179–197.

2 Fruits of Burden–The Organisation of Women Temporary Workers in Chilean Agribusiness
Stephanie Barrientos

INTRODUCTION

Over the past 20 years, rural women in the central region of Chile have experienced a radical change in their situation. Traditionally they played a subordinate position within the rural division of labour, with their primary role in the home and much of their work being unremunerated. Today women play a key role at the forefront of Chilean agricultural export production as independent waged temporary workers. Every year tens of thousands of women, the *temporeras*, are mobilised to work in the fruit sector, sustaining Chile's prominence as an exporter of out-of-season fruit to the north during its winter months. Many of these women have entered the labour force for the first time, are able to earn some of the highest wages in the sector and are dependent on their wage labour for their own survival and that of their families. Outside the season, however, there is very little alternative work for them, and they are subject to high levels of unemployment and poverty. Agribusiness has simultaneously reversed and exploited the traditional division of labour, as women have to combine productive and reproductive work in the season, but are forced to return to their traditional role in the home during the winter, remaining a reliable source of labour to be tapped again every year.

Their position at the centre of agribusiness gives these women a potentially powerful bargaining position, but despite this they have remained a marginal and fragmented group. They suffer poor working conditions, exposure to dangerous chemicals, long working hours, low pay and lack of services, especially childcare facilities. State policy and traditional trade union organisation within the transition to democracy have been unable to address many of the central issues facing the *temporeras*. But alternative forms of grassroots organisation have emerged which raise the possibility for the greater empowerment of temporary women workers. This chapter examines the contradictory ways in which employment in agribusiness has both disempowered and empowered women temporary workers. It asks why, despite their role at the centre of export production, these women have remained at another level marginalised and hence a disempowered force. Further, it examines why, despite the return to democracy, the state and trade unions have been unable to address the main problems of the *temporeras*. Finally, it considers whether emerging grassroots organisation, which breaks down the division between the productive and reproductive roles of these women, will be able to challenge the pervasive dominance of global agribusiness and enhance their empowerment.

THE EXPANSION OF FEMALE EMPLOYMENT IN FRUIT

The origin of this large female labour force lies in the counter-reform strategy in agriculture under the Pinochet dictatorship during the 1970s. Under the traditional hacienda system, which dominated Chilean agriculture until the 1960s, women had played a highly subordinate role. Chile is traditionally a very 'macho' society, in which women's role is seen as in the home, taking responsibility for reproductive and household tasks. There are no in-depth studies of the specific role of women in agriculture at this time, but evidence suggests that women's primary functions were as unremunerated family workers, occupied in specific tasks such as kitchen garden cultivation and caring for small livestock. When their labour was required at harvest time, they could be drawn into field work, but employment on the hacienda was usually under their husband's contract for which he received remuneration (Lago 1987, Bradshaw 1990). The agrarian reform programme initiated in Chile in the 1960s under President Frei and continued under Allende began to break down traditional forms of agrarian organisation and land tenure. Land was transferred from the haciendas and large farms to co-operatives of peasants. Again, it was primarily male heads of household who benefited from the reform process, and women were not direct beneficiaries of the reform (Lago 1987; Bradshaw 1990; Venegas 1995).

After 1973, the military dictatorship reversed the policy of land reform, initiating a counter-reform in agriculture. However, this did not involve a return to the traditional agrarian system, and only a small proportion of the old landowners were able to retrieve their land.

The capitalist policies of the military led for the first time to the creation of a free land market, in which much of the fertile land was bought up by capitalist farmers, creating medium-sized farms called *parcelas*.[1] Simultaneously the free trade and export-led growth strategy of Pinochet stimulated the rapid expansion of fruit production and exports by the new breed of professional farmers. As a result of this process of counter-reform, large numbers of peasant families were forced off the land into rural and urban shantytowns to eke out a subsistence based on waged labour. All members of the family were forced to take any paid work to stave off the ravages of poverty as part of a household survival strategy. Necessity thus forced large numbers of women to enter the wage labour force for the first time. Fruit production generated the requirement for a large number of cheap seasonal workers, and women were often seen to meet the specific needs of agribusiness (Venegas 1992a; Díaz 1991; Barrientos 1996; Waylen 1992).

The result of this process was the explosion of Chilean fresh fruit exports during the 1980s. Between 1985 and 1994, the volume of fruit exports grew by 175 per cent, accounting for 10 per cent of Chilean exports in 1993 (Asociación de Exportadores 1994). Chile is now a major provider of out-of-season fresh fruit to the northern hemisphere during its winter months (particularly grapes, apples and pears). The whole industry is characterised by its use of modern production techniques and selected seed varieties, with high levels of technological investment in computer-controlled drip irrigation systems, packing plants, atmospherically controlled storage and transport systems. This is high-tech agribusiness, which has involved the complete transformation of the fruit regions from traditional to advanced agriculture based on capitalist ownership and wage labour. The major problem with fruit, however, is its seasonality. To maintain these levels of output on an annual basis, the fruit sector generates a massive surge in employment at the height of the season. No reliable figures are available, but estimates put the seasonal agricultural labour force at 250,000 workers. Over half this employment is female, approximately 138,000 women workers in 1993 (Barrientos 1996).

Women are drawn into fruit work at the height of the season, usually from December to March. Some are employed in the fields, particularly in pruning, where the employers are usually the medium-sized capitalist farmers who bought land under Pinochet. These farmers rely on a small number of export firms for assistance and as a channel for their exports. Once harvested, much of the fruit goes straight into the

large packing houses which are now scattered across the central region
of the country and are owned by the large export firms. These export
firms are increasingly owned by large corporations and multinationals
(Gómez and Echeñique 1988; Gómez 1994). The majority of female
employment is in the packing houses. Here they carry out the work of
selecting, cleaning, preparing and packing the fruit in a highly presen-
table form for the external markets. Compared to the primarily male
temporary workforce in the fields, women in the packing houses are
able to earn some of the highest incomes in the sector, although they
also work the longest hours, often late into the night, and are subject to
the most flexible working practices (Barrientos 1996).

The women themselves come from a variety of backgrounds, and
form a fairly heterogeneous group. There is very little migration of
fruit labour, except at the beginning of the season, when some fruit
workers migrate from the centre to the north, where the season starts
earlier and there is a shortage of labour. However, once the season is in
full swing in the centre and the south of the fruit-growing region, local
labour is used. Evidence suggests that a significant proportion of the
women come from urban residence (both rural towns and cities), as
opposed to peasant households. This is in sharp contrast to other
developing countries, where internal migration is an important source
of urban and rural labour (see, for example, Davin in this volume). It
reflects the high degree of urbanisation which has already taken place
in Chile, and the degree of centralisation of the population within the
fruit-growing regions where production is concentrated. A result is the
anomaly of 'reverse migration', with many workers being bussed to
work in agriculture from the towns on a daily basis. [2] Whilst there are
regional variations, case studies have also found that the majority of
women are or have been married, and have children. The average age
of the women temporary workers is approximately 30 years (25 years
for men). There is also a higher incidence of women from female-
headed households amongst the *temporeras* than the national average
of 14 per cent female-headed households (Rodriguez and Venegas
1991; Venegas 1992a). This profile of the *temporeras* in Chile is different from the stereotype of younger, single women being employed in
agribusiness. I would suggest this is a result of the intense demand for
female labour at the height of the season, combined with specialisation
in agribusiness in the central region of Chile, and the increased feminisation of the labour market generally. [3]

Women are thus concentrated into the new forms of employment
generated by export requirements, and have been directly integrated

into modern agribusiness. As a result, they have been catapulted from a subordinate role in the traditional agrarian system to the forefront of the modern agro-export sector. Agribusiness has played an important role in breaking down the traditional barriers to women's empowerment. But agribusiness itself, particularly in the form of the large corporations and multinationals, wields immense economic and financial power, and any changes implemented have been to suit its driving need for profit-maximisation and market dominance. In relation to this, the women employed as temporary workers remain a subordinate and fragmented force. But agrarian change has generated new conditions, in which the options and constraints facing women workers have been transformed. This has led to a contradictory situation in which temporary women workers have both been disempowered in terms of their subordinate relation to international capital, and empowered in terms of the new opportunities they face. This is an example of the contradictory nature of the process of empowerment, as discussed by Jo Rowlands (see this volume), and raises the issue of how women themselves can be integrated into the empowerment process in the context of globalisation. We shall explore this contradiction by considering first the marginalisation of the *temporeras*, and then considering the ways in which they have gained.

THE DISEMPOWERING EFFECT OF AGRIBUSINESS

The disempowering effect of working in agribusiness is associated with the control agribusiness has in determining the pattern and conditions of employment. The women sustain an immense double burden in combining their productive and reproductive work, and are driven by the need to earn sufficient income for their families to survive given the short time each year they can earn an income. Women working in the packing houses will normally start work at around mid-day, when the first of the day's harvest arrives, and often continue until well into the night. Shifts of 12–16 hours are not uncommon. The packers are paid by piece rates for fruit that passes quality control, which increases the intensity of their work as they try to earn as much as possible. In the 1993–4 season the Comisión Nacional Campesina (CNC) estimated that on average temporary fruit workers earned the equivalent of US$134 per month. The most productive women packers are able to earn above the average, but they have to work the longest hours, and they work a shorter period each year than men, who are concentrated in the fields. Women also face greater job insecurity, and have the most flexible employment in terms of pay, hours of work and type of work (Venegas 1992a; Barrientos 1996).

Women also face a number of medical problems as a result of working in fruit. There is a high use of pesticides, fertilisers to sustain the intensity of cultivation of a limited number of fruit varieties for export and hormones, which are used to control production to meet the tight output schedules of the exporters. All workers in fruit are exposed to these, but women who work in the confined space of the packing houses suffer some of the highest levels of exposure (Thrupp 1995). There are numerous work-related health problems, including back pain from standing for long periods of time, nausea, infertility and an increased incidence of malformed babies. Many of the women do not have contracts of employment and are not covered by health insurance while they are working (not that they can afford to take time off work), but often the problems do not become obvious until after the season is completed and they have little or no recompense (Díaz 1991).

In addition to the problems of poor working conditions, many of the women still bear the burden of domestic responsibilities once they return home. Although there is evidence from surveys of some men taking on a small proportion of domestic tasks, the primary domestic responsibility still falls overwhelmingly on the women. Despite working the longest hours in fruit, Venegas (1992a) found that on average women worked an additional 3 hours once they returned home, having to wash, cook and clean to meet their families' needs for the next day. Fruit work is also concentrated during the summer school holidays, and there is little childcare provision other than family members and friends, so that the juggling act is constant. In contrast to the intense strain of work during the season, women suffer boredom and isolation in the home during the long winter months. There are high levels of unemployment amongst all temporary fruit workers, but the women suffer the longest and severest levels of unemployment in comparison to men. The incidence of poverty amongst temporary fruit households is also very high. The strain and tensions all these problems cause is associated with increased domestic violence (Díaz 1991; Venegas 1992a. Barrientos 1996).

Despite the crucial role female labour thus plays in sustaining fruit exports, and their large numbers, the *temporeras* remain a largely marginalised group within Chilean society. This marginalisation is reflected in a number of ways. Chileans are aware of the existence of the *temporeras*, and yet within the 'schizophrenic' culture which the gross inequality of dictatorship and liberalisation has created, the middle and upper classes block out any problems arising from arduous work or poverty. The focus is always on success, never its costs, particularly if those costs are borne by women. This is reflected in the long sections of the press given over to analysing the fruit sector (for example, the leading newspaper *El Mercurio* carries a weekly agricultural supplement, *Revista del Campo*, which devotes a whole section to fruit exports), yet the problems of the *temporeras* will rarely get a snippet. Socially, in the macho rural culture, where sexism, racism and classism predominate, and the producers and exporters are virtually all wealthy men, the *temporeras* are presented as 'housewives' entering fruit work for 'pin money', whose problems are of no concern (PREALC 1990). The fact that the majority of these women are wholly dependent on their income from fruit work for the survival of themselves and their families is ignored.

THE EMPOWERING EFFECT OF AGRIBUSINESS

However, despite the problems, suffering, arduous work, low pay, insecurity, double day and their marginalisation, I also want to examine another aspect, which underlines the contradictions within the transformation they have experienced. Numerous researchers and case studies have found that large numbers of these women *like* working in fruit, do not want to return to their previous situations, and given the alternatives would not want to take up different work. One important survey found that 92 per cent of the women temporary workers interviewed replied that they liked fruit work (Rodriguez and Venegas 1991). The advantages fruit work has brought to tens of thousands of women has also had an important impact on their potential empowerment.

Under the traditional rural system women always worked, and were bought into production in the fields if needed in harvesting. But women's work was often 'invisible', on the peasant plot or in employment on the hacienda. They had little or no independent source of income, except for employment in domestic service, which was and is viewed by many of the women as another form of ill-paid and isolated servitude. Fruit work has transformed this situation, if only for 3–6 months of the year. At the height of the season, large numbers of women enter waged employment in their own right. As they are able to earn some of the higher wages in the fruit sector in the packing houses (albeit through high productivity and long hours), they have thus not only become independent wage earners, but in many cases the main income earner of the household for the duration of the season (Venegas 1992a; Barrientos 1996).

Fruit work has thus provided a partial form of liberation from many of the shackles of the traditional gender division of labour. It has allowed women the identity of a wage worker in their own right, given them greater independence, let them become a major contributor to the family income and has enhanced their bargaining position within the household. It has also had a major effect on the socialisation of women beyond the confines of their extended family and immediate community. Large numbers of women, often from diverse back-grounds, are bought together within the fields and packing houses, allowing the development of a network and social communication (Venegas 1992a; Vogel 1995). At an individual level, therefore, agribu-siness has provided a form of empowerment by enhancing a sense of self-esteem, and at a social level it has provided a context in which women have new opportunities to organise collectively to enhance their power.

But the process of change has not been even. Whilst on one level breaking down traditional gender relations, agribusiness has also recreated the gendered division of labour in a new form to meet its requirements. Women are employed in large numbers at specific times of the year only to undertake particular functions, partly reflecting their perceived 'nimble fingers', but primarily to meet the massive surge in demand for labour at the height of the season. Agribusiness relies on their return to the home in the off-season 'blue months', where the traditional division of labour still predominates, to provide a reliable source of labour which can be re-tapped year after year. But at the height of the season, women are brought together in large numbers, in one of the country's key export sectors, giving the women themselves potential power. This power, though, has not yet been translated into a coherent force, either economically, socially or politically. Therefore, it is a contradictory position for women, on the one hand being marginalised and disempowered, on the other being empowered. However, much of their potential empowerment remains untapped, which is reflected in their low level of union organisation and lack of influence on state policy.

UNION ORGANISATION AND WOMEN TEMPORARY WORKERS

To be translated into an effective force, empowerment needs to go beyond the experience of fragmented individuals and be expressed through the organisation of those women into a coherent group. The traditional form of organisation of labour in relation to employers has been through workplace-based trade unions. Rural trade unions grew rapidly during the 1960s and early 1970s during the period of agrarian reform. But given women were often denied independent employment, and even under the agrarian reform women were seen as subordinate to men, these unions were primarily male-dominated (Bradshaw 1990).[4]

After the 1973 coup, trade unions were effectively outlawed through extensive military repression, especially in the countryside, where the conflict between traditional landowners and trade unions under agrarian reform prior to the coup had been intense. With the growth of fruit production during the late 1970–80s, the new producers and exporters often had a preference for female labour, because women did not have a tradition in union organisation or working practices and were less likely to rebel against the low paid, insecure work provided (Kay and Silva 1992). The fruit growers and exporters did particularly well during the period of dictatorship, when free market conditions were enforced, experiencing their most spectacular rates of growth during the 1980s, largely on the basis of the cheap and flexible temporary female labour force which liberalisation and high levels of rural poverty generated for them.[5]

With the return to democracy, trade unions have been fully legalised and have recovered some of their membership. The number of unionised workers increased from 10 per cent of the occupied labour force in 1988 to 15 per cent in 1991 (although it has fallen slightly since). However, democracy has not removed the deep effects of years of repression, especially in agriculture. Amongst temporary workers in the fruit export sector, union membership is very low, with only 1 per cent belonging to trade unions (Falabella 1993). Hence the strength of traditional trade unions as a form of labour organisation is extremely weak in this sector. There are a number of explanations for this low level of membership. Despite reform of Pinochet's Labour Code, trade unions still do not have a legal right to collective negotiation on behalf of temporary workers, thus they have no incentive to join them. Producers and exporters often know who the activists are and can effectively blacklist them. This is especially so in rural communities where the same labour is re-employed annually, and given women are more likely to work close to home than men, they are particularly vulnerable. Thus with no job security, and under conditions of chronic poverty, where the pressure of maintaining a family is paramount in women's priorities, union activism remains a risky venture. The ability to join a work-based trade union is also limited by a number of other factors, especially for flexible female labour. Whilst some women return to the same employers year after year, the work is temporary, insecure and there is a high labour turnover. Women also work the longest hours and have the burden of the double day with extremely long, uninterrupted hours of work. This means that women workers have virtually no time to participate in trade union activity during the season, have long periods away from the workplace and no certainty of returning to the same employer. The high flexibility of labour, use of non-traditional working practices and deregulation of labour all run counter to traditional forms of labour organisation and expectations, based on more stable working practices. Rodriguez and Venegas (1991) found that only 29 per cent of women temporary workers had a good opinion of trade unions, and 59 per cent had no opinion or had no real knowledge of trade unions, suggesting that many women do not relate to traditional rural unions at all.

Interviews suggest that many women, who have traditionally been excluded from formal rural employment and trade union representation, do not necessarily aspire to traditional agreements. On the contrary, many women workers embrace the flexibility that fruit employment offers. In addition, the needs of women relate not only to their pay and conditions within the workplace. There are a whole series of issues such as employment in the off-season, childcare and domestic responsibilities, education and technical training, social and financial support which are also of prime importance to women, which hierarchical male unions do not relate to. It is a long struggle to change entrenched traditional male attitudes and practices within the rural unions, particularly their focus on the productive role of their members in the workplace, in isolation from the reproductive role which is of major concern to women trying to balance work and domestic responsibilities (Bradshaw 1990).

The trade unions have also failed to have the legal right to collective negotiation extended to the *temporeros*, even though most permanent workers have benefited from this right under the transition to democracy, and so the formal power of the employers in agro-exports remains supreme. The male hierarchical structure of traditional unions is an anathema to the notion of empowerment of women at the grass-roots, and the women themselves are often able to exert their power through other more 'subversive' means. The fact that they are working at the forefront of one of Chile's key export sectors, with a product which is highly perishable, gives them potential economic power. As the women themselves are aware, at the height of the season, when the producers and exporters are working to stringent schedules, and the sun is at its fiercest, they only have to fold their arms for a short time for the fruit to be at risk. This gives them a strong but temporary bargaining position in relation to their employers, and ultimately more formal agreements would be required to consolidate gains. But it is an indication of the potential empowerment which exists, independently of any union organisation, arising out of the dynamics of change resulting from the dominance of agribusiness.

Traditional peasant unions are, however, being forced to make gradual changes to their perceptions of women workers, largely as a result of the active and forceful participation of some of the women at the base. The Comisión Nacional Campesina (CNC) has an active Women's Department, which was established in 1986. It campaigns vigorously on issues relating to the *temporeras*, attempting to change traditional attitudes and policies within the union sector, as well as applying pressure for policy changes by the state and employers towards the *temporeras*. These relate especially to issues of pay and conditions, social and welfare provision, crèches and childcare facilities, and the use of pesticides and chemicals which are seriously affecting the health of those working in fruit. They are an important source of information on the problems faced by women working in agriculture, and provide information and support to a large number of unions in the rural sector. In addition, the Women's Department of the CNC works closely with NGOs, women's groups and other national and international organisations to promote the problems of women working in agriculture, and especially the *temporeras*. However, union representation is only one aspect affecting the empowerment of women, we must also examine state and grassroots organisation relating to the *temporeras*.

STATE POLICIES AFFECTING THE TEMPORARY FRUIT WORKERS UNDER THE TRANSITION TO DEMOCRACY

The transition to democracy, initiated in 1990, marked a significant social and political change in contrast to the extremely repressive conditions under the military. Aylwin's government, and that of his successor since 1994, Eduardo Frei, is based on a coalition of Christian Democrat and Socialist Parties called *Concertación*. The central plank in the government's policy has been 'Equity with Growth', with the aim of reducing the high levels of poverty and inequality endured under the dictatorship, and addressing the problems of disadvantaged groups (especially women and youth). Women's organisations played an important role in helping to undermine the military dictatorship, and the democratic government has formally taken up the issue of women's oppression. It has set up a unit under the Ministry of Planning (SERNAM) with the specific function of addressing the problems of women, and has charged other government organisations with addressing the specific needs of women in combating urban and rural poverty (Matear 1995). Within *Concertación*, however, there are different perceptions of the role of women, with the dominant Christian Democrats still taking a more traditional view of women's role in society.

The government has combined this social strategy with a full acceptance of the neo-liberal model as the basis for attaining economic expansion. It has continued to promote export-led growth, based on primary goods (copper, fruit, forestry and fish). In embracing the free market approach, it further reduced import tariffs, extended privatisation and, with certain provisos, has continued the policy of deregulation of the economy. The government's concentration on the need to maintain healthy economic indicators has met with success since 1990, with high levels of growth averaging over 6 per cent per annum in 1990–3, and low unemployment and inflation (Economist Intelligence Unit 1995). As a result, Chile has been acclaimed as an economic miracle, and proof of the benefits which can be gained from combining economic liberalisation and democracy. However, there is a question as to the extent the government can genuinely enhance the position of the *temporeras* given its committment to the fruit exporters at the heart of its export-led strategy.

The dual policy of equity and growth has only had a limited impact on the temporary fruit workers, despite acknowledgement of their problems by the government. Policies affecting the fruit workers can broadly be grouped into two areas: (i) social policies and (ii) changes to the labour code. These two areas reflect the dual role women have in combining their productive and reproductive roles as workers in a key export sector, but they have been addressed quite separately. Whereas traditional unions have tended to focus on women's productive role through organisation based within the workplace, the state has tended to focus on the women temporary workers' reproductive role through extending social policies for them. A number of government organisations have been proactive at the level of social policies, and various projects have been initiated by the government. The main project involves the provision of childcare facilities, which is minimal for temporary workers. By the 1993/4 season 40 kindergartens in 6 regions had been set up under a programme co-ordinated by SERNAM. They operate during the height of the season and are available to children aged 2–12 years, opening from 8 am to 7 pm. They not only provide children with food, recreational and play facilities, but also cover health needs and extend information and support to the women on their rights, health, sexuality and other related issues. This is an important initiative, but these centres offer limited provision given they are only available in the school holidays (occupying school premises), and close at 7 pm even though the majority of women are in packing and work late into the night. By 1993 only 2011 mothers had been able to benefit from this provision, a tiny proportion of the total number employed. An additional programme has been co-ordinated by JUNJI, providing day-care for pre-school children aged 2–5 years (Barría 1992; Matear 1995). SERNAM and other government organisations have also become involved in some of the community-based organisations supporting the *temporeras*, which I shall discuss in the next section.

The second key area where government policy has affected the temporary workers has been through the reform of the Labour Code, which affects women as productive workers. It was under this code that Pinochet had deregulated labour markets, facilitating the extensive use of cheap, temporary and highly flexible labour in fruit production, and curtailed trade union rights. President Aylwin's reform of the Labour Code has enhanced the legal status of trade unions, recognised temporary workers as a specific category, and introduced tighter rules covering the formalisation of contracts of employment. Legislation has also improved regulations covering the provision of adequate and hygienic lodgings (mainly affecting male migrant labour to the north), the adequate and hygienic provision of facilities for food consumption and provision by the employers; and the provision of transport for employees over 3 km away where public transport is absent (Venegas 1993).

Despite all these and other more general reforms, the democratic government has consistently failed to address one central issue: after five years of democracy, temporary workers are still denied the legal right to collective negotiation by trade unions. Under the reformed Labour Code, employers are only legally subject to collective negotiation where there are 15 or more permanent employees. Given the vast majority (over 80 per cent) of fruit employment is temporary, this applies to very few employers, and anyway the percentage of female permanent employment in fruit production is negligible. In 1995 a proposal was put to Congress to grant a legal right to collective negotiation at the beginning of the season only, but it is unlikely that this proposal will be enacted if it is opposed by the right (reflecting the all-powerful interests of agribusiness). As a result this largely female temporary fruit workforce has not had the legal right to collective negotiation over key problems which affect them as productive workers. Many aspects of their pay and conditions of work remain unaddressed, despite more than five years of democracy.

Even where legislation does exist covering their working conditions, case studies have found that over 50 per cent of women temporary workers have no contract of employment at all, and are thus not formally covered by legislation. They do not have contracts, either because their employer has not provided one or because the workers themselves see no point in having 20.6 per cent of their pay deducted for health and pension insurance, which as temporary workers they are never likely to be able to make sufficient contributions to genuinely benefit from (Díaz 1991; Venegas 1992a and 1993). The majority of women temporary workers, therefore, do not even have the privilege of the minimal legal protection which should be available to them. With lack of enforcement by the government, this female labour force remains marginalised and highly exploited in one of the most important export sectors of the economy. Despite playing an important part in sustaining the growth of the economy, they have not benefited in a fundamental way from the policy of equity.

This raises the question of whether a policy of equity with growth within the framework of the neo-liberal economic model is capable of addressing the overall needs of women workers, given economic considerations take precedence. It also raises the question as to whether government policies initiated from the top can genuinely enhance the empowerment of women, especially if this runs counter to the prevailing economic power of agribusiness. By extending social provision to the *temporeras*, the state is taking an important step towards recognising the burden women carry in the summer, which did not exist previously. At the same time social provision such as nurseries maintains the supply of female labour to agribusiness, and are in the employers' interest as well. On the other hand, the failure to extend to temporary fruit workers the basic legal right of collective negotiation gives the women little legal power to combat the adverse conditions they have to endure in work, or lengthy hours they have to work to make a basic income. The policies of the government, it could be argued, focus on facilitating the supply of a flexible female workforce, whilst doing little to ameliorate the high exploitation of labour. For the government, extending legal negotiating rights to the temporary workers could reduce the comparative cost advantage of Chilean fruit in a volatile and competitive global market, undermining one of the lynchpins of the neo-liberal economic model. By separating out policies relating to the women's productive and reproductive roles, and only partially addressing the latter to enhance the female supply of labour at the height of the season, government policy has failed to address genuinely the burden women endure, or the gender division of labour recreated by agribusiness. The needs of the temporary women workers remain subordinate to the needs of agribusiness and maintenance of the neo-liberal export model.

NEW FORMS OF ORGANISATION AMONGST THE *TEMPORERAS*

Trade unions and the state both rely on traditional male hierarchical structures, which assume a rigid gendered division of labour between work and home, and stable working practices of permanent employment. They have thus both proved limited in their ability to address the new highly flexible forms of work, based on a reconstructed gender division where women play a key role in the waged labour force at specific times, but where monocultivation itself generates an intense seasonal dislocation between employment and unemployment, and women are forced back into the home out of season. New forms of employment in fruit require new forms of labour organisation, and women as the key workers in the sector have a major role to play.

Some interesting developments have taken place at the grassroots, where the organisation and empowerment of women temporary workers appears to have some potential. Given there are clear problems with workplace organisation, an alternative location for organisation of temporary labour lies within the local communities where the work is located. Community-based organisation can act as a focal point during periods of employment and unemployment, irrelevant of movement between different local employers. Community-based organisation can act as a forum for women to formulate their own needs and voice their own demands in relation to employers, trade unions and the state. It allows women to cross the divide between the different aspects of their life: it allows the combining of demands relating to pay and conditions with other issues such as childcare and social provision; and it provides continuity for a fragmented workforce throughout the long periods of unemployment, when time for labour organisation is more feasible and the need to find alternative sources of income is paramount.

An important co-ordinating force in the setting up of community-based organisation has been the NGOs. These played an important role in Chile during the years of military dictatorship and structural adjustment (Barrientos 1993), although community-based organisation in which women played a key role was always much stronger in the urban sector during the recession of the 1980s than in the countryside. Since the return to democracy, community-based organisations nationally have declined in number, and NGO funding has been reduced quite radically. However, many remaining NGOs have not only played a community role, but have also acted as a link between community, women's organisations, trade unions and the state. Local NGOs working in fruit have developed a number of small but successful projects based on community organisation, providing an important service to local workers. These act as a point of communication and support for temporary workers, especially women. They offer a range of services to temporary workers, including childcare during the fruit season, information on legal and welfare rights, health education, communal purchasing, education and training and capacitation in seeking non-fruit income during the blue months, and women's support groups. In addition, there are a number of smaller projects relating to specific aspects, such as the training of temporary workers in the off-season.[6]

The success of these projects has been recognised by the government, which has also set up its own centres in the Valleys of Maipo and Cachapoal, attempting to co-ordinate with local NGOs, trade unions and employers (although the latter have proved less forthcoming). These centres were modelled in part on centres such as the *Casa de Temporeros* in Santa María, an NGO-funded centre for temporary workers in the Aconcagua Valley, north of Santiago. The purpose of the centres is to provide permanent premises and institutional support for the provision of services and information to local temporary fruit workers. These services include childcare, help with the provision of food and basic necessities, information on state services and legal rights, education and training, and support for small projects to provide out-of-season employment and incomes, often through the formation of *microempresas* (Venegas 1993).

The traditional trade union leaders are sceptical about the potential of projects such as these, and have kept their distance. But if these types of activity, which are important in providing immediate support for temporary workers, are to play a greater role in providing the basis for independent labour organisation they need also to be linked to the workplace, and in this way can provide a more integrated basis for responding to women's triple roles in work, the household and the community. An example of the potential of such organisation can have is in the small but important fruit commune of Santa María in the Aconcagua Valley, where a local inter-firm union was established in 1989, linking workplace demands with social, self-help and out of season projects. The membership of this union was 21 per cent of the local fruit workers by 1993, much higher than the national percentage (Falabella 1993). Most of the membership are temporary workers, with a large female membership and strong representation of women in the leadership.

Despite their potential, these projects have a number of problems. By being located within the community, they reach women living within close proximity of their employment only, and they do not relate easily to the large numbers of fruit workers who are bussed into the fruit regions during the season. There are also problems in trying to confront age-old structures based on a clear division between work, home and the community. Community-based organisations tend to be fragmented, being set up by different NGOs or groups in different localities, and there is insufficient co-ordination between them. Although some NGOs remain in Chile, their funding has been greatly reduced, and there is little independent sources of funding for these types of projects, which require at a minimum a building or centre which can provide essential services and a meeting place. Where these projects combine involvement of the state, trade unions and NGOs, there is often a problem of dialogue between them, each having its own agenda, which does not necessarily reflect the voice of the women at the grassroots. In addition to this, there is an inherent problem of party political conflict within Chile, where hierarchical and heavily male-dominated political parties are each represented, especially within the trade unions and state, by their own 'line' over which there is little or no compromise. These tensions reflect the issue of who is empowering whom within the process of empowerment. Government and traditional union organisations tend to perceive empowerment as a 'top-down' process, in which they strive to retain control. NGOs working at the grassroots attempting to mediate between the different levels of organisation are caught up in this contradiction, and as Elsa Dawson discusses in this volume, it is not always easy to assess the extent to which the women themselves are genuinely being empowered, such that they have a primary impact on the decision-making process reflecting their needs and aspirations.

Despite these problems, and the limitations of community-based projects to date, they do provide the basis for the organisation of the women themselves. Although they suffer from heterogeneity, fragmentation and marginalisation, fruit work has bought large numbers of women together in paid employment, giving them a common identity as *temporeras*. At the height of the season these women have great potential economic power, as the producers, exporters and state are only too aware (a one hour stoppage at a crucial moment can be devastating for an individual producer). To date, the legacy of political repression, the power of agribusiness and the persistence of a macho culture have succeeded in maintaining these women in a fragmented and subordinate position, reflected in their lack of a legal right to collective negotiation. However, if new forms of community organisation which break down the social and political isolation of the women temporary workers could be harnessed to their potential economic strength as workers in a key export sector, this could help provide the basis for enhancing their empowerment in the future, and might force a change in the labour laws. To be effective in relation to agribusiness, therefore, the process of empowerment needs to incorporate mechanisms for collective forms of power, both within the *temporeras* as a group, which community organisation facilitates, and simultaneously collective forms of power over the agro-export employers, which union organisation facilitates. Agribusiness has thus generated the potential for the enhanced empowerment of women workers.

CONCLUDING REMARKS

In conclusion, therefore, the all-prevailing force of agribusiness in the fruit-growing regions has had a contradictory effect. On the one hand,

```
            Castlegar 365-1229
            ***************




                Selkirk College
                   Library


atron's name:BARISOFF, SHAUNA LYNN

   title:Privatization, law, and t
   author:Cossman, Brenda.
 tem id:B001079359
      due:7/11/2005,23:59

   title:Women and empowerment : i
   author:Afshar, Haleh, 1944-
 tem id:B001128917
      due:7/11/2005,23:59
```

it has released women from their traditional, invisible role as rural workers, making their work more visible and bringing them together during the season, and in that sense the market itself has acted as a facilitator of empowerment. On the other hand, it has reinforced a gendered division of labour in which women endure the double burden of domestic responsibility and waged work. Their burden includes the extremes of working 16 hours a day in the summer and having no means of support for the family during the winter. But these extreme pressures have also bought the contradiction between women's productive and reproductive roles to the fore.

State policy and traditional trade unions have tended to focus either on women's productive or their reproductive role in isolation from each other. New forms of organisation amongst the *temporeras* have been community-based, transgressing the division between work and home, and addressing the extremes of work and unemployment these women face. They provide the potential for new forms of labour organisation based in the community, in which the women workers are empowered to address the issues which are key to them, challenging the traditional hierarchical norms of state and trade unions. Ultimately, though, the government must extend the right of collective negotiation to the *temporeras* if they are going to be able to confront and consolidate their position in relation to the immense financial power of agribusiness. But achieving this itself will be a reflection of the ability of the women's organisations to exert an influence over the state, and is thus an essential element in the process of empowerment itself.

NOTES

1. For a discussion of the process of agrarian reform and counter-reform, see for example: Gómez and Echeñique (1988); Hojman (1990 and 1993); Jarvis (1992); and Kay and Silva (1992).
2. Rodriguez and Venegas (1991) found that overall 30 per cent of women *temporeras* (27 per cent of men) came from towns of 15,000 inhabitants or more. However, there are regional differences, with a higher urban residence in the centre around Santiago, Gómez and Echeñique (1988) found that in the Aconcagua Valley north of Santiago 20 per cent of temporary workers (women and men) came from peasant households, 52 per cent came from towns and villages, and 28 per cent from cities. In 1993, 84 per cent of the

total population were estimated to be urban residents in Chile (World Bank1995).
3. The female participation rate in Chile has been rising rapidly since 1980, increasing from 28.7 per cent in 1980 to 38.5 per cent in 1993 (ILO 1994). A recent study of agribusiness in Mexico, where there is increasing specialisation in agro-exports and feminisation of the labour market, has also found the majority of women workers were over 21 years with children (Barrón 1994).
4. Much of the information for the section comes from information and interviews with members of the Comisión Nacional Campesina Women's Department.
5. Whilst women can earn better wages than men within the sector, Chilean fruit labour is still cheap relative to fruit workers in other countries. For example, it was estimated in 1988 that Chilean workers earned 20 times less than Californians doing similar work (Díaz 1991).
6. Much of the information regarding local community based organisations comes from interviews with *temporeras*, members of local NGOs and trade unions active in the field.

REFERENCES

Afshar, H. and C. Dennis (eds) (1992) *Women and Adjustment Policies in the Third World*, Basingstoke: Macmillan.
Asociación de Exportadores de Chile (1994) *Estadísticas de Exportaciones Hortofrutícolas, 1993-4*, Santiago.
Barría, L. (1992) *Políticas y Programas del Gobierno 1990/92*, Santiago, Ministerio de Agricultura, INDAP.
Barrientos, S. (1993) 'The Other Side of Economic Success: Poverty, Inequality and Women in Chile', in B. Evers (ed.), *Women and Economic Policy*, Oxford: Oxfam.
Barrientos, S. (1996) 'Flexible Work and Female Labour – The Global Integration of Chilean Fruit', in R. Auty and J. Toye (eds), *Challenging the Orthodoxies*, Basingstoke: Macmillan.
Barrón, A. (1994) 'Mexican Rural Women Wage Earners and Macro-economic Policies', in I. Bakker (ed.), *The Strategic Silence*, London: Zed Press.
Bradshaw, S. (1990) 'Women in Chilean Rural Society', in D. Hojman (ed.), *Neo-liberal Agriculture in Rural Chile*, Basingstoke: Macmillan.
Cruz, M.E. (1992) 'From Inquilino to Temporary Worker, From Hacienda to Rural Settlement', in C. Kay and P. Silva (eds), *Development and Change in the Chilean Countryside*, Amsterdam: CEDLA.
Díaz, E. (1991) *Investigación Participativa Acerca de las Trabajadoras Temporeras de la Fruta*, San Bernardo: Centro El Canelo de Nos.
Echeñique, J. (1990) 'Las Dos Caras de la Agricultura y las Políticas Posibles', *Proposiciones*, 18: 145–58.
Economist Intelligence Unit (1995) 'Chile Country Report 1994–5', London.
El Mercurio, various issues, Santiago, Chile.

Elson, D. and R. Pearson (1981)' "Nimble Fingers Make Cheap Workers", An Analysis of Women's Employment in Third World Export Manufacturing', *Feminist Review*, Spring, 87–107.

Falabella, G. (1993) 'Reestructuración y Respuesta sindical. La Experiencia en Santa María, Madre de la Fruta Chilena', *Revista de Economía y Trabajo*, PET, July–December, 1 (2): 239–60.

Fempress/Mujeres, various issues, Santiago.

Gómez, S. (1994) 'Algunas Caracteristicas del Modelo de Exportación de Fruta en Chile' Serie Estudios Sociales No. 59, November, Santiago: FLACSO.

Gómez, S. and J. Echeñique (1988) *La Agricultura Chilena, Las Dos Caras de la Modernización*, Santiago: FLACSO.

Hojman, D. (ed.) (1990) *Neo-liberal Agriculture in Rural Chile*, Basingstoke: Macmillan.

Hojman, D. (1992) *Chile: The Political Economy of Development and Democracy in the 1990s*, Basingstoke: Macmillan.

Hojman, D. (ed.) (1993) *Change in The Chilean Countryside*, Basingstoke: Macmillan.

International Labour Organization (ILO) (1995) *World Labour Report Data Base*, Geneva.

Jarvis, L. (1992) 'The Unraveling of Agrarian Reform' in C. Kay and P. Silva (eds), *Development and Change in the Chilean Countryside*, Amsterdam: CEDLA.

Kabeer, N. (1994) *Reversed Realities, Gender Hierarchies in Development Thought*, London: Verso.

Kay, C. (1993) 'The Agrarian Policy of the Aylwin Government: Continuity or Change', in D. Hojman (ed.), *Change In the Chilean Countryside*, Basingstoke: Macmillan.

Kay, C. and P. Silva (eds) (1992) *Development and Change in the Chilean Countryside*, Amsterdam: CEDLA.

Lago, M. S. (1987) 'Rural Women and the Neo-liberal Model in Chile', in C.D. Deere and M. Léon (eds), *Rural Women and State Policy. Feminist Perspectives on Latin American Agricultural Development*, Boulder: Westview Press.

Matear, A. (1995) 'The Servicio Nacional de la Mujer (SERNAM): Women and the Process of Democratic Transition in Chile 1990– 1993', in D. Hojman (ed.), *Neo-liberalism with a Human Face? The Politics and Economics of the Chilean Model*, Institute of Latin American Studies, University of Liverpool, Monograph Series No. 20.

Moser, C. (1993) *Gender Planning and Development, Theory, Practice and Training*, London: Routledge.

Petras J. and F. Leiva, with H. Veltmeyer (1994) *Democracy and Poverty in Chile, The Limits to Electoral Politics*, Boulder: Westview Press.

PREALC (1990) *Ciclos Ocupacionales y Disponibilidad de Mano de Obra Temporal en Dos Comunas del Valle de Aconcagua*, No. 344, Santiago.

Rodriguez, D. and S. Venegas (1989) *De Praderas A Parronales, Un Estudio sobre Estructura Agraria y Mercado Laboral en el Valle de Aconcagua*, Santiago: GEA.

Rodriguez, D. and S. Venegas (1991) *Los Trabajadores de la Fruta en Cifras*, Santiago, Universidad Academia de Humanismo Cristiano, Grupo de Estudios Agro Regionales.

Rowbotham, S and S. Mitter (1994) *Dignity and Daily Bread, New Forms of Economic Organising among Poor Women in the Third World and the First*, London: Routledge.

Stichter, S. and J. Parpart (eds) (1990) *Women, Employment and the Family in the International Division of Labour*, London: Macmillan.

Thrupp, L.A. (1995) *Bittersweet Harvests for Global Supermarkets: Challenges in Latin America's Agricultural Export Boom*, Baltimore: World Resources Institute.

Venegas, S. (1992a) *Una Gota al Dia... Un Chorro Al Año. El Impacto Social de la Expansión Frutícola*, Santiago: GEA.

Venegas, S. (1992b) *Mujer Rural: Campesinas y Temporeras*, Santiago: Ministerio de Agricultura, INDAP.

Venegas, S. (1993) 'Programas de apoyo a temporeros y temporeras en Chile', in S. Gómez and E. Klein, *Los Pobres del Campo, El Trabajador Eventual*, Santiago: Organización Internacional del Trabajo.

Venegas, S. (1995) 'Las Temporeras de la Fruta en Chile', in *Mujer, Relaciones de Género en la Agricultura*, Santiago: Centro de Estudios para el Desarrollo de la Mujer.

Vogel, I (1995). 'Gender and the Labour Market: Women's Experiences of Labour Force Participation in Chile,' in D. Hojman (ed.), *Neo-liberalism with a Human Face? The Politics and Economics of the Chilean Model*, Institute of Latin American Studies, University of Liverpool Monograph Series No. 20.

Waylen, G. (1992) 'Women, Authoritarianism and Market Liberalisation in Chile, 1973–89' in H. Afshar and C. Dennis (eds), *Women and Adjustment Policies in the Third World*, Basingstoke: Macmillan.

World Bank (1995) 'Workers in an Integrating World', *World Development Report*, New York: Oxford University Press.

3 Gender and Rural–Urban Migration in China
Delia Davin

Migration is one of the most important economic, demographic and social phenomena in China today, involving the transfer of tens of millions of people from villages where they are employed – or underemployed – in agriculture, to cities, towns, or other rural areas, where they hope they will find better economic opportunities. Migration has allowed the supply of cheap labour to remain buoyant in China's industrialising coastal regions, despite the extraordinarily rapid growth of the economy and of employment in these areas. Here, I focus on the gender aspects of this migration, attempting a preliminary discussion of the impact of migration on gender relations and the lives of women in the villages of the sending areas. Does the experience of migration empower the female migrant (usually a young woman), who may work long hours in poor conditions, but often earns more than anyone back home? When male migration leaves a woman without a husband in the village, is she empowered by being in charge of the household and the land, or disempowered, left to struggle with a heavy work burden in a sector of the economy characterised by low capitalisation and low productivity? It is too early to answer these questions fully, but we can begin to explore their dimensions.

The possible impact and implications of the internal migration in China are enormous and complex. The flow most commented on is, of course, of the migrants from the sending areas to the areas of destination. But equally important to China's development are the flows in the other direction, back to the sending areas, of cash remittances, information through letters, and returning migrants bringing new skills and ideas.

As this large-scale migration is still quite new, there have been few studies of it, and fewer still which cover gender issues. Much of what I have to say will therefore be rather speculative.[1]

CHINA'S 1990 CENSUS

Migration is 'a selective process affecting individuals with certain economic, social, educational and demographic characteristics' (Todaro 1976: 26). It is widely acknowledged that migration tends to involve a rather narrow range of economically active people in terms of age, and, sometimes, in terms of gender, altering the demographic balance of the sending areas. In many developing countries, it is mostly males who migrate to seek employment. In China, judging by evidence from the 1990 census which provided information on migration (Population Census Office, 1991 and 1993), the sexes are comparatively evenly balanced: of all migration recorded by the 1990 census, 57 per cent was male and 43 per cent female. However, this picture is likely to be somewhat misleading and does not reflect the complexity of the situation.[2]

Marriage in China almost invariably involves the bride moving to her husband's home. Moreover, it is still the norm for the woman to marry into a different village, possibly some distance away. Females who move within their own province are most likely to be marriage migrants. Comparatively few marriages would involve moving across provincial borders (Goldstein and Goldstein 1990).

In rural–urban migration, the focus of this chapter, men outnumber women in all categories, whether they come from cities, small towns or the countryside, and whether their destination is a small town or a city. Women made up 46 per cent of the total of migrants from the rural areas (Messkoub and Davin forthcoming). Although some of these migrants are also no doubt marriage migrants, we know that the great majority of rural-to-urban migrants move to urban areas in search of work. The 1990 census enumerators had to record the reason for the move under one of nine categories. The third of these categories – that of work/business/trade/commerce – is the most important nationally, accounting for almost 29 per cent of all inter-provincial movement and 42 per cent of movement by rural migrants. Thus the census confirms all the other evidence we have that economic migration is of major importance in migration between provinces in China.

GENDER ASPECTS OF MIGRATION

Changing sexual division of labour

It is generally recognised that where migration alters the sex balance in a sending area, it has the potential to alter the sexual division of labour. Parnwell says that a common response to migration is for the old, the very young or women to be drawn into work they would not otherwise have done (Parnwell 1993). He omits to point out the possibility that men may take on what is normally thought of as women's work, where there is heavy migration of women. Such developments will inevitably be affected by culture. For example, in Africa male migration from the rural areas normally results in a greater female participation in agriculture; in Pakistan, where the seclusion of women is favoured, it is more usual for a male relative to farm in place of a male migrant.

The data of China's 1990 Census, which show that the numbers of male and female migrants are not vastly different, probably masks considerable differences at the micro-level. In many cases, male and female migrants go to different places and find different types of work. Some flows are dominated by one sex or the other: for example, most migrants from Anhui to Beijing are women who go to do domestic work; and migration flows from some counties in Sichuan are dominated by young women who go to work in the new export industries of south-east China (Wan Shanping 1992). In other areas, many men leave the rural areas to do construction work, transport work or trading, while women remain in the villages.

As we could expect in such areas, there are many reports of the breakdown of the sexual division of labour. Women may take over most of the agricultural work, even doing tasks which traditionally were always performed by men. By contrast, in Anhui it has been reported that men cook, clean and even sew when the female members of their family have gone to work in the cities (Wan Shanping 1992).

Migration and childcare

All over rural China, old people take care of children whose parents are busy elsewhere. In some cases, the mother may be in the city, although young unmarried women outnumber married women among the migrants. Where a young father has migrated, the wife may have to work on the land and may look to the older generation for help with the children. Although old women certainly do more childcare than old men, men undoubtedly do more than they did in the past.

It is common practice in many developing countries for the children of migrants to be left in, or sent back to, the sending areas, where childcare is cheaper. However, in China, there are unique factors which encourage this. Under the household registration system, migrants to urban areas, even if they have obtained temporary residence permits, do not have the same rights as people with permanent urban household registration. Specifically, they cannot send their children to school in the urban areas, and do not have rights to free or low cost healthcare there.

These restrictions induce many migrants to send their children back to their home areas when they reach school age, even if they have not already done so earlier. Even migrant women who marry urban residents may face this problem, as the children's household registration follows that of their mother. I interviewed one new mother from Sichuan, who had married a man from Nanjing where they both worked. Her child's registration was in the remote village from which she had migrated. She was already saving to purchase permanent residence for her child in Nanjing, which she thought she would need to do at the cost of several tens of thousands of yuan, when the child reached school age. She had asked her mother if she would consider caring for the child later, but the mother had given notice that she could not on the grounds that she would have to care for her son's baby, 'a child of her own family'.

Other mothers return to the sending area to care for their child or children. In Sichuan I interviewed one grandmother, who cared both for her son's child, and for her daughter's child during the day. Her two sons and her daughter-in-law were working in Guangdong Province as was her daughter's husband. Her daughter had also worked there until the birth of her son. She was forced to stay in Sichuan after the birth of the baby because there were no childcare facilities at her Guangdong factory and her mother-in-law was dead. Her mother was prepared to care for the child during the day while she worked in her in-laws' fields but had refused to take total responsibility for him. She said, 'I can do that for my son and my daughter-in-law because we are all one family and they send money back home. My daughter is married so she belongs to another family.'

CIRCULATION AND THE INFLUENCE OF RETURNING MIGRANTS

Chinese migrants maintain close ties with their home villages. In Sichuan we were told repeatedly that between 70 per cent and 90 per cent of them return home at least once a year, usually at Spring Festival. Such ties are, of course, commonplace elsewhere in the developing world, but again the Chinese experience is shaped by legal institutions.

We have already seen how even legally registered migrants lack certain rights in the urban areas. One of the justifications offered for denying them rights to the urban system of social security is that their security is supplied by their right to land back in their villages. Rural migrants retain a link with their villages through their right to that land, which is cultivated for them, usually by other family members, in their absence.

Migrants also lack other types of security in the urban areas. They are usually on quite short-term contracts and can be fired if their enterprise runs into problems. They are sometimes rounded up and bussed out of town by urban authorities, who feel that they pose too many problems. Although a temporary residence permit affords some protection, it costs money and in many towns must be frequently renewed at the police station. Only the most successful migrants could consider purchasing a permanent residence permit which was said to cost 20,000–100,000 yuan in Beijing, or 4,000–20,000 in Shanghai in the early 1990s (*Jingji Wanbao* 1994; *Wenzhaibao* 1993).

Negative images of migrants are constantly put forward in the media, and open hostility is not infrequently shown to them on the street. Many migrants live in poor shanty-type accommodation which they must hesitate to improve given the risk that it could be razed to the ground in an anti-migrant drive (*Wenhuibao*, August 1994). All in all, migrants are not made welcome in the city, and not surprisingly most see their sojourn there as temporary.

All these factors contribute to a situation in which most rural–urban migration in China is of the so-called circulation type, where each year a number of young migrants depart for the city; most will return, probably permanently, in a few years' time, and their place be taken by other young hopefuls.

Obviously the effects of this circulation migration are likely to differ in important ways from migration which is very long-term or permanent. Notably, circulation produces greater and more continuous flows of information, skills, capital, innovation and life-style influences back to the villages with all sorts of implications for developments there.

THE INFLUENCE OF YOUNG FEMALE RETURNEES

Young women who leave the villages and come back after a few years' experience working in the towns are likely to have the greatest influence on gender relations and assumptions in their home areas. Although the final decision on their initial migration will normally be taken by a male head of household, they inevitably take some part in reaching this decision. Their very departure challenges the traditional concept of woman as the 'inside person' responsible for the home. The cash remittances sent home by some female migrants make them the biggest contributors to the shared family income.

Even when they are less significant, remittances always make a considerable difference. Few families appear to rely on them for subsistence; rather, they are able to set them aside for house construction, financing events such as weddings and investment in small 'sideline' production. We know from the work of Salaff in Hong Kong, Kung in Taiwan and Bell on Wuxi silk-workers that the mere fact that daughters become important wage-earners in the family does not mean that they are necessarily accorded equal status with their brothers (Salaff 1981; Kung 1983; Bell 1994). The boys, after all, remain in the family all their lives, unlike the girls, who marry out.

But girls do gain something from their contributions. They apparently feel a sense of self-esteem at repaying their families for their upbringing; they may be able to negotiate greater personal autonomy; they are likely to marry rather later than non-migrants; and they acquire savings, clothes and other personal property during their sojourn in the urban area (Wan Shanping 1992). In exceptional cases they may even use their earnings to purchase greater personal freedom. I interviewed one Sichuan migrant to Guangdong who had made a marriage arranged by her father which turned out unhappy. She said that during her father's lifetime she could do nothing about it. When he died, she applied for a divorce, which her husband was willing to agree to provided that she left her son with him and paid 7000 yuan for child support. She had found a factory job in the south at 600 yuan a month, specifically in order to save this sum. Once it was paid, she was looking forward to 'being able to save for my own future and help my mother'.

Young women who have worked in the city are easily identifiable on their return to the villages. They wear bright-coloured, more fashionable clothes, more expensive (and impractical) shoes and sport modern hairstyles. No doubt their appearance inspires other village girls to attempt to go to the city. Researching in Anhui, Wan Shanping found that the desire to buy clothes was an important motive for female migration. To what extent are these changes merely superficial? Have they changed in ways which are likely to bring changes to their villages?

There is evidence that a sojourn in the city can influence both the roles and attitudes of women. Most female migrants earn a wage which they receive into their own hands. Such is the gap between the poor counties and the booming coastal area that their monthly wage may be double, or even treble, the average per capita in their home villages. The knowledge that they are able to earn so much money must increase their sense of self-esteem. Even when they save and send most of their earnings back home, the experience must give them a sense of power and autonomy which working as part of the labour force of a peasant household could not give them. Later they are likely to carry into their marriages an expectation at least of some control over their new family budget.

Migrants to the towns are likely to be influenced by urban lifestyles and customs. The strongest influence will perhaps be on the young rural women who work as maids, because living within an urban family they become most intimately aware of a different way of life. However, factory workers who live in dormitories, too, are able to observe from real life, from magazines and from the television and films. They take back with them to the villages notions of love, more companionate modes of marriage, home comforts and luxuries, smaller families, and so on.

In all probability, for many individuals this will result in conflict and difficulty. Control over arranged marriages has long been an area of struggle in the Chinese rural family. In many areas, parents still expect to choose partners for their children and would certainly insist on a right of veto. The influence of urban ideas about courtship and love on whole cohorts of young women is likely to exacerbate such struggles, as peasants of the older generation will still see marriage as an important affair for the whole family. Older people are also likely to shake their heads at the extravagance of the young, when returnees seek to furnish and equip their houses, or dress themselves and their children, according to their new tastes.

The returnees may experience considerable difficulty in resettling in the countryside and feel deep frustration at the things they cannot change. Wan Shanping noted the dislike felt by young women who had lived in the cities for rural latrines; they found it hard to re-accustom themselves to these, and to other hardships which for most of their lives they had taken for granted.

THE FERTILITY OF RETURNEES

Much concern has been expressed in China by officials and in the media about the fertility of migrants (*Beijing Wanbao* 1994). Migrants in the urban areas are perceived as having too many children, because they are 'difficult to control' and 'no one is responsible for them'. Such concerns are perhaps understandable, for they are voiced by harassed urban officials, anxious to keep within their low birth quotas. The one-child family rule is strictly enforced in the cities and urban fertility is very low. The situation in the countryside is quite different. First, the regulations are less strict – peasant couples whose first child is a girl are usually allowed a second, and in a few areas, even a third birth is permitted. Secondly, the regulations are more commonly ignored in the rural areas.

However, there are other ways of looking at the problem. Many migrants come from poor remote areas of China, where fertility is still comparatively high. If they move as families to the urban areas, their fertility may indeed be higher than that of local people, but it is likely to be lower than it would have been had they remained in the villages. The difficulties associated with giving birth to, and bringing up, children in areas where they do not have rights to health and education, and the opportunity costs for the mother whose earning power will almost certainly be reduced, will be powerful inducements to migrants to restrict the size of their families.

Some migrant couples in urban areas may even have fewer children than the locals (*Yangcheng Wanbao* 1994). In the more common situation where married migrants leave their spouses in the villages their fertility will be reduced by separation, while single people who migrate tend to postpone marriage, at least by a year or two (Wan Shanping 1992). Finally, migrants to the urban areas will be influenced by the different aspirations of the urban population regarding family size, and are likely to be both more receptive to, and more knowledgeable about, birth control.

There are many reports of young women who have brought back capital to their villages with which they set up shops and even small manufacturing enterprises (Wan Shanping 1992). If such developments are general and sustained, they will contribute substantially towards changing gender relations. As managers in such enterprises, individual women will attain greater autonomy and respect, and also offer a new role model to other village women.

CONCLUSION

It is certain that the demands and expectations of young women who return to their villages after a period spent living in the urban areas will be affected by urban norms. This may lead to initial conflict, but it is likely that these women empowered by their experience and their savings, will successfully retain greater personal autonomy. As norms begin to change, there will be knock-on effects for non-migrant women. The impact of male migration on women in China is less certain. More time and fieldwork will be needed to assess it.

Migration will also create cash-flows into the villages, leading to a higher level of material consumption. Although women will remain disadvantaged by the marriage system and other customs, their earning power as migrants, and the money which they send and bring back to the villages, will help them to realise at least some of their demands. The economic, social, cultural and educational gap between the poor countryside and the prosperous urban areas of China will remain wide for the foreseeable future, but migration in the form it takes at present in China has the potential to return human and financial resources to the villages, and thus helps to prevent the gap becoming even wider.

ACKNOWLEDGEMENTS

Research on which this paper is based was carried out in 1994 in Sichuan Province, funded by grants from the Nuffield Foundation and from the Academic Development Fund of the University of Leeds, and travel grants from the Ford Foundation and the British Academy. Delia Davin would also like to thank her co-researcher, Dr Mahmood Messkoub of the School of Economic and Business Studies at the University of Leeds, and the Institute of Social Studies at the Hague.

NOTES

1. I should however acknowledge my debt to the many Chinese colleagues who have been generous with their time and their research data and especially to members of the Sichuan Academy of Social Sciences, to Ms Tan Shen, of the Chinese Academy of Social Sciences, and to Wan Shanping whose

MPhil on the migration of Anhui maids to Beijing has been extraordinarily useful to me (Wan Shanping 1992). I am also very grateful to the many Chinese with whom I have discussed migration, migrants themselves, officials, colleagues, students and chance acquaintances.

2. Although the 1990 census was based primarily on *de facto* rather than *de jure* residence, the instructions given to enumerators probably resulted in the omission from the migrant totals of millions of temporary migrants. Moreover, it seems probable that some migrants without any sort of residence papers might have sought to avoid enumeration, although I am uncertain how these omissions might have affected the figures for male and female migrants respectively.

REFERENCES

Beijing Wanbao (1994), 'Changing District in Shanghai Opens School for Migrant Labourers to Teach Law, Hygiene and Birth Control', 23 May.

Bell, L. (1994) 'For Better for Worse: Women and the World Market in Rural China', in *Modern China*, 20:2.

Goldstein, S. and Goldstein, A. (1990) in C. Nam W. Serrow and W. Sly (eds), *International Handbook on Internal Migration*, Westport, CT: Greenwood Press.

Jingji Wanbao (1994), 'Beijing to Charge 20–100 Thousand Yuan for Urban and Suburban Residency', 22 June.

Kung, L. (1983) *Factory Women in Taiwan*, New York: Columbia University Press.

Parnwell, M. (1993) *Population Movements and the Third World*, London: Routledge.

Salaff, J. (1981) *Working Daughters of Hong Kong: Filial Piety or Power in the Family?* Oxford: Oxford University Press.

Todaro, M. (1976) *Internal Migration in Developing Countries: A Review of Theory, Evidence, Methodology and Research Priorities*, Geneva: ILO.

Wan Shanping (1992) 'From Country to Capital: A Study of a Female Migrant Group in China', unpublished MPhil thesis, Oxford Brookes University.

Wenzhaibao (1993), 'Farmers Buy Residence Permits, at Cost of 4–20 Thousand Yuan, Popular again since 1992', 15 April.

Wenhuibao (1994), 'Putuo (Shanghai) Sends Hundreds of Migrants Home, Dismantles 5,000 square metres of Shacks', 19 August.

Yangcheng Wanbao (1994), 'Guangdong Finds Population Makes Fewer Babies than Natives Contrary to Previous Theory', 25 July.

Population Census Office, *10 per cent Sampling Tabulation in the 1990 Population Census of the People's Republic of China*, Statistical Publishing House and Population Census Office (1993) *Tabulation of the 1990 Population Census of the People's Republic of China* China Statistical Publishing House.

For a more detailed discussion of migration as reflected in the census, see M. Messkoub and D. Davin (forthcoming) 'Migration in China: Results from the 1990 Census', in T. Cannon (ed.), *China: Economic Growth, Population and the Environment*, Basingstoke: Macmillan.

4 The Grameen Bank Experiment: Empowerment of Women through Credit

Lutfun N. Khan Osmani

INTRODUCTION

In patriarchal societies, the subordinate status of women signifies a lack of empowerment – in the sense that they are unable to take part in the decision-making processes on an equal footing with men, either within the household or in the society at large. This lack of empowerment is manifested, *inter alia*, in the relative weakness of their bargaining power in situations characterised by 'co-operative conflict', i.e. situations in which it is in the interest of both men and women to co-operate, but in which a conflict of interest is also involved. Most intra-household decisions, including those relating to the allocation of household resources, involve such co-operative conflicts. In situations like these, the party with superior bargaining power can influence the outcome of the co-operative effort in their own favour. The inferior bargaining power of women, entailed by their lack of empowerment, thus biases the allocation of scarce household resources such as food and health-care against them, resulting in inferior nutritional status and poorer survival chances of women relative to men.[1]

This is especially true of those societies of Asia and Africa which Kandiyoti (1988) has characterised as 'classic patriarchy'.

It is said that women's lack of empowerment in these societies emanates to a large extent from their relative lack of participation in the so-called 'gainful' economic activities. By implication, it is generally believed that their increased participation in the economic sphere will lead to, or at least facilitate, their empowerment (e.g. Boserup 1970). This is a plausible hypothesis, but its validity needs to be tested empirically. In particular, one must consider the alternative hypothesis that women's earnings may be appropriated or at least controlled by

67

men, especially in those societies where women's subordination is so deeply rooted in socio-cultural norms that men's control over women is taken for granted even by women themselves. It is possible that in such cases women may not get empowered enough to take part in intra-household decision-making processes with the same bargaining power as men, even after becoming economically active.

In this chapter I examine the relationship between women's participation in economic activities and their empowerment in the sphere of intra-household decision-making. This examination is based on the experience of poor rural women in Bangladesh who have increasingly been able to enter the economic domain with the help of credit from the Grameen Bank.

First, the nature of the Grameen Bank, its difference from other banks, its lending process and the reasons for its success are briefly described. Then, a theoretical framework is presented, which makes it possible to assess the impact of the Bank's activities on the empowerment of women. Next, the impact is assessed based on a field survey conducted by the author in 1993. Finally, conclusions are presented.

THE GRAMEEN BANK

Grameen is a Bengali word, meaning 'rural'. Grameen Bank (GB) therefore means a rural bank. It started as an experimental model, with the modest aim of ensuring a secure source of income for a small number of assetless people. It subsequently received the status of a semi-government organisation in 1983. It has been expanding very fast since then. Starting from a handful of villages in a small area, it now covers over 15 per cent of all villages in the country, and is still expanding.

Grameen Bank is a target group-oriented credit institution which provides credit to rural households owning less than 0.5 acre of land. Normally, such poor households have very limited access to the formal credit market for several reasons: (1) they are incapable of providing collateral which is required as security for the granting of a loan; (2) the loan-seekers, the vast majority of whom are illiterate, are hardly capable of maintaining accounts which are necessary for the preparation of bankable projects; and (3) their repayment capacity is low because their propensity to consume is high at their subsistence level of living.

It differs from other banking institutions mainly in three ways. First, it confines its operations exclusively to the poorest of the poor. Second, it provides credit without any collateral. Poor rural women are particularly helped in this way as they are never able to provide collateral except through their husband, because any asset possessed by the poor family is owned by the husband. And finally, loanees do not have to go to the bank; agents from the bank communicate with them for banking operations. The latter is particularly helpful for the women as the existing sociocultural norms restrict women's mobility (though the trend is changing gradually). In fact, the Bank has made a special point of giving priority to women while allocating credit. As a result, it has over the years turned out to be essentially a bank for the poor women in rural areas. As much as 98 per cent of its borrowers now happen to be women.

Grameen Bank is going from strength to strength because it has been able to ensure an excellent repayment record (see, for example, Hossain 1988). Almost 99 per cent of its loans are repaid on time. Several factors have contributed to this excellent recovery performance: (1) personal interest and close supervision of activities in the field by the managing director/founder of the bank; (2) dedicated service of the bank workers, who have a keen interest in providing service to the poor; (3) providing loans for activities that generate regular income; (4) the system of repayment by small weekly instalments; and (5) group formation.

The practice of group formation helps in two distinct ways. First, it acts in lieu of tangible collateral. It is only natural that the borrowers might have the propensity to default in the absence of collateral. But this problem is tackled by the 'group liability' system as everyone is denied credit as punishment for default by anyone belonging to the group. In this way, peer group pressure is generated, inhibiting each member from defaulting. Second, as the group is formed by the borrowers themselves, it helps the Bank to select more desirable customers. The borrowers choose other members on the basis of mutual trust and personal understanding. As a result, a kind of homogeneous group is formed with the same level of skill (Osmani 1992).

The economic impact of the Grameen Bank has been extensively studied in recent years (e.g. Rahman 1986; Kumar 1987; Hossain 1988; Hossain and Afsar 1989; Pitt and Khandker 1994; Khandker *et al.* 1995). It has been observed, for instance, that the Bank has helped improve the living standard of at least 90 per cent of its loanees (Hossain 1988), and has successfully reached the target group, i.e. the poorest of the poor, especially landless rural women.[2]

But raising income is not the only way in which the Grameen Bank has benefited the rural women of Bangladesh. Apart from giving loans, the Bank also engages in a whole range of welfare activities and consciousness-raising programmes. Borrowers are given advice regarding family planning, first aid as well as personal and community hygiene. There are also free evening schools for them and their children. All borrowers are required to achieve the minimum literacy level of being able to sign their names, something that the majority of rural women cannot do. All these, together with the opportunity to engage in income-earning activities, ought to contribute towards the empowerment of women. It is the objective of this chapter to investigate the extent to which such empowerment has actually happened.

THEORETICAL CONSIDERATIONS

Whether or not women's involvement in income-earning activities will empower them to improve their position within the household depends crucially on the nature of the intra-household decision-making process. We therefore need a theoretical framework to describe the various determinants of a household's decisions regarding the allocation of resources among its members – in particular, between men and women.

One such theoretical framework is provided by the bargaining model used by economists in various contexts. This model is particularly useful for understanding the decision-making process within the household because it can capture one important aspect of the relationship between male and female members. This feature has been described as 'co-operative conflict' i.e. the simultaneous existence of co-operation and conflict (Sen 1990). In the household, different advantages are gained by different people through co-operation with each other. And yet conflicts exist owing to people's divergent interests. It may be in the interest of the husband, for example, to enjoy a greater share of the household resources and a lower share of the household activities as compared with his wife. Conflicts may thus exist in the background of co-operative behaviour, well hidden under conventional norms.

In such a situation, the actual division of household resources will depend on a process of implicit bargaining, and the person with greater bargaining power will enjoy the larger share of resources. The fact that traditionally men have exercised control over household resources and enjoyed a bigger share of the fruits is because they have had greater bargaining power as compared with women. This means that if the income-earning activities of women can in some way improve their bargaining power, then there is a good chance that their relative disadvantage will be reduced.

What then determines the bargaining power? In general, relative bargaining power, and hence the allocation of resources within a household, will depend on three characteristics of the bargaining parties: (1) their status quo or breakdown position, (2) perceived interests, and (3) perceived contribution to household resources.

Breakdown Position

The breakdown position represents how well each person can do without any co-operation. In other words, it represents the fall-back position in the event that co-operation breaks down, and as such plays a critical role in determining the strength or vulnerability of a person in the bargaining process. Given other things, if the breakdown position of a person is worse, then the outcome of the bargaining process will be less favourable for that person.

There are many reasons why the breakdown position is weak for women, especially the women of Bangladesh, as compared with the male members of the household:

1. Women's breakdown position is worse because of their gender-specific problems, e.g. the demands of pregnancy, childcare etc., which adversely affect their bargaining position everywhere, although in some societies more than in others.
2. There are some socially generated asymmetries between men and women, for example, in ownership of assets, acquisition of education and training; in access to certain kinds of economic activities (for which women are considered to be too fragile to be suitable), all of which undermine their breakdown position.
3. Their breakdown position is further undermined by certain social conventions. For example, a divorced woman is generally looked down on in the Bangladeshi society, especially in the lower stratum. Divorce is always assumed to be the fault of the woman in so far as she could not identify herself with the interests of her husband's family. Even her parental family often blames her and refuses to offer her any moral or material support. As a result, no matter what, women always try to co-operate in order to keep the

family together, rather than face the horrors of a divorced life, thereby weakening their bargaining power.

Perceived Interest

The outcome of the bargaining process will also depend on how clearly a person perceives his or her own interests. A person whose perceived interests take little cognisance of his or her own well-being may receive a worse deal in the bargaining outcome. This is particularly true in Bangladesh. Many women do not even realise their deprivation. Thus, it has been observed that 'if a typical Indian woman was asked about her personal "welfare", she would find the question unintelligible' (Sen 1990). Socialisation within this culture since childhood has led to these norms being internalised by women. In intra-household bargaining, therefore, women fare worse than men by being too willing to sacrifice their own interests.

Perceived Contribution

Given other things, bargaining power is greater for the person who is perceived to be making a larger contribution to the overall wealth of the family. Perceived contribution is different from actual contribution. In an integrated production system it is not always very clear who is actually producing what. It is even less clear in the case of women. Though women usually work harder and longer hours, they are not perceived to be making much contribution since their work does not normally make a direct financial contribution to the family as does men's. Since co-operative outcome goes in favour of those whose perceived contribution is greater women fare worse in the bargaining process.

This analysis shows that anything that can improve the breakdown position of women, or enhance their perception of self-interest, or increase their perceived contribution to the household, will strengthen their bargaining power and will thus enable them to improve their position within the household. One hypothesis is that women's involvement in income-earning activities will empower them on all three counts. In the first place, such involvement should improve their bargaining outcome directly by strengthening their 'breakdown' position as they become economically more independent. But it will also help indirectly by augmenting their perceived contribution to the household economy as they begin to earn money income in the same way as men. Finally, as women find that their contribution to the household is being valued more, they will become conscious of their importance, which, along with the exposure to the outside world that will come from work experience, will sharpen their perception of self-interest. This too will empower them to try to mould household decisions in their favour. Therefore, women's access to income-earning activities of the kind financed by the Grameen Bank should empower them in various ways to circumvent their present weakness in intra-household bargaining. It is from this theoretical perspective that we have attempted to analyse the findings of our field survey in the following section.

THE FINDINGS OF FIELD STUDY

The survey was initially designed to cover a sample of 100 households, with equal numbers of borrowers and non-borrowers. But several households had to be left out from the final enquiry for a number of reasons, so that we were finally left with 78 households equally divided between the two groups. In choosing the borrower (or project) households, the main criterion was that they must have had a fairly long association with the Grameen Bank since the beneficial effects, if any, should be more readily observed in such borrowers. In choosing the non-borrower (or control) households, great care was taken to ensure that they were as similar as possible to the borrowers in terms of socio-economic status except to the extent that they were not involved with the Grameen Bank or any other project of a similar nature.

Some of the salient characteristics of the two groups are compared in Table 4.1. As can be seen from this table, there is no statistically significant difference between the two groups in terms of land owner-ship, one of the basic determinants of socioeconomic status in rural Bangladesh. There is, however, a significant difference in terms of land holding, the project group having a significantly higher average hold-ing, but as we shall argue later, this is more likely to be a consequence of involvement with Grameen Bank than a difference in initial condi-tions. They are also very similar in terms of two other determinants of socio-economic success, namely, educational achievement, which is extremely low for both groups, and the size of labour force in the household.

Table 4.1 Comparative Characteristics of Borrower and Non-Borrower Households

Characteristics (per household)	Borrower	Non-Borrower
Annual household income (Tk)	18,948.00	12,285.00**
Annual per capita (ad.eq.) income (Tk)	4884.00	3435.00
Household size (persons)	4.79	4.21*
Household size (adult equivalents)	4.62	4.00*
Labour force in the household (persons)	2.10	1.92
Proportion of non-farm workers	0.79	0.46**
Proportion of self-employed workers	0.87	0.50**
Land owned (acres)	0.26	0.15
Operational land holding (acres)	0.49	0.31**
Schooling of husband (years)	1.49	1.79
Schooling of wife (years)	1.10	0.69

Note: The superscripts* and ** indicate that the difference between the two groups is statistically significant at 10 per cent and 5 per cent levels of significance respectively.

One very important difference between the two groups lies in the nature of their major occupations. In comparison with the control households, a far larger proportion of workers of the project households are engaged in self-employed non-farm activities as opposed to farming or wage labour. This finding corresponds with many earlier ones (e.g. Hossain 1988), which showed that people who were already engaged in self-employment in the non-farm sector had a greater propensity to associate with the Grameen Bank and other credit-giving agencies than those involved in farming and wage labour. In so far as this occupational difference may affect the economic achievement of the two groups, we shall try to allow for this effect while assessing the impact of involvement with the Bank.

The most obvious contrast between the two groups lies in the levels of their income. Despite having similar land ownership, educational achievement and size of labour force, the annual income of borrower households is on the average 50 per cent higher than that of non-borrowers. And even after adjusting for the fact that borrowers have a higher household size, their per capita income is still 40 per cent higher. This is an immediate indication of the income-raising effect of Grameen Bank's credit. In order to assess this effect more clearly, after adjusting for other possible effects, we have carried out a multivariate regression whose results are reported in Table 4.2.

Table 4.2 Regression on Per Capita Income

Variables	Coefficient	T-value
Household's land holding	−4.68	−0.42
Adult equivalents	−1333.65	−4.35**
Occupation dummy	2317.01	2.71**
Sample dummy	1641.47	1.91*
Constant	8320.04	6.52**

$R^2 = 0.31$; n = 78
F-statistic = 8.12; Significance of F = 0.0000

Note: Occupation dummy takes value 0 for households whose head's main occupation is agriculture (including farming and fishing) and 1 for those whose main occupation is non-agriculture. Sample dummy takes value 0 for control households and 1 for project households.
The superscript** indicates significant at 5 per cent level.

In addition to using a dummy variable for distinguishing between borrowers and non-borrowers, we used an occupational dummy, household size (in terms of adult equivalent) and landholding as additional variables. The occupational dummy was used in order to allow for the fact that self-employed non-farm workers are more predominant among borrowers, and the other two variables were used since the two groups differ significantly in these two respects as well. All but landholding turn out to have significant effects on per capita income. The most significant finding in the present context is that even after adjusting for other variables such as occupational pattern, household size and the amount of landholding, the borrowers appear to have a significantly higher per capita income than the non-borrowers. This confirms many previous findings (e.g. Fuglesang and Chandler 1986; Hossain 1988; Malkamäki 1991) that access to credit from the Grameen Bank has enabled many poor families to increase their income-earning capability.

In this chapter, our main concern is to see how this enhanced capability to earn income affects the situation of women *vis-à-vis* men. However, before we can discuss the gender dimension, it is necessary to consider certain features of the loans taken, and the way these were used by the women borrowers. We present some of the important features in Tables 4.3–4.5.

Table 4.3   Some Basic Information about Loans

Average length of GB membership	7.9 years
Average amount of first loan	Tk 1769
Average amount of present loan	Tk 7885
Average amount invested from present loan	Tk 3477
Average excess of loan over investment	Tk 4408
Average percentage of excess loan	50 per cent
Percentage of borrowers taking excess loan	85 per cent

As can be seen from Table 4.3, we do have a sample of fairly experienced borrowers with an average of nearly 8 years' association with the Grameen Bank. Over this period, the size of loan has increased nearly fourfold. However – and this is of crucial importance for the purpose of our present analysis – a large part of this increased loan is not invested in the activity for which it was meant. On the average, almost half of the money borrowed is not invested in the specified manner, and as many as 85 per cent of borrowers borrow more than they invest. Thus the practice of diverting borrowed money to other purposes is both widespread and large-scale in nature.

Table 4.4 sheds some light on the reasons of such diversion. When the first loans were taken, nearly eight years ago, 74 per cent of the loans were used for purposes such as rice husking, cow and goat fattening, poultry raising, etc. These are some of the activities in which the poor women of rural Bangladesh have always been involved, albeit on a small-scale, as part of household activity. So, in practice, the initial loans from the Grameen Bank enabled poor rural women to pursue their traditional activities on a slightly larger scale and geared more to the market than before. Over time, however, the financing of such activities has declined in importance; at the time that this research was undertaken, only about 15 per cent of loans were taken for these purposes, and only 3 per cent of the sample borrowers envisaged taking any future loan on these accounts.

At the same time, the activities that have gained in importance are the ones from which the women of Bangladesh still shy away. Thus, for example, fishing has emerged as an important credit-financed activity in the survey villages, but this is almost entirely a male-dominated activity. This means in practice that the money borrowed by the wife is utilised for buying nets and other equipment for the fisherman

Table 4.4 Purpose of Loan (number of loans taken for different purposes as percentage of total number of loans taken)

Major purposes of loan	First loan	Present loan	Future loan
Rice husking, cow/goat fattening, poultry raising	74.0	15.0	2.6
Buying nets for fishing	0.0	12.0	2.6
Land acquisition, construction of dwelling	0.0	20.5	90.0
Others	26.0	51.0	5.0

husband. Another emerging activity is to take other people's land in mortgage. In this case, the Grameen Bank borrower acts as a financial intermediary, passing on the loan to others in exchange for mortgaged land; but once again it is the husband who will actually work on that land. Until recently, Grameen Bank did not allow such financial intermediation; so the borrowers would take loans for some purpose allowed by the Bank, but would actually use a part of the money for land acquisition. That such acquisition accounts for a large part of the phenomenon of loan diversion mentioned earlier is confirmed by Table 4.5. But the Bank has recently legalised loans for land mortgage and other new activities such as construction of dwelling house. It is interesting to note that an overwhelming majority of borrowers plan to take future loans for these purposes (Table 4.5).

Table 4.5 The Uses of Excess Loan (number of borrowers using excess loan for various purposes as percentage of total number of excess borrowers)

Use of excess loan	Percentage of excess borrowers
To acquire land (purchase/mortgage)	57.6
To meet emergency cash needs	54.5
To acquire other assets	54.5
To meet daily household needs	42.4
To repay other loans	39.4
To construct/repair dwelling	12.1
Other uses	6.1

A common feature of all these new activities is that women are no longer involved directly. Thus, as the size of loan has increased over time, the women borrowers have found it increasingly difficult to use the money themselves. Obviously, the cultural norms prevailing in rural Bangladesh and the lack of opportunities are responsible for this. Given the restricted mobility of women outside home, the range of activities in which they can engage is necessarily small; as a result, their absorptive capacity is small i.e. their capacity to utilise credit is severely restricted. So the only way in which they can make full use of the increased volume of credit is by asking their husbands to undertake some credit-financed activity. What is emerging is a kind of joint enterprise in which the woman provides finance and the man provides labour and entrepreneurship. Similar results were found by Goetz and Sen Gupta (1996). It is important to keep this in mind when assessing the gender impact of the Grameen Bank.

We have mentioned that according to the bargaining model of the household, women's position *vis-à-vis* men should improve as a result of their involvement in income-earning activity. The picture now gets slightly complicated if such activity turns out to be a joint enterprise between men and women. However, the basic insight of the model should still hold since the woman plays a crucial role in the joint enterprise by dint of her access to credit. One should therefore expect that women's perception of their contribution to the family will improve as will her breakdown position, leading to greater bargaining power and as a result better access to resources and decision-making processes. There are some indications in our survey that this is indeed happening.

As can be seen from Table 4.6, there is no difference between borrowers and non-borrowers in terms of the proportion of women who feel that they work just as hard as their husbands, if not harder; but there is a very significant difference in the proportion of women who value their work no less than their husbands'. Among the borrowers, only about 3 per cent feel that the husband contributes more to the family, as compared with 23 per cent among non-borrowers. Obviously, women's perception of their contribution to the family is a lot stronger among borrowers as compared with non-borrowers.

Their breakdown position is also much stronger (Table 4.7). The borrower wives in our sample personally own significantly higher amounts of both land and non-land assets as compared with non-borrower wives. It is interesting to note that this difference between the two groups is not entirely a difference of initial conditions. It is true that the borrower women started off better by inheriting more land; but the crucial point is that the gap has widened over time as the borrowers have improved their land ownership while non-borrowers have lost theirs. This improved access to assets as well as their experience of involvement in income-earning activity has apparently given them the confidence that in a crisis they will be capable of looking after themselves. Thus, although the percentage of women who hope that parents/brothers will support them in such times is not significantly different as between the two groups, an overwhelming majority – some 82 per cent – of the borrowers feel capable of supporting themselves, while only 28 per cent among non-borrowers do so (Table 4.7).

Table 4.6 Comparison between Borrower and Non-borrower Women in Terms of Perceived Contribution and Perceived Interest (percentage of women with given attributes)

Attributes	Borrower	Non-borrower
Thinks she works no less hard for the family than husband	51.3	56.4
Thinks husband contributes more to the family	2.6	23.1**
Thinks unequal access to food in the family is fair	78.3	87.5
Thinks unequal access to education in the family is fair	26.3	38.5
Thinks unequal access to healthcare in the family is fair	5.3	5.3
Thinks unequal role in decision making in the family is fair	0.0	10.0**

Notes: The superscript ** indicates that the difference between the two groups is significant at the 5 per cent level, according to the chi-square test of association of attributes.

Table 4.7 Comparison between Borrower and Non-borrower Women in terms of Breakdown Position

Variables	Borrower	Non-borrower
Value of non-land assets owned by herself[a] (Tk)	2002.56	247.00**
Land owned by herself at present (acres)	0.16	0.04**
Land received through inheritance or previous marriage	0.11	0.07*
Percentage of women who think parents/brothers will support in a crisis	22.90	13.90

Table 4.7 (Contd)

Percentage of women who think they can support themselves fully if left alone	82.10	28.20**

Note: The superscript** indicates that group differences are significant at the 5 per cent level.

[a] Non-land assets include ornaments, furniture, cattle, cash savings, savings with the Grameen Bank, equipment and miscellaneous items.

While both perceived contribution and breakdown position have apparently improved as a result of access to credit from the Grameen Bank, there is a question mark over the other determinant of bargaining power, namely, perception of self-interest. As Table 4.6 shows, of all the criteria used to judge the women's perception of their self-interest, only one indicates a positive impact. Thus, not a single borrower thinks it fair that men and women should have an unequal role in decision-making within the family, whereas 10 per cent of the non-borrowers find nothing unfair in it. But by all other criteria, there is no difference between the two groups. For example, an overwhelming majority of borrowers (78 per cent) feel that unequal access to food within the family between men and women is fair, and in this respect they are no different from the non-borrowers. There is also no difference between the two groups in terms of the proportion of women who feel that unequal access to education and healthcare is fair. Obviously, centuries of cultural conditioning cannot be undone by less than a decade's involvement in income-earning activities.

Nevertheless, the changes that have occurred in the women's perception of their contribution to the family and in their breakdown position are not without value. Our data suggest that these may have resulted in empowering them and in giving them better access to resources and decision-making within the family. Thus, in Table 4.8, we note that a larger proportion of borrower wives receive money to spend from their husbands, and they can also spend this money as well as their own money much more freely compared to the non-borrower wives.

The two groups also differ in some aspects of reproductive behaviour. For example, there is a significant difference between them in terms of control over the decision to have children. When asked whether they ever had to give up the idea of having a baby because of their husband's opposition, only 3 per cent of the borrowers said they did, as compared with 13 per cent of non-borrowers.[3] This indicates that borrower wives have more autonomy than the non-borrower wives. Moreover, 61 per cent of the borrowers themselves claim that their role in decision-making with regard to family planning has improved after joining the Grameen Bank.

Table 4.8 Comparison in terms of Autonomy, Access, and Consumption Between Borrowers and Non-borrowers

Variable	Borrower	Non-borrower
Receives pin money from husband	95.0	82.1*
Can spend pin money freely	75.7	34.4**
Can spend own money freely	95.0	73.0*
Wife insisted on and adopted family planning measures	49.0	31.0
Wife could not have baby because of husband's opposition	3.0	13.0*
Wife claims to have gained weight on family planning after joining GB	61.0	n.a.
Claims males and females have equal access to food in her family	56.3	22.6*
Claims males and females have equal access to healthcare in her family	90.0	51.0**
Claims males and females have equal access to education in her family	39.0	25.0
Claims husband and wife have equal role in decision-making in her family	82.0	36.0**
Wife's meal score[a]	26.23	23.62*
Husband's meal score[a]	26.62	22.82**
Difference between the couple's meal scores[b]	0.38	−0.79*
Wife's annual consumption of personal effects (Tk)	719.97	606.69
Husband's annual consumption of personal effects (Tk)	534.10	458.97
Household's annual non-food consumption(Tk)	2317.79	1958.62

Notes:
(a) Meal score is defined as follows. Information was collected on how many times during the three days preceding the enquiry each member of the family (excepting breast-fed infants) had eaten eleven broad categories of food. Meal score was obtained by adding the number of times each food category was eaten. Thus meal score for person i is $\sum n_{ij}$, j= 1,...11, where j stands for category of food.
(b) Husband's meal score minus wife's meal score.
The superscripts * and ** indicate that the group differences are significant at the 10 per cent and 5 per cent levels respectively.

We also find that the proportion of women who claim that men and women have equal access to food, healthcare and decision-making processes within the family is higher among borrowers as compared with non-borrowers.

Apart from the respondents' claim about access to resources, data were also collected on the actual consumption pattern of individuals in the family. This is currently being analysed, but some preliminary results are worth reporting. As can be seen from Table 4.8, there is no significant difference between borrowers and non-borrowers in terms of non-food consumption (personal effects). By contrast, members of borrower households do have better access to food compared to non-borrowers.[4] However, it is surprising to note that the borrower women's access to food relative to their husbands is not better than that of non-borrowers. In fact, it is in the non-borrower households that wives seem to have better access to food relative to their husbands.[5] Thus, borrowers do not seem to have been empowered enough to alter the traditional pattern of intra-household allocation of consumption.

CONCLUSION

The evidence presented in this study demonstrates that access to credit from the Grameen Bank has gone some way towards empowering poor rural women in Bangladesh by improving two determinants of their bargaining power – viz. their perceived contribution to the family and their breakdown position. However, the success is far from complete. There is some evidence to suggest that the third determinant of bargaining power – perceived self-interest – may not have improved much. Besides, our evidence on the outcome of the bargaining process involving intra-household decision-making also gives mixed indication about the empowerment of women. Thus we find that the borrowers have gained greater autonomy in certain spheres of decision-making (such as freedom to spend money, reproductive decisions, etc.) and they also claim to have gained better access to food and healthcare. However, actual measurement of food and non-food consumption does not reveal superior outcome for the borrowers as compared with non-borrowers.

Two reasons can be cited for this incompleteness in empowerment. In the first place, even a prolonged exposure to income-earning activities in one generation cannot be expected to neutralise centuries of cultural conditioning completely. Secondly, low absorptive capacity of women, i.e. their limited ability to utilise large volumes of credit in the prevailing cultural conditions, increasingly requires them to lean on their husbands in order to make full use of the credit they obtain; but in the process any improvement that might occur in terms of their empowerment may conceivably get diluted.

ACKNOWLEDGEMENTS

The author wishes to acknowedge her indebtedness to Maria-Lisa Swantz, Kumari Jayawardena, Lal Jayawardena, Ulla Mustanoja, Erkki Koskela, Valentine Moghadam, David Canning and Renee Prendergast for guidance and encouragement at various stages of the work, and to several participants at the annual conference of the Development Studies Association held in Dublin in September 1995 for helpful comments on an earlier draft of the paper. However, she alone is responsible for any remaining inadequacies and errors. She is also grateful to the Finnish Academy for providing financial support and to Professor M. Yunus, the Managing Director of the Grameen Bank, for facilitating the field survey.

NOTES

1. See, for example, the evidence presented in Chen *et al.* (1981), Chen (1991), D'Souza and Chen (1980), Harriss (1990), Kabeer (1991), Papanek (1990) and Sen (1984).
2. The success of Grameen Bank has inspired many replications in other countries, some of which are discussed in Hulme (1991).
3. The borrower women's desire to have more children seems to go against the hypothesis that women's involvement in income-earning activities contributes to reduction of fertility. However, the hypothesis is more likely to be true in the case of wage-employed women rather than self-employed women, as in the present case, who work mainly from their home.
4. Access to food is defined in terms of a 'meal score' indicating the number of meals consumed. For more details see Table 4.8.
5. This apparent anomaly is perhaps explained at least in part by the fact that the husbands of the non-borrower women are mostly agricultural wage-labourers who have some of their meals in their employers' households and these were not recorded in our survey.

REFERENCES

Boserup, E. (1970) *Women's Role in Economic Development.* New York: St. Martin's Press. 2nd edition 1986, Aldershot: Gower.

Chen, L.C., Huq, E. and D'Souza, S. (1981) 'Sex Bias in the Family Allocation of Food and Health Care in Rural Bangladesh', *Population and Development Review*, vol. 7, no. 1.

Chen, M. (1991) 'A Matter of Survival: Women's Right to Work in India and Bangladesh', (mimeo), Cambridge, MA: Harvard Institute of International Development.

D'Souza, S. and Chen, L.C. (1980) 'Sex Differentials in Mortality in Rural Bangladesh', *Population and Development Review*, vol. 6, no. 2.

Fugelsang, A. and Chandler, D. (1986) *Participation as Process: What We Can Learn from Grameen Bank, Bangladesh*, NORAD, Norway.

Goetz, A. M. and Sen Gupta, R. (1996) 'Who Takes the Credit? Gender, Power and Control over Loan Use in Rural Credit Programs in Bangladesh', *World Development*, vol. 24, no. 1.

Harriss, B. (1990) 'The Intrafamily Distribution of Hunger in South Asia', in J. Dreze and A. Sen (eds), *The Political Economy of Hunger*, Vol. 1, WIDER Studies in Development Economics, Oxford: Clarendon.

Hossain, M. (1988) *Credit for Alleviation of Rural Poverty: The Grameen Bank in Bangladesh*. Research Report 65, Washington, D.C.: International Food Policy Research Institute.

Hossain, M. and Afsar, R. (1989) 'Credit for Women's Involvement in Economic Activities in Rural Bangladesh'. Research Report 105, Dhaka: Bangladesh Institute of Development Studies.

Hulme, D. (1991) 'The International Transfer of Institutional Innovations: Replicating the Grameen Bank in Other Countries', in R. Prendergast and H. W. Singer (eds), *Development Perspectives for the 1990s*, London: Macmillan.

Kabeer, N. (1991) 'Gender Dimensions of Rural Poverty: Analysis from Bangladesh', *Journal of Peasant Studies*, vol. 18, no. 2.

Kandiyoti, D. (1988) 'Bargaining with Patriarchy', *Gender and Society*, vol. 2, no. 3.

Khandker, S., Khalily, B. and Khan, Z. (1995) *Grameen Bank: Performance and Sustainability*. World Bank Discussion Papers No. 306, Washington, D.C.: World Bank.

Kumar, J. K. (1987) *To Chase a Miracle: A Study of the Grameen Bank of Bangladesh*, Dhaka: University Press Limited.

Malkamäki, M. (1991) *Banking the Poor: Informal and Semi-Formal Financial Systems Serving the Microenterprises*, Institute of Development Studies, University of Helsinki, Finland.

Osmani, S. (1992) 'Credit for the Poor and the Grameen Bank Model: A Theoretical Analysis' (mimeo), Helsinki: WIDER.

Papanek, H. (1990) 'To Each Less than She Needs, From Each More than She Can Do: Allocations, Entitlements, and Value', in I. Tinker (ed.), *Persistent Inequalities: Women and World Development*. Oxford: Oxford University Press.

Pitt, M. and Khandker, S. (1994) 'Household and Intrahousehold Impacts of the Grameen Bank and Similar Targeted Credit Programs in Bangladesh'. (mimeo) Washington, D. C.: World Bank.

Rahman, R. I. (1986) 'The Impact of Grameen Bank on the Situation of Poor Rural Women' (mimeo). Working Paper No. 1, Grameen Bank Evaluation Project, Dhaka: Bangladesh Institute of Development Studies.

Sen, A. K. (1984) 'Family and Food: Sex Bias in Poverty', in A. K. Sen, *Resources, Values and Development*, Oxford: Basil Blackwell.

Sen, A. K. (1990) 'Gender and Cooperative Conflicts', in I. Tinker (ed.), *Persistent Inequalities: Women and World Development*, Oxford: Oxford University Press.

5 Localities of Power: Gender, Parties and Democracy in Chile and Brazil

Fiona Macaulay

What is the relationship between democracy and the empowerment of women in society? How does democratisation as a political process interact with other political and economic processes, such as decentralisation and neo-liberalism, in dis/empowering women as citizens and autonomous agents? How do political actors such as parties, state bureaucrats and women's movements, with their discrete ideologies, organisational practices and public policy demands, exert influence on these processes? This chapter examines the recent transition to democracy in two Latin American countries, Brazil and Chile, in order to explore the complex and contradictory ways in which women's agency has been encouraged or inhibited, as certain dimensions of women's citizenship (social, political, economic, sexual) have been promoted or suppressed. The degree and nature of women's empowerment is further qualified by the collectivities in which women are located (family, community, nation) and by the literal and metaphorical spaces of power (household, municipality, nation state). In the process of consolidating democracy in Brazil and Chile, important differences of interpretation, strategy and policy choices have emerged as sites of struggle between the actors indicated above. Do parties regard women as the objects or subjects of their programmes? How do they consult women about their needs/interests? Might a higher presence of women within the parties or the political system substantially affect policy on gender relations, and thus multiply or accelerate processes of empowerment?

INTRODUCTION[1]

Over the last decade, military and authoritarian governments in Latin America have been replaced by a 'third wave' of democratic governments. Some countries have reinstalled a pre-existing democratic system (Chile and Uruguay), others are creating and consolidating a new democratic polity after decades of instability and authoritarianism (Brazil, Paraguay). One of the features of the 1980s, the decade of transition, was the very high level of grassroots and popular movement activity in defence of human rights, minimum standards of living and political participation. Women founded and led the many committees for the relatives of the disappeared, responded creatively to the recessionary effects of the debt crisis, inflation and structural adjustment (Fisher, 1993), and raised feminist demands, spurred by the United Nations Decade for Women and the ratification of the UN Convention on the Elimination of All Forms of Discrimination Against Women (CEDAW) by the majority of countries. The transition to democracy ushered back in the traditional political actors – political parties and elites – and, whilst there was a crucial moment of opportunity in which women's groups were able to apply leverage and press demands with the key players (Alvarez, 1990; Waylen, 1993), that strategic conjuncture passed very rapidly and it seemed as if women were to be excluded once more from the realm of 'real' politics, i.e. the parties and national government.[2]

This chapter examines some of the reasons for that closure, but also suggests that although women would appear to have been disempowered in the national political arena, there are other spaces available and emerging, specifically in sub-national arenas. The nascent process of decentralisation in Brazil, Chile and elsewhere in South America has the potential both to facilitate gender-relevant public policy-making and implementation, and to empower women as political agents who are individually and collectively both the subjects and objects of that public policy, and of evolving notions of citizenship. A shift to the local alters the terrain of power and politics, but whether this empowers women is dependent on a number of factors, including the structural/institutional context and the attitudes of the main actors (parties, political elites, women's movement) to local arenas.

The analysis focuses on political parties and their relative permeability to gender demands and women's agency. As key interlocutors between civil society and the state, their history, ideology, internal culture and organisation and insertion in the political/electoral system all have a strong bearing on the way in which they limit and construct understandings of gender relations, transform those concepts into public policy and enact them, locally and nationally. The chapter presents the innovative examples of the Workers' Party (PT) city governments in Brazil, their unique methods of popular consultation and policies on gender which will be contrasted with the Chilean political parties and their relationship with sub-national government and with the national women's ministry, SERNAM. This chapter also implicitly addresses inadequacies in several interlocking existing literatures, such as that on democratisation in Latin America (O'Donnell *et al.* 1986; Diamond *et al.* 1988 Higley and Gunther 1992;), and on women in politics (Chaney 1979; Jaquette 1994), by focusing not only on the question of gender relations and public policy, but specifically on sub-national arenas of government. It explores the points of articulation between political parties, national state agencies and local political actors such as organised civil society, grassroots movements, political parties, NGOs, and private and public agencies delivering social services, and suggests the spaces and modes of interaction within which empowerment is possible.

COMPARATIVE PERSPECTIVES

Brazil and Chile both experienced prolonged authoritarian rule (20 and 16 years respectively) which ended in the 1980s. The process of transition in each case presents both common and divergent elements, including its duration and the role played by the political parties and by organised civil society. Brazil's transition was gradual (10 years) and followed a system of collegiate military rule in which the party system had been maintained throughout albeit under draconian controls. Pinochet's rule was ended abruptly, by a plebiscite and then free elections prior to which parties had been completely excised from the political scene.

The role of the political parties during and after the transition varied. In Brazil, the current parties have few historical continuities with the past and, apart from the Workers' Party, may be characterised as rent-seeking, ill-disciplined and non-ideological, concerned more with power than programmes (Mainwaring 1992). In Chile, the party system which was reinstalled in 1989 looked remarkably like that ousted in 1973, including clear left, right and centre ideological cleavages, and disciplined parties with identifiable social bases. Chile had enjoyed over a century of stable, inclusionary democratic government before 1973. Brazil had to invent a democracy it had never really had, with new parties and social groupings emerging in a highly unequal and exclusionary society and polity. The relative weight of 'tradition' in both cases produced both negative and positive outcomes for women's ability to maintain visibility as political actors and influence public policy as will be seen.

Both countries have important left-wing parties, one historic and currently sharing government (the Socialist Party in Chile in coalition with the Christian Democrats), the other a radical new party leading the opposition (the PT in Brazil). The genesis, history and present circumstances of each have offered contrasting opportunities for the development of a progressive agenda with respect to grassroots democracy, in particular women's effective participation as equal citizens. Analyses of the future of the Left in Latin America point to its revaluation of democracy-as-a-good-in-itself, and to local government as a site for that good (Castañeda 1993). The degree to which the centre-left is willing to question the boundaries of citizenship, democracy, gender relations and spheres of government is highly variable however.

Both had significant, heterogeneous, organised grassroots movements, whose protests and activities helped precipitate the breakdown of authoritarian rule in both cases. Not only did women form the bulk of the membership and leadership of many of these groups, but they also stimulated visible and well-organised women's and feminist groupings. One of the contradictory effects of authoritarian rule was the empowerment of women initially through necessity and the absence of masculinised actors (trade unions and parties), further encouraged by supporting organisations such as NGOs, the Church and international organisations. In the transition period these movements were successful in establishing machinery within the state for the promotion of gender equality, by lobbying opposition parties, and using women's involvement in the pro-democracy movements as leverage (Jaquette 1994). As the two countries have passed through the transition and begun to consolidate democracy, different factors have produced divergent results in terms of public policy on gender relations, at both national and local level, and with respect to wider relationships between civil society, political parties and the state.

Finally, the consolidation of democracy has prompted a process of decentralisation and 'modernisation' of the state apparatus, considered further below, in which the historical development of the state, and the ideological alignments and political practices of the main parties become salient.

LOCATING POLITICS

Interest is growing in sub-national spheres of administration and government, and territorial restructuring of the state in Latin America (Goetz and Clarke 1993; Fox 1994;) including gender issues (Raczynski and Serrano, 1992; ISIS, 1993) as realignment of centre–local relations is an emerging feature of the consolidation period. Having secured the stability of the economy and the central polity, a devolution to the local is the next stage in promoting efficiency in allocating resources and good governance. This process can be approached from a number of angles: technical (subsidiarity, efficiency, good governance); welfarist (safety nets and targeted anti-poverty programmes); or political, as an articulation space for civil society to express collective demands, press competing claims and negotiate with the state and its mediators, the political parties. The different actors involved – multilateral agencies, national governments, parties of differing ideological inclinations and grassroots movements – all hold divergent perspectives and expectations. A deepening of democracy, or indeed attention to gender relations, is not a necessary precondition or expected outcome of decentralisation, which was initiated in Chile under authoritarian rule. However a non-political view of the process obscures underlying gender biases in the apparent neutrality of the stewardship or techno/ bureaucratic model of municipal administration. A 'developmentalist' approach that targets women locally and seeks to 'integrate' them into the economy may fail to recognise them as *political* citizens whose claims overs resources or access to power may conflict with those of others, particularly where power is distributed as a finite resource in a zero-sum game.

I here propose a combination of temporal and spatial perspectives on gender, integrated with a comparative politics approach to gender and democratisation.[3] In examining women's exclusion/inclusion as citizens and political agents in the democratisation process it is useful to distinguish between three main phases: breakdown of authoritarian rule; transition to democracy; consolidation of democracy (Waylen 1993). In the first women were active and highly visible in protest movements and popular organisations reacting to human rights abuses or economic adversity. Women's ability to occupy oppositional space then interdicted to traditionally male political expression (parties, trade unions) afforded them some leverage in the second phase with the main opposition parties (Fisher 1993; Radcliffe and Westwood 1993; Jaquette 1994). They gained a purchase in the state, with new women's ministries and agencies, but found themselves rapidly squeezed out of the conventional channels of representation as men in the parties scrambled after the big national prizes of power and resources. It is in the third period of consolidation, where decentralisation has renewed interest in the participation of civil society and in deepening this new democracy, that I argue there is an opportunity to (re)empower women as citizens, and facilitate debate and policy on gender relations at all levels of society.

In approaching local government and politics (for present purposes effectively urban politics) a number of interlinked considerations emerge. Women form the majority now in the urban centres of Latin America, where the sexual division of labour concentrates women and their families, especially if single parents, in lower income brackets and more marginal areas. Women were very active in social movements in the 1980s, especially territorially based groups articulating consumer demands (infrastructure, services). The exclusion of civil society and social movements from the central political arena in the transition period maps onto an effective exclusion of women. Recent feminist work on cities and the urban environment highlights the spatial dimensions of gender inequality and the exclusion of women as citizens from the public spaces of the city (Massey 1994). The city cannot be gender-neutral. The key problem areas of urban management will present special gendered characteristics, e.g. transport, the provision of social services, the spatial division of the city into residential, productive, service sectors which may bear no relation to women's real needs or movements in the city.

It is important to insist on the *differentiated localities of power*. Political structures, at local, national and supranational level, are saturated with gender discourses, even if in the last two instances women as physical bodies may be notable mainly by their absence (Peterson 1992; Marchand, 1994). The physical space in which politics is enacted, or performed, is fundamental to the constitution of its meanings, and offers differential access to the subjects, or actors. The female-led social movements that emerged under military rule managed, in stepping 'out of character', moving in an alien space, performing familiar yet contradictory roles (mother-as-protestor), to wrongfoot the military regime in their responses.

There are a number of discursive binary mappings of gender (that is, around feminine/masculine polarities) onto social and political relations, which need to be confronted, and debunked. These include: community/nation, periphery/centre, social/political, object/subject, local/national, administrative/political, home/workplace, consumption/reproduction, space/time, being/becoming, stasis/narrative (Massey 1994). Of course, these are not fixed or exclusionary categories. The local arena is a hybrid one, poised between community and state, private and public, the household and the town hall, and thus offers a cross-over space for women just as the process of decentralisation is throwing up hybrid agencies and social actors, blurring boundaries between private and public sector, elected and non-elected bodies.

Insights have been borrowed from recent feminist work in political science and in geography, notably in critiques of liberal democracy (Pateman 1989) and on 'locality', space, place and gender (Massey 1994). Transformations in state and government around gender relations are situated within analyses of the *politics of space* and the *spatiality of politics* in examining the interplay of the 'new localism' and 'emerging local politics' of Latin America with the production of social policies aimed at reducing gender inequality. Decentralisation is taken here as the main process, political parties and civil society as the main actors and shifts in gender power relations as the potential outcomes. The 'variable construction of gender relations in different local/cultural space-places' is linked by Massey to anti-essentialism, that is, deconstruction of the universal (male) citizen and political subject (Massey 1994: 178). Women have been historically constructed as lacking in political agency at national level and relegated to the shadow world of community-home-private-local. However, if political actors take a consciously political view of local/municipal administration/government as a contested space in which spatial underpinnings of the public/private split, of gender subordination and control are embedded in the environment, what impetus will that give to the deepening of democratisation in Latin America? Under what conditions is a decentring of the locus of politics accompanied by a decentring of the subject allowing the entrance of non-traditional political subjects/groupings/constituencies? Recent feminist work on the state has foregrounded notions of permeability, fluidity, opportunity spaces within the state, historically and geographically differentiated sites of struggle. The state is neither neutral, nor monolithically patriarchal or capitalist. It has some degree of autonomy, its institutions, agencies and practices interact constantly with, are influenced by and exert influence on society, social processes and social relations, including gender. Where, then, are these opportunity spaces for women to press claims on resources, to influence policy, to be political protagonists? As the social is subordinated to the political, so the feminine has been to the masculine and the local to the national. The politicisation of the local arena has the capacity to interrupt the naturalised feminisation of local-community-place. The slogan of the Chilean women's movement under Pinochet, 'Democracy in the house and in the country', neatly elided the personal and political, the private and the public space.

BRAZIL, MUNICIPAL ARENAS AND THE WORKERS' PARTY

The Workers' Party (PT) is arguably the only party in current Brazilian politics which functions as such, in the accepted sense of aggregating and representing social interests, pursuing an ideologically informed programme of social and governmental policies, and exerting internal discipline over members and elected representatives, following clearly defined democratic structures and procedures (Keck 1992). What, then, is the degree of programmatic coherence to their commitment to both popular democracy and the empowerment of women in their local government administrations?

The PT has only ever governed until recently at municipal level.[4] They won two cities in 1982, a large state capital in 1985, 36 cities in 1988, rising to 53 in 1992, including several state capitals and large industrial centres. The number of cities governed represents only 1 per cent of Brazil's municipalities but accounts for some 10-15 per cent of the population. Three of the largest cities in Latin America moreover were governed by PT women mayors.[5] The party has engaged in much self-reflection as to its aims and performance in local government with respect to its two chief principles – popular participation and prioritising marginal sectors, including women (Bittar 1992; Macaulay 1996) – not least because the municipal administrations offered a showcase for their 'good governance' on which to build their electoral base and implement radical, oppositional policies in reaction to a centre-right national government.

There is an active feminist lobby within the PT, at local and national level, institutionalised in a women's secretariat and a 30 per cent quota for women in all internal decision-making bodies won at the First Party Congress in 1991.[6] Women activists and feminists migrated to the party in the late 1970s and early 1980s from three sources: the pre-1980s opposition party (MDB),[7] the feminist movement, and the grass-roots organisations (Base Christian Communities, Cost-of-Living, Amnesty, Creche, Healthcare, Neighbourhood and other movements), and in some local branches women dominate the party. For example, the party leadership and representation in Santos, site of successful innovation in local government, is female-dominated, a feature attributed to the absence of men in the military period (Santos was subject to harsh repression of its dockworkers' unions). Since the party was formed in 1980, the bulk of the local political organisers have been women with a track record in the amnesty movement. At other levels of government women have been well represented. In 1994 the PT elected two women out of five senators, and overall has a percentage of women elected to executive and legislative posts (17 per cent) around treble that of the other main four parties.

The PT operates radical conceptions of political subjectivity, citizenship and social plurality, a vision that derives from their unusual and heterogeneous support base arising from the confluence of social forces at the time of its formation ('new' anti-corporatist trade unions, backed by the progressive Catholic church, who nurtured the frequently female-led grassroots movements). The PT embraces a rainbow coalition of groups with diverse subject positions – women, gays and lesbians, Blacks, shantytown dwellers, rural workers and so forth. This has two effects. First, it *decentres the political subject*, rejecting any 'privileged' viewpoint, such as that of the masculine proletariat.[8] Second, it leads to the necessity of open, participatory debate, and the centrality of citizenship (in contradistinction to historical modalities of corporatism, and welfarism). The PT's relationship with these movements has aimed to empower, support and represent, but not to co-opt or supplant them.

Policy on women has evolved from token expressions about women's equality to a commitment to tackle gender relations and promote citizenship for all based on equality-in-difference. Social services are defined as duties of the state and rights of the citizen. Alongside its commitment to equal rights, health care, employment, etc., the party has integrated more 'radical' proposals on sexuality and reproductive rights, presented in terms of sexual citizenship.[9] The PT's programmatic coherence, combined with its policies on gender relations, plus its insistence on participation in government, make its experiences in local government pathbreaking. Approaches vary from the highly traditional in very small towns ('the mayor's wife deals with women's issues'), to extremely radical experiments such as in Santo André (see below). The range of public policy varies from setting up a women's refuge, projects to combat violence against women, literacy classes for women municipal workers and sex education, to mental health projects and training schemes. Generally, the PT will establish either a women's council or a women's secretariat/coordinating committee, or a combination of the two, reflecting debates in the women's movement as to the advantages and disadvantages of working within, or outside, the state, and on the Left about the nature of popular participation, and mechanisms for encouraging and institutionalising such participation.

Brazil took the lead in the region in the mid-1980s in establishing agencies and mechanisms within the state, at federal, state and then municipal level for promoting gender equality, and in forming channels for the permanent input of women's organisations and representatives. These Councils on Women's Rights were the results of the women's movement taking advantage of the 'opportunity space' within the state (Alvarez 1990). The PT has always taken a position of preferring women's secretariats, that is entities within the machinery of government, with executive powers, legal status and budget facilities, able to engage on equal terms with other state agencies. Women's councils are intended to provide a forum for the representatives of civil society, in an advisory capacity. Ideally, both should exist and perform mutually reinforcing roles. Policy without participation sets up women as objects of the political agendas of others, be that individual parties or developmental regimes. Participation without access to power and the means to implement demands leaves women's movements weak and ineffective.

Brazil has a federal structure and the relative autonomy of the three tiers of government was greatly enhanced by the 1988 Constitution, offering institutional opportunities for transforming the municipal into a site of both resistance to national policies and of radical new constructions of participation.[10] The Brazilian municipalities are among the most autonomous local governments in the world. They are political entities, not merely administrative or deconcentrated agencies. The municipalities draw up their local constitution (Organic Municipal Law)[11] and each city of over 20,000 inhabitants is required to draw up a Master Plan. There are additional provisions for Popular Councils, participatory budget discussions and legislative instruments such as referendums and 'popular initiatives'. The PT has used such mechanisms for expressions of citizenship, commitments to gender equality, and for popular consultation, making explicit the contested nature of urban space and resources. In Santo André this resulted in the full integration of gender into the planning and running of the city. The Organic Law of Santos passed under PT mayor Telma de Souza enshrines the principles of gender equality of the sexes, the PT credos of 'transparency', 'morality' and 'administrative decentralisation', and commits the municipality to guaranteeing welfare provision to women, including healthcare, tackling violence against women and reproductive choice. Article 188 states: 'It is the duty of the public health service to provide medical attention for the practice of abortion in the cases provided for under the Penal Code.[12] In São Paulo they reiterated national commitment to outlawing all forms of labour discrimination (e.g. pregnancy tests) and allocated resources to following up grievances, and blacklisting those firms from city contracts. In Goiânia the Municipal Law commits the city to encouraging women and men to share domestic labour.

The PT challenges the fluid, contingent and normative features of the urban environment, and recognises that town planners and municipal leaders are engaged in the process of continually creating and determining the physical environment in which social relations are reproduced and power exercised or opposed. Every decision to consult particular groups, to allocate resources in a particular way, to certain groups or areas of the city, impacts on social relations and the physical and political dimensions of these relations. Women's Councils and the expression of female-dominated social movements in other councils (health, housing, neighbourhoods) acknowledge women's capacity as citizens to compete with others over resources. The PT's municipal governments have responded to women's practical and strategic needs in a variety of ways. Indirectly, the centrality of the politics of everyday life, of neighbourhood/consumption as well as workplace/production issues, of citizenship, of 'popular empowerment' in the PT's rubric, demasculinises the business of politics. The PT's policy of decentralising municipal services has a greater impact on the practical gender needs of women than of men, as does a gender-alert approach to city planning, or commitment to 'desegregate' the city (Singer 1993; Bittar 1993). Tackling housing, public transport, integrating the city (bringing workplace, residency and commercial and public services closer together), providing infrastructure, have also had indirect impacts on the quality of life for women, given sexual and spatial divisions of labour. Many initiatives undertaken by the women's secretariats tackle gender-specific issues. The São Paulo team set up a shelter for battered women and persuaded a city hospital to fulfil its legal obligation to perform abortions for those women entitled to them.

Reappropriation of the urban space by the marginalised is one of the tenets of PT municipal administration. One of the images that dominated Luiza Erundina's campaign in São Paulo in 1988 was of her being arrested whilst participating in a land occupation with a grassroots housing group. The examples of the Madres de la Plaza de Mayo, and human rights groups, illustrate symbolically and literally how forbidden territory may be breached and occupied (the street, the Plaza). Other initiatives in this area include sexual harassment awareness training of the Municipal Guard; offering literacy classes and other services to the lower ranks of municipal employees, mainly low paid women workers, such as street cleaners, and giving them channels to enter debates on municipal policies; consideration of spatial security, e.g. licensing street traders, which include many women in São Paulo, and gender-sensitive management of public areas.

Santo André was the boldest experiment, which illustrates both the opportunities and constraints faced by the PT in trying to enact radical models of citizen participation and access. The mayor invited a feminist geographer to draft the city's new Master Plan, *from a gender perspective*, that is, to presume that gender permeated every aspect of the city's activities, rather than constituting an optional policy 'add-on'.[13] This Plan was not approved by the Municipal Chamber for party political reasons and the PT lost the next elections; however, the process and approach have provided a model which is being taken up and modified in other PT administrations. Their experience here underscored a number of important issues about both public policy on gender and local democracy, such as the political will of the chief executive, the importance of appointing gender-aware administrators (the woman administrator managing the Master Plan knew and brought in the feminist academic), the need for strategy and networking between gender-aware technical staff. Feminist women in each city department formed an informal 'Women's axis', to promote interdepartmental collaboration on the insertion of gender policy in all areas of public policy. However, despite executive level commitment to gender issues, it took two years to establish a local Women's Council. In the absence of an autonomous articulated women's *movement*, the coordinating group contacted and catalogued all existing women's groups, and organised a women's forum for some 800 women, in which the draft Master Plan was debated.[14] The Santo André experiment, which involved a steep learning curve, is valuable in demonstrating how political commitment may empower women in the administration to 'think' gender strategically and practically, setting up structures which then empower other women, bringing them in as political actors with preferences to be expressed.

In summary, whilst Brazil's central initiatives on gender equality have been stymied for the past few years, as the National Women's Council was rendered inoperative by political manoeuvring and the gains made in the 1988 Constitution have yet to pass into law and the Civil Code, the use by the PT of local administrations as sites both in which to oppose national government and in which to pursue a radical agenda has opened new spaces for women as political subjects.

CHILE, THE PARTIES AND THE WOMEN'S MINISTRY

By contrast to the above there are a number of features in the Chilean polity, both historical and conjunctural, that tend to impede greater participation and a political role for women in local government. Historically, centre–local relations in Chile have been characterised from early this century by marked centralism. Local government was a site for a vertical power brokerage, by which local officials satisfied individual and community demands by mediating with the central party or state apparatus (Valenzuela 1977). Brazil's regional clientelism is well known (Nunes Leal 1977), but periodic oscillation between assertion of central control, and local/regional challenges in a multi-focal polity, plus its federal structure, have resulted in sub-national arenas of government being used as sites of political contestation and challenge to the centre. Both the Christian Democrat Party (PDC) and the Socialist Party (PS) espoused ideological models of society that were strongly centripetal, the former with an organic, quasi-corporatist frame, the latter described as the 'centralist, Jacobin, statist tradition of the Left' (Castañeda, 1993: 371) linked with the then still dominant model of the dirigiste, developmentalist state. Under military rule (1973–89) an authoritarian form of decentralisation was instituted, devolving greater responsibility, but not resources or power, to the municipalities for social service provision, notably health and education. Central control was amplified under Pinochet, and his programmes of decentralisation, privatisation of social policy delivery and 'clearance' of shantytowns to the urban margins, creating wide inequalities between one local council and another in terms of resources and infrastructure, were designed to demobilise, fragment opposition and disperse certain functions of the state. Local government was utterly depoliticised, either as a site for party patronage or as a site for political contestation, and reconstructed as a locus for 'good house-keeping', a concept whose gendered connotations are explored below.

The democratic governments of Aylwin (1989–93) and Frei (1993–) have done little to reverse this trend. Whilst the popular mobilisations of the 1980s created the conditions in which to negotiate and mobilise for the No vote, the spectre of the Popular Unity period loomed large and the involvement of civil society was traded for a political strategy of maximum consensus and stability, centred on the political class. It is now a commonplace to note the displacement in these transition periods of civil society (in which women are active in many spheres) by the parties (from whose elites they are generally excluded). However, in the Brazilian transition, despite frequent laments about the demise of popular movements, there have been a great many mobilisations (e.g. for direct elections, for the impeachment of President Collor) which the PT has encouraged and benefited from politically. The anti-mobilisation model has predominated to date in Chile, and has affected the women's movement as much as local neighbourhood organisations. There are, however, signs of change. Modernisation of the state has now become the slogan of the Frei administration. Chilean democracy is considered to be stable and consolidated, the centre-left coalition won a landslide victory for the presidency and maintained their position in Congress and the Senate. The economy is booming and healthy, so attention is being refocused on further measures to democratise society and streamline state structures. There has also been considerable disgruntlement from the grassroots organisations and from the municipalities signalling a potential shift in state-political party-civil society relationships.

The political prize in the transition period was national power and so parties paid scant attention to local administrations, activists or members. On the centre-left there is little internal party debate or communication, no forum for discussing problems of local administration. The inertia of the dominant parties in this area is permitting the Far Right of the political spectrum to move into this vacuum. The Independent Democratic Union (UDI) is colonising this space with 'democratic' gimmicks, e.g. local plebiscites and intensive, clientelistic work with women in the poor areas. The party receives a higher percentage of votes from women than any other party, has around 60 per cent female membership and no women at all on its executive. As a traditionalist Catholic party, it advocates extremely traditionalist gender relations. The centre-left has signally failed to appreciate gender-related policies, or indeed popular participation, as potential political issues at local level. The former is delegated to the National Women's Ministry. Popular participation has been restrained first, by the dominance of the anti-mobilisation model, and second, by the parties' centralist traditions which have failed to replace centre–local clientelism, or the authoritarian stewardship model, with structures of local consultation that can be independent of party co-optation. If current institutional arrangements discourage citizen participation in general, women remain even more marginalised as long as the parties do not view local government as a site for political contestation.

'Developmentalist' policies targeted at women have however been enacted locally. From the mid-1960s onwards, working-class women were organised first by the Christian Democrats, then under Pinochet, in top-down structures operated at local level, in the hundreds of Mothers' Centres all over the country, receiving political and moral 'instruction' from the military regime's upper- and middle-class lady volunteers of the Women's Secretariat. These have persisted in modified form whilst more militant women's groups and grassroots feminist organisations have found themselves cast adrift, as the new National Women's Service (SERNAM), along with national feminist NGOs, monopolises state resources. SERNAM is hindered in its municipal level activities by political and institutional blockages that hamper effective policy implementation and input from the intended beneficiaries of their services, that is, local women.

In short, national and local government in Chile remain delinked, and exist as parallel spheres. Alliances are built horizontally not vertically. The newly formed Association of Chilean Municipalities has been set up as a cross-party alliance to fight the municipal corner against the national parties' monopoly of resources and political initiative. Parties regard the municipality as unimportant or subject to national policy. Present arrangements for local administration are widely deemed to be inadequate, as the electoral system of indirect election of mayor splits the mandate frequently between opposing parties, the ratio between councillors and population is one of the most skewed in the continent (Nickson 1995), local officials are inadequately trained and local 'participatory' mechanisms (the Social and Economic Councils) are inoperable. All these conspire to depoliticise the local arena, where women are marginalised on all fronts, in elected office (viewed now as a party political 'prize'), as citizens with political claims (at variance with the combined stewardship/clientelist model) and in the popular movements whose institutional expression has been much limited.

In Chile, the municipal arena has been more explicitly gendered than in Brazil. Interviews with women mayors in Chile of all hues, from the governing coalition to those appointed under Pinochet, revealed that women constructed themselves discursively, and allowed themselves to be designated, as distinctively gendered actors, as the optimal house-keepers of *la casa grande* ('the big house'), i.e the municipality. In a polity where there has historically been a fierce contest for national power, with strong, ideological parties, class-based constituencies, and an early extension of universal male suffrage, women were viewed as trespassers in a masculine realm. They were assigned an 'appropriate sphere', that of the home-from-home municipality. This is underscored by the two-stage extension of the vote,[15] and by the surprisingly high number of women mayors (10 per cent) appointed under Pinochet as stewards and matrons of the nation's local household. This number has dropped after the first democratic elections in 20 years in 1992. In Brazil, women have in the past been elected mayor either through old-fashioned family links, 'standing in' for a male relative who cannot stand for immediate re-election, or clientelistic local relations, often running their own Evita-style charity (Blay 1979), that is, they are elected as men's proxies, not as feminised political actors. By contrast to the dynasty-based politics of Brazil, the PT activists and represent-atives, however, do not come from an identifiable political caste, and the women PT mayors elected to date have tended to have strong organisational ties to local grassroots consumer movements. They do not justify either their candidacies or their behaviour in gender terms, but rather in party-political/ideological ones, although they are not unaware of the pressures to adopt masculine modes in the political world. Ultimately, I argue, this affords them greater leeway for adopt-ing a political and contestatory stance on gender relations, and for viewing the municipality as an arena of empowerment not of con-straint.

In effect, women argued themselves into a corner. Purporting to have special feminine qualities (sensitivity, warmth, human touch, pragmatism, time management, efficiency, probity), either from bio-logy or acculturation, that made them better town hall managers meant that the parties were happy to leave them there. It did not in the end constitute much of a power base either, as the women appointed by Pinochet who then joined UDI still faced an internal battle to win candidacies against men who viewed the post of mayor in certain localities as a political prize. This mapping of feminine onto municipal depends on viewing the local as apolitical, a site of the 'social' and 'developmental', not 'political'. Such notions also underpinned the organicist, authoritarian view of local government, and genuine political contestation, as well as an emergence of women as political actors, rather than as housekeepers, remain blocked by such constructions. Initiatives on gender equality remain top-down and executive-led, channelled principally through the National Women's Service (SERNAM). SERNAM was established in 1990 under the new democratic government of Aylwin, as a result of pressure from women involved in the feminist movement and linked to the now governing *Concertación* coalition. SERNAM is not an executive agency, although its head has the rank of minister. It is subsumed within the Ministry of Planning, has an operational budget but otherwise must work with other ministries and agencies for the implementation of projects on the ground. This involves negotiating with other ministries and adjusting their work to the rhythm of bureaucratic activity in the ministries in order to integrate gender projects in the other core areas. In some cases (for example, training), NGOs will be contracted to carry out the work. Certain of its programmes depend crucially on the political will of the municipal authorities to take up and support some of the key programmes such as the Female Headed Households, women's legal advisory centres, or education and prevention of domestic violence.

SERNAM faces a number of obstacles in implementing its policies. These include the labyrinthine nature of the state administration, specifically the overlapping of the functions between ministries, and between national, regional and municipal entities and partial access to key ministries owing to their secondary ministerial status. Their influence on a ministry's work is still dependent on the strategic location of feminist sympathisers who act as gatekeepers to facilitate access, which also holds true of ministerial appointments. For example, the appointment of Jorge Arrate to the Labour Ministry provided an executive-level commitment to collaboration with SERNAM (not only was he then leader of the Socialist Party but he is also the partner of the ex-vice-president of SERNAM, Soledad Larraín). This underscores frequent observations about the insular composition of the Chilean political elite, which has at once given leverage to SERNAM in its initial stages, but also made its interventions contingent upon personal and factional, rather than programmatic, backing.[16] Appointments within SERNAM have been made not solely on the basis either of feminist sympathies, organic linkages with the wider women's/feminist movements, or technical capacity, but also in order to reflect the balance of parties and factions within the governing coalition. In the first four-year period, three key posts were held by the wives/partners of leaders of the three parties of the governing coalition. This has alienated SERNAM both from the grassroots and from the right-wing opposition, for different reasons. Although, arguably, SERNAM is designed as a policy-generating body, not as a representative one, it is viewed by many as middle-class and elitist. There is no equivalent in Chile to the three tiers of Women's Councils in Brazil (national, state, municipal) which could provide such representivity and feedback.[17] The popular women's groups have become marginalised as policy consumers, whilst feminists have moved into the NGOs and a comfortable coexistence with SERNAM. The Right, meanwhile, is dismissive of 'jobs for the girls', and questions the need for an additional state entity to do what the free market, along with welfare safety nets and charity, is supposed to achieve alone. In the absence of substantial differences between the governing centre-left coalition and the opposing centre-right bloc on macroeconomic or foreign policy, the Right has chosen to make the private arena of family, morality and sexuality its main platform. This, combined with the Christian Democrats' church links, has made the topics of divorce and reproductive choice virtual taboos. SERNAM has been in no position to press for notions of sexual citizenship, and none of the major parties admits such debates into the political field.

Additional blockages lie in the unevenness of gender-awareness in all of its working partners: ministries, parties, municipal authorities, bureaucratic agencies and NGOs. SERNAM suffers from a lack of programmatic backing in the *Concertación* parties who have delegated responsibility so completely to SERNAM as to have no party agenda for gender issues to be implemented at municipal level (although they may nationally). For example, the head of regional development in SERNAM, herself a PDC activist, admitted that there was no greater likelihood of a PDC municipal administration adopting a SERNAM programme than any other party. In 1990, SERNAM wanted a fully fledged regional structure, but negotiations with the Right to get SERNAM approved meant concessions on cost-cutting and staff reduction. SERNAM identifies its regional presence as a weakness and is developing strategies to compensate. A more effective presence in the municipality will depend on structural/administrative changes, and a shift in attitude within the parties and SERNAM itself.

What we see occurring, then, is a piecemeal application of policies on women, despite the centralism of the administration, with little popular input at local level from the women at whom the projects are targeted.[18] Much depends on the political will of the individual mayor, in a manner quite divorced apparently from the party in government in the municipality, even when these are parties of the *Concertación* who formally back SERNAM and its policies. The municipality of Santiago for example initiated a number of collaborative projects using the services of the NGO *Instituto de la Mujer*. The Mayor, Jaime Ravinet, is prominent in the PDC, and is the President of the Chilean Association of Municipalities. His party however does not have a coherent programme for local government, or for increasing popular participation. The presence of a long-time feminist activist and academic, and member of the political elite (Claudia Serrano) opened the strategic doors. Maria Antonieta Saa, a radical feminist and Partido por la Democracia activist appointed mayor of one of Santiago's poorest districts, Conchalí, ran a successful participatory administration, working with NGOs, providing training for women grassroots leaders, and establishing citizens councils. This however she would and could have done with or without SERNAM or her party's backing.[19]

In conclusion, SERNAM as an institutionalised governmental policy-making body has managed to empower women in Chile in specific ways that are constrained and shaped by the institutional context (contests between the political parties, ideologies, historical legacies). SERNAM has enjoyed latitude to empower women as economic actors in a neo-liberal marketplace, whose foundations are left unquestioned. For example, a gendered division of labour still persists, even as the economy restructures (see Stephanie Barrientos' chapter on the *temporeras* in this volume). While economic and social citizenship are promoted, political empowerment has been conflictive due to the highly competitive nature of party politics and the demobilisation model, and sexual citizenship remains a taboo topic. High levels of national consensus over economic policy and international relations have shifted party debates to the field of morality and the private. Thus, empowered individually in a limited way in the market place, women are still constrained by collective constructions of family, from SERNAM's programmes targeted at Female Heads of Household, through the meso level of municipality as *'casa grande'* to the meta-narrative of nation-as-family. Rational self-interest in a neo-liberal market economy appears to require the sacrifice and guardianship of women in the private sphere as a social counterweight.

CONCLUSIONS

In the two cases examined, certain elements emerge as significant for an opening of politics to greater participation by civil society, and empowerment of women individually and collectively. The first is the central mediating role played by the political parties, and encompasses their history, organisational culture, ideological orientation, relationship with grassroots membership and activists, social composition of membership and elite, relationship to the central government and attitude to local/municipal government. The second is the availability of constitutional and legal instruments such as municipal constitution, or master plan, which can define the powers and status of consultative groups in civil society. Institutional arrangements may be limiting, for example electoral regimes, or empowering, for example, a federal system. A third is the socio-political context, including formal relations between the tiers of government, and between members of the political class at each level. This extends to a consideration of degrees of centralism, or regionalism, and national political culture, such as corporatism.

In Chile, gender policy initiatives come from the centre and have had great difficulty in permeating locally due to the strictures of a centralist state and polity, dominated by internally competitive and centralised parties. In Brazil a party with a programmatic commitment both to gender equality and to local democracy has been able to operationalise at local level gender policies which have been stymied at national level. It has also empowered women's participation in part due to the constituencies it serves and perceives as having collective interests. Participatory instruments have been used by women to claim power over resources, to change the rules of distribution of power, and to 'generate' empowerment, that is, to bring other women into contact with such channels, to organise, and encourage 'voice'. Bottom-up ideology and practice have reinforced the PT's ability to be less disempowering of women than parties generally are, and indeed to achieve the opposite. All of the foregoing is to argue for a consciously political, rather than technocratic, bureaucratic, managerial or welfarist approach to local government in so far as it is viewed as a site of political action in which women may act as citizens engaged in dynamic political interactions with the state at local level, rather than as strategically placed conduits of welfare policy aimed at family and community. Emerging local governments and decentralised administrations have the potential to empower, rather than manage, women.

NOTES

1. This chapter is based on my doctoral research, and I gratefully acknowledge the financial assistance of the ESRC in conducting fieldwork. I am also indebted to my many women interviewees in Chile and Brazil.
2. In the first free elections after military rule in Chile in 1989, the percentage of women elected to parliament (5.8 per cent) was nearly halved from its pre-1973 level. In Uruguay in 1984, no women at all were elected in the first democratic elections.
3. The temporal aspects of democratisation have predominated in the literature by the 'transitologists' (O'Donnell *et al.*, 1986), underpinned by a narrative-driven, linear, often voluntaristic, and elite-centric interpretation of political change. The spatial dimensions have been largely unexplored.
4. The PT has challenged twice for the presidency, narrowly losing in 1989, and leading the field until defeated by the opponent's anti-inflation plan in 1994. In 1994 it nearly doubled its congressional presence to become the fifth largest party, and won two governorships. It has succeeded in shifting the political debate to the centre-left, and in redefining the terms of that debate, e.g. foregrounding concepts of citizenship and social equity.
5. These included the Brazilian 'Thelma and Louise': Luiza Erundina in São Paulo (pop. 9.5 million) and Telma de Souza in Santos, Latin America's most important port. The third was Maria Luiza Fontenele in Fortaleza in north-east Brazil.
6. A PT deputy and well-known feminist, Marta Suplicy, put a bill through Congress obliging all parties to include a minimum of 20 per cent women in their lists for the October 1996 municipal elections. The PT is key in articulating a cross-party grouping of women legislators in Congress to support such measures. The bill was accompanied by a public campaign urging women to affiliate to parties in order to be eligible to run.
7. The Brazilian Democratic Movement which after 1980 became the PMDB.
8. The PT differs from the traditional Left in taking 'reproductive' issues (in Marxian terms) as seriously as 'productive' conflicts. Its association with consumer and identity-based groups has been influential.
9. The 1994 party manifesto contained commitments to the equal rights of gays and lesbians and to public policies such as initiatives to combat violence against women, and the establishment of a Women's Secretariat with the status of a Ministry. After heated debate at the May 1994 Party Congress a draft commitment to decriminalising abortion was converted into a commitment to reducing its incidence via health and sex education and to opening a public debate on the issue.
10. The women's movement, led by the National Women's Council, mobilised around the drafting of the 1988 Constitution, making it one of the most progressive in the region in terms of commitment to women's equality (Verucci 1991). Many of its provisions however have not been operationalised (e.g. penal and labour codes have not yet been formally altered to reflect them), and the Constitution underwent a messy revision process in 1994 in which many of these hard-won rights came under threat.

11. The federal system in Brazil determines that every tier of government – national, state and municipal – should formulate its own constitution, the lower echelons subject of course to the higher-level documents. Thus, when the National Women's Council was effectively dismantled after 1989, the State Women's Council of Sao Paulo took on the text of the CEDAW, to which Brazil is a signatory, and transformed it into a state-level charter for women, to which municipalities in the state became party.

12. *Lei Orgânica do Município de Santos*, p. 85. Abortion is permitted in the case of rape or danger to the woman's life.

13. The blueprint entitled *Mulher e Espaço Urbano* begins 'The city, a product of every society and its contradictions, reproduces spatially the situation of social discrimination experienced by women, as in the city the division of space and time present the same divisions as exist in society' (p. 3).

14. Interview with Ivete Garcia, city women's officer during the administration.

15. Women were granted the vote in municipal elections in 1934 but had to wait until 1949 for national suffrage.

16. Ann Matear's comments have been valuable in this section.

17. SERNAM has a formal regional structure, albeit under-resourced, which inserts gender concerns into the regional development plans. It has no formal presence at municipal level, but implements its programmes in conjunction with local city councils, using NGOs are service providers and financed by local funds and central transfers.

18. SERNAM's policies as enacted in the municipalities have a strongly welfarist flavour in the absence of channels of participation and 'voice'. In this they resemble the pre-1973 activities of the PDC via the Mothers' Centres, and those currently of UDI. Without the backing of the parties, it is hard to see how those in SERNAM who want to empower women politically could break this familiar mould.

19. She is a long-time left-wing militant, with a strong feminist profile. She represented women in the 'Civil Assembly' set up in the mid-1980s in opposition to the military regime, and was jailed as a result. She was one of two PPD women appointed mayor by President Aylwin, until the municipal elections called in 1992. It is symptomatic, however, of the scramble for scarce positions in the parties that, although she had a powerful electoral base in Conchalí, and the PPD (and PS) in principle operates a 20 per cent quota for women in its internal posts, she was nearly robbed of her candidacy for deputy in the selection process for the 1994 elections.

REFERENCES

Alvarez, S. (1990) *Engendering Democracy in Brazil: Women's Movements in Transition Politics*, Princeton: Princeton University Press.

Bittar, J. (ed.) (1992) *O Modo Petista de Governar*, São Paulo: Cadernos de Teoria e Debate

Blay, E. (1979) 'The Political Participation of Women in Brazil: The Female Mayors', *Signs* 5(1): 42-59.

Castañeda, J. G. (1993) *Utopia Unarmed: The Latin American Left after the Cold War*, New York: Vintage

Chaney, E. (1979) *Supermadre: Women in Politics in Latin America*, Austin: University of Texas Press

Diamond, L., Linz, J. J. and Lipset, S. M. (eds) (1988) *Democracy in Developing Areas: Latin America*, Boulder: Lynne Rienner.

Fisher, J. (1993) *Out of the Shadows: Women, Resistance and Politics in South America*, London: Latin America Bureau.

Fox, J. (1994) 'Latin America's Emerging Local Politics', *Journal of Democracy* 5(2): 105-16.

Goetz, E. and Clarke S. (1993) *The New Localism: Comparative Urban Politics in a Global Era*, London: Sage.

Higley, J. and Gunther, R. (eds) (1992) *Elites and Democratic Consolidation in Latin America and Southern Europe*, Cambridge: Cambridge University Press.

ISIS (1993) *El Espacio Posible*, Issue No. 19 of *Ediciones de las Mujeres*, Santiago: ISIS International.

Jaquette, J. (1994) *The Women's Movement in Latin America: Participation and Democracy*, Boulder: Westview Press.

Keck, K. (1992) *The Workers' Party and Democratization in Brazil*, New Haven: Yale University Press.

Macaulay, F. (1996) "Governing for Everyone': the Workers' Party Administration in São Paulo 1989–1992', *Bulletin of Latin American Research* 15(2).

Mainwaring, S. (1992) 'Brazilian Party Underdevelopment in Comparative Perspective', *Political Science Quarterly* 107(4): 67-707.

Marchand, M. (1994) 'Gender and the New Regionalism in Latin America: Inclusion/Exclusion', *Third World Quarterly* 15(1): 63-76.

Massey, D. (1994) *Space, Place and Gender*, Cambridge: Polity Press.

Nickson, R. A. (1995) *Local Government in Latin America*, Boulder: Lynne Rienner.

Nunes Leal, V. (1977) *Coronelismo: The Municipality and Representative Government in Brazil*, Cambridge: Cambridge University Press.

O'Donnell, G., Schmitter, P. C. and Whitehead, L. (eds) (1986) *Transitions from Authoritarian Rule: Latin America*, Baltimore: Johns Hopkins University Press.

Pateman, C. (1989) *The Disorder of Women*, Cambridge: Polity Press.

Peterson, V. S. (ed.) (1992) *Gendered States: Feminist (Re)Visions of International Relations Theory*, Boulder: Lynne Rienner.

Raczynski, D. and Serrano, C. (eds) (1992) *Políticas Sociales, Mujeres y Gobierno Local*, Santiago: CIEPLAN.

Radcliffe, S. A. and Westwood, S. (eds) (1993) *'Viva': Women and popular protest in Latin America*, London: Routledge.

Singer, P. (1993) *São Paulo's Master Plan 1989–92: The Politics of Urban Space*, Washington DC: Occasional Paper Series No. 2 Comparative Urban Studies. Woodrow Wilson International Center for Scholars.

Valenzuela, A. (1977) *Political Brokers in Chile: Local Government in a Centralized Polity*, Durham, NC: Duke University Press.

Verucci, F. (1991) 'Women and the New Brazilian Constitution', *Feminist Studies* 17(3): 551–67.

Waylen, G. (1993) 'Women's Movements and Democratisation in Latin America', *Third World Quarterly* 14(3): 573–87.

6 The Syrian Woman: Reality and Aspiration

Leila Djabari

At the recent Copenhagen summit Dr Boutros Boutros-Ghali, Secretary-General of the United Nations, declared that

> The elimination of abuses of the rights of women is a basic prerequisite towards the abolition of poverty in the world, because women are the poorest of the poor.

The echoes of this declaration strike a deep chord in our spirits and in our consciences. Why is a woman the poorest of the poor? And how can we get her out of this trap? This is the first task if we are to embark on the process of empowerment.

I shall confine my analysis to an overview of the legal situation of Syrian women in particular and Arab women in general. This is because in my opinion the main abuses of the rights of woman and her inequality with man is rooted in her role within the familial context. This has led to a failure to secure rights in other spheres. The laws relating to personal status in Syria place the woman within her family, in a situation of subordination and effective dependence on her *patron* and on the males of the family. This gives man discretionary authority over her activity which may accord with male interests but is not, in most cases, in either the public interests, or the family's interest, or in the personal interests of the woman herself.

For example, parental rights are granted only to the father. The children are his children only. Parental authority is his alone and falls to other males of the family after him. The mother's rights are limited to nursing the children in the early years under the supervision and in the interest of the father. Even a woman's authority over herself appears in law to be obscure and unrelated to whether she is mature or not. Similarly the law gives the husband the right to divorce his wife as he wishes. He may make the decision whenever he wishes and without conditions. In effect he may destroy the marital household at any time he wants, he may throw the woman out and deny her access to her children. The woman is given an implicit choice: submit to the arbitrariness of your husband and abandon your rights in other

110

spheres, or be deprived of access to your children. We see here the explanation for the woman's resignation to the forfeiture of her rights or her so-called submission.

Moreover the law does not recognise the working woman with regard to what she spends on herself, on her children or on her family from her own income. She is considered legally as provided for by her husband. She is assigned no rights in the property of the family or in the customary or abstract rights that exist in the family as a result of her membership of it. Her rights are restricted to her expenses and her dowry.

The law of personal status today does not differ in any way from what it was half a century ago, or even from what was inherited from the Ottoman era. It places the woman in a role totally inconsistent with the spirit of Syrian legislation which is based on principles of human rights in their loftiest and most up-to-date sense. In this legislation the Syrian woman enjoys a status of freedom and of total equality with the Syrian man in every walk of life. It may be that this legislation is rare in being totally free of discrimination against women. Our constitution specifies this equality and lays down in Article 46 'the obligation of the State to provide opportunities to achieve this equality in practice, and to work to abolish restraints that inhibit the development of women and their participation in the building of the community'. It also grants woman her political rights in full, as candidates, as electors and as able to fill the highest political offices. And the Labour Law guarantees for women opportunities and conditions of employment that are equal to those for men. She may enter any sphere of employment and she receives equal pay for equal work. There is no discrimination against applying for work or education at any level.

We know full well that a high status for women is a major criterion for assessing the modernity of a state. Political empowerment for Syrian women requires them to be involved in the progressive development that the country is going through. The political leadership in Syria must exert all efforts, seriously and honestly, to qualify women and to reinforce their freedom in their personal life. The General Women's Union – a leading mass organisation, enjoying a widespread geographical membership and receiving large official and financial support – works towards directing women's efforts into taskforces. The Union is active in raising awareness of women's issues, in providing crèches for working mothers and in campaigning for the elimination of female illiteracy. It also establishes centres for women to get professional qualifications so as to increase financially worthwhile employment opportunities for them. It works with other Arab and international women's organisations in devising and implementing study programmes relating to women. It monitors the media to ensure that attention is paid to women's issues. Women's committees in other mass organisations (dealing with workers, peasants, professionals, etc.) collaborate with the Union in these areas. Cooperative societies have also spread throughout the country and they have a very high proportion of women members.

In spite of all this there are still abuses of the rights of woman in everyday life in Syria. Indeed, the situation in general has deteriorated. What lies behind this inconsistency? How is it possible for the laws of personal status to diverge from the general principles of our legislation?

The reason is that these laws of personal status derive from the religious codes of the followers of the three Semitic religions and their different subdivisions. Different confessional groups have proliferated in all Arab countries. Adherents of each confession submit their family concerns to the religious hierarchy, all of whose sources of authority and fundamentals differ. The law of personal status is not uniform and makes a distinction not only between men and women individually, but also between different groups of men and women. This conflicts with the concept of equality among citizens enshrined in most constitutions of the Arab world, manifested most clearly in the principle of equality before the law. Some Arab countries, with complete confessional cantonisation, such as Sudan and Lebanon, suffer particularly in this respect.

This established personal law is derived from medieval-patriarchal concepts of the rights of man and, because of its source, has added to it religious sanctions. Consequently, they are characterised by inflexibility and are no longer consistent with modern developments or progressive changes in the nature and functions of the family, either internally or in relation to the community. These laws have likewise failed to keep up with developments in international law or to adjust to international agreements issued in accordance with the latest concepts of the rights of man. We may also add that these laws have not absorbed the 'agreement on the abolition of all forms of discrimination against women', issued by the United Nations in 1986. Only six Arab countries have accepted this agreement, four of which have expressed reservations about Clause 16, which codifies the principle of equality between men and women in families, arguing that such matters lie within the framework of 'Islamic Arab heritage'. Perhaps Tunisia is the only Arab country that fulfils these requirements and more, for it has had a modern Family Law since the 1950s and has unequivocally developed in line with the most up-to-date concepts of the rights of man. All other countries, including Syria, still flounder in endless sterile debates. Proposals for schemes for adjusting or developing these laws all end up in failure or, in one country or another, some success is achieved in a point of detail.

Customs and traditions in these countries produce a climate hostile to women. The situation has deteriorated following the spread of medieval-patriarchal concepts in the region at the present time. This perpetuates what seems to be one long, unending night, at a time when elsewhere there have been the most enlightened ideas concerning the reform of laws relating to personal status in general and the removal of discrimination against women in particular. For example, in spite of the increase of the number of women judges the area of sharia law remains deliberately and persistently closed to us. In Syria, as in Iran, and elsewhere in the Middle East, sharia judges must all be men. These male judges can even keep women away from sessions that reach decisions relating to marital separation.[1] It cannot be concealed from anyone the damage done to women claimants when nobody in the legal process can represent their point of view, particularly as the judge is empowered to make an arbitrary judgment.[2] If we take into account the quite shocking ignorance of most women of the details of law because of the style in which these laws are drafted, we realise the importance of having women present in the processes of sharia law, as legislators, judges and arbiters.

Rulings from other personal laws have reinforced the negative impact on the lives of women. I will briefly enumerate the most important.

- *In the penal code* crimes of 'honour' such as adultery stipulate for the same crime double the penalty for women. There is discrimination against women in the matter of where the crime has been committed. Crimes against honour take no account of the humanity of women as far as the penalty is concerned: the priority is to avoid scandal. Perhaps the most serious of these laws is Article 548 of the Syrian Criminal Code which permits a murderer, or one who causes harm, the plea of mitigation if he has come across his wife or a close female relation in suspicious circumstances with another. This article has wide implications. It is the same with articles that offer mitigating circumstances to the man who kills to 'purge a dishonour' or to 'exact revenge'. And Article 523 criminalises spreading information or increasing awareness of contraception. These rules are common to all Muslim legislation across the Middle East.[3]

- *In the law relating to nationality* women are still not allowed to transfer their nationality to their children. This too is common to all Arab countries.

- *In commercial and property law* in Lebanon there is discrimination against women with regard to their competence to act on legal matters. And the law dealing with juridical authority in Iran and Egypt does not allow women to act as public prosecutor. Violation of the principle of equality is even greater in the field of applied law, that is in administrative orders. These may discriminate against women and violate their freedom in a way that is in conflict with the Syrian constitution. For example, Permanent Law 876 of 1979 permits husbands and women's *patrons* to prevent a woman travelling, by submitting a direct request in writing to the security authorities, bypassing the courts of justice. There are many similar instances of discrimination against women in administrative rulings of less significance, but all are in effect offensive. Furthermore custom violates women's rights that are established in law and the sharia.

The most important of these concerns the right of inheritance and the right to own agricultural land. In spite of the Koranic law that states that women shall inherit half of what a man inherits, custom has removed this right altogether. In no part of the Arab world do women in rural areas inherit land. What happens is that she 'resigns' her right to one of her male relations, whether she wants to or not. The violation of this established principle is a cause of anger and resentment. Fathers seize their daughters' dowry on their marriage in violation of the law and of sharia. This happens in Jordan and among Bedouin communities.

Given these serious legal discrepancies, the first step towards empowerment for women in the Middle East is to reform the law on personal status and strive to eliminate all discrimination against her in all aspects of life. Many Muslim feminist lawyers and activists in Syria, Iran and elsewhere in the Middle East are working for a family law that is contemporary and uniform, one that regards the small family unit consisting of father, mother and their children as the basis for legislation, a law that regulates relations among them, protects them and assists in providing security for them. The law should guarantee equal and mutual rights and duties between married couples both during the time of their marriage and in the event of its dissolution. It should consider the moral and material interests of all. The law should guarantee freedom of choice and total consent on the ratification of marriage and at its dissolution. Both should be validated in the presence and by the decision of a judge. The law should decree equality of father and mother in parental rights and duties. The law should safeguard the rights of the children and take into consideration their spiritual, emotional and educational interests. The special bond between mother and child should have priority. Anything that gives marital relations the character of an arrangement whereby the woman is a waged hireling of the man should be removed. She should emerge from the reformed laws with social status albeit with educational obligations. This reform should be accompanied by the abolition of all discriminatory laws such as those I have touched upon above.

We also aim to improve study and research in women's issues of whatever kind, in order to remove infringements of those rights in various social and professional sectors.

I would like here to proclaim the importance of encouraging research by women in these fields, and the need for unofficial women's organisations to take a role. In this respect I welcome the first issue of *Bahithat*, a specialist journal produced by a collective of Lebanese women researchers. It is a pioneering effort, worthy of imitation in each Arab country.

To sum up, we wish to bring the day-to-day life of women in our country into line with her excellent status in legislation. We wish her to balance those efforts required to mobilise women to work for the development of our country and those efforts required to remove the restrictions to that development.

Our situation as Syrian women is the same as that of women all over the world: faithful guardians of life and its joys. Consequently we have a fundamental interest in achieving the rights of humankind in accordance with the loftiest concepts of humanity, and with all that strengthens democracy, freedom, peace and equality among the children of humanity.

Thank you.

Translation from the Arabic by Peter Clark

NOTES

1. For a comparative study of the Iranian case, see this volume, chapter 7 and H. Afshar (1996) 'Islam and Feminism: An Analysis of Political Strategies' in M. Yamani (ed.), *Feminism and Islam, Legal and Literary Perspectives* (Reading, MA: Ithaca Press).

2. For detailed discussion, see also Ziba Mir-Hosseini (1993) *Marriage on Trial. A Study of Islamic Family Law* (London: I. B. Tauris).

3. For a similar case, see chapter 7 on Iran in this volume.

7 'Disempowerment' and the Politics of Civil Liberties for Iranian Women

Haleh Afshar

This chapter addresses the question of power as a process (Rowlands, this volume) and looks at the political struggles of women in post-revolutionary Iran to gain the 'power to' disentangle the disempowering policies of the state and undermine its control over their destiny.

The process of Islamification in Iran has resulted in blatant inconsistencies between women's civil liberties and legal rights granted to them by the post-revolutionary personal and criminal laws (Afshar 1985). Their civil liberties are based on a conception of political freedom which recognises and respects women as independent political actors. But the post-revolutionary state has constructed laws which classify all women as dependent and define their role in the context of their unequal familial obligations. Thus in Iran as elsewhere in the Muslim world, their political rights are undermined by the catchall of an ascribed 'Islamic' identity.[1] Under the guise of religiosity Iranian women have been deprived of hard fought-for and shortly held constitutional equal rights. The advent of Islamification created a national identity of a 'Muslim woman' who was required to abandon all her civil rights in order to assume her maternal and domestic duties. But, Iranian women's active resistance has demonstrated that such 'disempowerment' cannot be easily or permanently imposed.

WOMEN AS EMBLEMS OF ISLAM

Islamist Iranian women actively participated in the Revolution and supported the rejection of secularism as an imperialist Western implant. In advocating a return to Islamic values, they sought to return to the historical roots and recapture both the purity and the vitality of Islam at its inception. These women, who form part of the Islamist elite in the country today (Moghissi 1996) freely embraced the imposition of the veil and the introduction of strict dress and moral

117

codes. They willingly accepted the burden of representing the public
face of the revolution.

Thus for some 15 years the success of the revolution has been
measured in terms of its ability to maintain a high profile presence of
veiled women who have been proudly paraded as the emblem of
Islamification (Afshar 1992). It is fair to say that with the removal of
rations, the absence of welfare or any kind of safety net for the
dispossessed, female dress codes are almost all that is left to demonstrate that Iran is a revolutionary Islamic state (Behdad 1995).

Islamist women had expected greater returns for their rigorous
defence of the faith. As the revolution matures, the women's struggles
to regain some of the civil liberties, which they lost in the early post-
revolutionary days, has redoubled. In this there is a tacit alliance
between the elite Islamist women and secular lawyers and activists
who accept the veil as a necessary price to pay in order to be able to
participate in the battle for women's liberation.

ISLAM A GOAL

Those women who had fought for Islamification had engaged critically
with Western feminists' analysis of women and their positions within
the family and had chosen to reject the 'White', 'Western,' feminist
options (Rahnavard, n.d., 1995; Rezayi 1979). They argued that the
complementarity offered to women by Islam was preferable to and
more practical than the Western-style civil liberties gained by feminists
fighting for nearly a century in Iran. According to the Islamist women,
some 14 centuries ago Islam had recognised their legal identity and
economic and political independence as existing and remaining separate from that of their fathers and/or husbands and sons. The Islamic
marriage was conceived as a matter of contract between consenting
partners (The Koran 4:4, 4:24), and one that stipulated a specific price,
mahre, payable to the bride for the sexual services provided. This was
to be paid before the consummation of marriage. Islam demands that a
husband maintain his wife in the style to which she has been accus-
tomed (2:238, 4:34) and pays her for suckling their babies (2:233).
Daughters and wives have been given inalienable rights of inheritance
and retain their own entitlement to their property regardless of their
marital status.

The Islamist women state that a different and preferable form of
liberation can be found by returning to the sources of Islam. They

defend gender complementarity rather than equality as a cause and a means of serving their faith and living fulfilling lives. They note that Islam demands respect for women and offers them the opportunity of being learned, educated and gainfully employed, while at the same time providing an honoured space for those who choose to become mothers, wives and home-makers. They state that, unlike capitalism and much of feminist discourse, Islam recognises the importance of women's lifecycles; it offers them different roles and responsibilities at different times of their lives and at every stage they are to be valued respected and financially rewarded for that which they do.

THE ISLAMISTS' STRUGGLES

The problem has been that far from offering such an idyllic alternative, the Islamic revolution has exacerbated the subordination of women, without in return giving them many of their Islamic rights (Afshar 1989). As a result Islamist Iranian women have been obliged to engage on a hard and long battle to challenge the male hegemony in their own country and demand the recognition of a woman-centred inter-pretation of the faith. Over the past decade and a half they have fought for and won the right to a presence within the political domain, the right to retain a toe-hold in the judiciary and to revise some of the more Draconian aspects of the post-revolutionary divorce laws.

Throughout, religious discourse has been at the heart of the demands for improved civil rights (Afshar 1996). It is only elite Islam-ist such as the veteran Parliamentarian Maryam Behrouzi who have succeeded in gaining some ground. They have done so by locating their demands centrally with Islamic teachings and denigrating secularism. Thus Behrouzi for example declared:

> The revolution brought about by Islam 14 centuries ago had been eroded over the centuries and with it all the rights that Islam had stipulated for women... without the Islamic revolution we would have had a more limited view of women and we would not have had the advantages that we have now. When we make a comparison we find that Islam has the first and the last word. I am of the view that if there was no question of women's liberty maybe we would not have appreciated the Islamic gift and not valued it as much. But seeing what is available today in terms of liberty and equality, in

terms of women's rights, in terms of women's values ... we see that
by comparison with other religions Islam is fairer.

(*Zaneh Rouz*, 4 May 1994).

Given the conviction that Islam is good for women, the Islamist
women take a non-confrontational approach applauding the principles
and lamenting the failures of the state to achieve the high Islamic goals.
Thus, for example, Behrouzi states that the Islamic Republic has
already granted women many civil rights:

Imam [Khomeini] changed the whole root of the matter by changing
the general attitude to women. He stated that women are free to be
educated, to work, that women are free and should be involved in
politics and Islam sees men and women as equal and heaven knows
that he helped women more than men.

This great change has resulted in women ... becoming complete
persons equal to men, who are complete human beings, with equal
rights and this is no longer in question ...

At last in Islamic society women have the freedom to speak, on
the radio, on the television, in international meetings and to defend
Islam, not only women's rights but on all issues. They give their
views on politics, on economics they make public speeches, their
advice is sought and their presence shows that the Islamic society has
accepted the presence of women. This is the result of the revolution.

(*Zaneh Rouz*, 4 May 1994)

SECULARISTS

Secularism has no formal place in the women's political arena in the
post-revolutionary state. Women Marxists and members of the resistance groups in Iran have, since and before the revolution, paid with
their lives for their convictions (Moghissi 1994). Yet, despite the high
price, many continue the struggle and end up in prison and torture
chambers of the regime (Rejali 1993).

Secular free-thinking women working in the public domain are
under constant pressure and surveillance and frequently dismissed for
minor dress code transgressions. In some provinces such as Mazan-
daran the Islamic revolutionary *Komiteh* banned not only the wearing, but also the sale of, un-Islamic garments which are described as:

translucent stockings, or stockings with arrows, pictures or in bright colouring and short length coats, i.e. above the knee, or outer garments made of material with any designs or markings on the collar, bodice or arms.

(Iran Bulletin, 1993)

Schools and universities have instituted harsh moral and dress codes and imposed strict separation of sexes. This is particularly problematic in mixed colleges and universities. Employees of Tehran University even received a directive demanding that 'they should not walk in a speaking manner'!

In the summer of 1993 a woman professor sacked because she was caught shaking hands with a male colleague was accused of committing 'adultery while standing up', *zenayeh istadeh*! A male and female student in Tehran Teachers' Training College were seen talking to each other. They were immediately expelled and a court sentenced them to be lashed for the crime of 'adultery by interview', *zanayeh mosabeheyi*! It is worth noting that they appealed to the Chief Justice who quashed the sentence. Nevertheless, the college refused to re-admit them and insisted on condemning their 'immoral' conduct *(Iran Bulletin,* 1993).

Yet there is a large tranche of feminists who still choose to disregard the strict dress code and segregation rules and pay a heavy penalty for their opposition. Women students at the Shahre Rey Open University boycotted classes in protest against harassment during body and bag checks. The revolutionary guards reacted by instituting a campaign for reinforcement of the dress codes. Their tactics ranged from killing to public denouncements. They pursued and shot a 17-year old girl, Bahareh Vojdani, in a telephone booth for 'inadequate Islamic attire'. In the first two days of the campaign, in August 1993, they arrested 15,000 young girls; 300 were brought before an audience in the Teachers Hall to recant their transgression in public *(Iran Bulletin,* 1993).

Nevertheless the resistance has continued. Death by fire has become one of the most dramatic and prevalent methods chosen by some women to show their opposition. They refuse to be the silent standard bearers of national honour and the public face of Islamification.

A classic example was Professor Homa Darabi, who set herself on fire in 1994. A popular teacher and respected researcher, Darabi had been dismissed in December 1991 from her post as the Chair in Child Psychiatry for 'non-adherence to Islamic dress code, *hijab*'. Although the decision was overturned by the Employment and Grievance

Tribunal in May 1993, the University refused to reinstate her. Darabi was a long standing feminist. In 1960 she was imprisoned for organising the Iranian National Front's student demonstrations in Tehran University demanding equal rights for women. After completing her studies, Homa Darabi continued her struggles while practising in a small village of Bahmanieh in northern Iran. Subsequently she went to the United States where she completed her studies. She returned to Tehran in 1976 where she was appointed to the Chair in Child Psychiatry and continued her anti-government resistance activities with the National Front.

On the 21 February 1994, Homa Darabi, tore off her head scarf and her Islamic long coat in a public thoroughfare near Tajrish Square in the Shemiran suburb of Tehran. Darabi passionately called for liberty and condemned oppression crying 'Down with tyranny, long live freedom, long live Iran!' She then doused herself in petrol and set herself alight.

Her death led to widespread protests in Iran and abroad. An estimated 10,000 people attended her memorial service on the 24 February 1994, at the Aljavad Mosque in Tehran. The meeting was held despite the government's intention to ban it.

EDUCATION

There is, however, a degree of tacit cooperation amongst some of the Islamists and those non-believers who for the time being accept the veil. They have joined hands in seeking to improve women's access to education and alter the blatant inequalities that they suffer under the post-revolutionary laws.

Using the Koranic instruction that all Muslims must become learned, they have fought to remove many of the bars placed on their education. The Islamic government is committed to compulsory, publicly provided, schooling, but it has not been very successful in providing it; not least because of critical shortage of funds (Afshar 1992: 206–13; Omid 1994: 158–61). At its inception the Islamic Republic instituted segregated schools and insisted that girls be taught by female teachers. Given the shortages of trained women scientists and mathematicians in Iran, this would have been a serious handicap for the younger generation of Iranian women. But this regulation was more or less universally flouted by private schools and even government schools chose to disregard it in most cases (Omid 1994: 157).

Initially, women were excluded from 54 per cent of the subjects taught at the tertiary level (Qahraman 1989; Afshar 1992) and were reduced to 10 per cent of the total student population in 1983 (Omid 1994: 162). Slowly and painfully many fought their way back. By 1991 they were still barred from 97 academic areas (*Zaneh Rouz*, 31 August 1991), but had managed to obtain some quotas specifically for them in many faculties. Eventually they were assisted by the Women's Cultural-Social Council. Despite its conservative membership it convinced the High Council of Cultural revolution to eliminate the prejudicial treatment of women in higher education and in the selection for degree courses.

In practice many leading religious figures had consistently fought against such discriminatory measures. So, for example when, at the inception of the revolution, Khomeini decreed that women must be barred from the Faculty of Law, some eminent religious leaders such as Ayatollah Mohamad Hosein Beheshti, the first post-revolutionary Head of the Judiciary, Ayatollah Mussavi Ardabili and Ayatollah Mohaqeq Damad set up informal classes for male and female postgraduate law students, to teach them Islamic law. This enabled many of the women who had graduated just before the revolution to acquire the necessary Islamic legal training. Given the shortages of male lawyers and the closure of the Faculty of Law for about three years, those amongst these women who were both educated and had good revolutionary credentials found themselves propelled into relatively powerful positions in no time at all. For example, Azam Nuri, the Director General of the Legal Department of the Ministry of National Guidance, *Ershadeh Meli*, was appointed to her post in 1979, when she was 24 years old.

In their battle for access to education, Islamist women and their supporters have been at pain to insist that Islam demands that women be well educated. In April 1994 Azam Nuri told reporters:

> Women must arm themselves with knowledge. They must seek to learn at any age under any condition be it at work or at home ... They must study. Our religion recognises no limit whatsoever for learning and the acquisition of knowledge. Once humanity is armed with knowledge it can remove all the problems.
>
> (*Zaneh Rouz*, 30 April 1994)

Another useful strategy is to refer to Khomeini, his life and his teaching for Islamic endorsement of female education. Even though in his life-time he instituted bars against women's education. His daughter Farideh Mostafavi Khomeini, declared in an interview:

> *Hazrat imam* was always concerned with and supported women's education. He personally taught my mother and asked my late brother to teach me. At the time when women were viewed as unsuited to education, the late saint Khomeini instructed my late brother to teach me, which he did for many years.
> I remember one day on the eve of an exam. The house was full of guests . . . I picked up my books and went to my father's room and said 'your room is quiet I've come to study here' . . . a little while later he came in with a tea tray. I was most embarrassed and said 'Sir, why have you taken so much trouble?' He smiled and said 'A person who studies is worthy of respect' . . . This clearly denotes the importance that the *hazrateh imam* attached to education.
>
> (*Zaneh Rouz,* 4 May 1994)

A third approach has been to use the phobia about contact between the sexes which has remained paramount for some government officials. This fear of immorality has contributed to the reinstatement of technical training for women. In 1993 the first women's institute for technical and vocational training was opened in Ahwaz with 1500 women registering. But the term technical was widely interpreted to mean not only courses in computing, electronics, technical drawing, repairs of household goods, accountancy, design, but also tailoring, knitting and cake making.

The arguments about segregated education proved most effective in the field of medicine. Even as recently as July 1993, Deputy Minister of Health Larijani restated the official view that:

> We must reduce to a minimum the contact between sexes. This is one of our serious principles and no amount of seemingly enlightened thinking would deviate us from this correct path. Medical centres, operation theatres must not be places where people expose their bodies to the opposite sex. Hence the urgent need to have all-women hospitals and clinics.
>
> (*Iran Bulletin,* 1993)

Islamists used this obsession with sexual transgression to obtain government funds to set up a special all-women Faculty of Medicine at Qom. At the same time, they also gained better access to other medical schools; in 1994 the government agreed to institute a 25 per cent quota for women in other medical schools and other medical fields.[2]

LAW AND THE JUDICIARY

The problems of segregation and fear of women have proved most intractable in the domain of law and judiciary. At the inception of the revolution, women judges were sacked and law schools closed to female students. The country was placed under Islamic jurisdiction. Nevertheless much of the pre-revolutionary Civil Codes survived and even family courts which had been closed down for a brief period were re-opened (Mir-Hosseini 1993).

Although the post-revolutionary state had intended to exclude women from the legal domain altogether, in the early days there were simply not enough men trained in Islamic law, to take over the new system. With the massive outmigration of educated men, those Iranian women who stayed behind filled the gap. So very early on Clause 5 was added to the law. This enabled women to be present as 'advisers' or as 'consultants' in almost every domain of law; they could even be advisers in formulating laws. They could be advisers in family courts; they could be advisers to prosecutors. The existence of this law enabled women who had been lawyers before the revolution to continue practising.

Women lawyers chose a number of other strategies to remain present as acting lawyers. Some re-registered in the name of their husbands, their brothers, their sons, who may or may not have been lawyers. The official lawyer was the husband, and the woman who had been trained as a lawyer became the 'adviser' and continued to function as she had always done. There were other women, particularly new graduates of the Faculty of Law, who were Islamic women who had been in the forefront of the revolution. They were trained by some of the leading religious leaders, as part of the new nexus of Sharia lawyers who were being trained. These women immediately stepped into powerful legal posts, as 'advisers' or 'consultants'. The availability of Clause 5 meant that although officially women were excluded from the domain of law, in practice they remained active and effective. But as the Islamic state tightened its grip and Sharia-trained men gradually emerged to take over, the religious institution, *ulama*, began a campaign to remove women from the domain of law. By 1993 they were arguing that the male lawyers no longer needed any 'advisers' and so the posts should be eliminated. In April 1993, *Majlis*, the parliament, was advised by its judicial committee, that all of these posts should be abolished altogether. Clause 5 had to be rejected. The arguments in the *Majlis* were very clearly articulated in terms of the necessity to remove women from the legal domain. It is worth noting that in 1993 for the first time since the revolution there were nine women Members of Parliament: that is a remarkable event in itself. There have always been women Members of Parliament; in the early days there were two, then there were three, but never more. Of course, there has never been a woman in the cabinet and so the glass ceiling operates in Iran, as it does in the West.

The women who are in Parliament have been able to organise effectively, and this particular case shows the variety of ways they have employed.

The veteran parliamentarian Behrouzi girded her loins and once more declared Islam to be exemplary in its provisions for women:

> We are seeking to benefit from Islamic laws in terms of securing legal and judicial protection; which thanks be to God we have been doing and we can have the very best economic, political, social and familial laws and lay claim to the best kind of equality, in fact something more than equality before the world.
>
> (*Zaneh Rouz*, 4 May 1994)

Then she went on to reassure the weary that women 'advisers' would not transgress the segregation lines:

> It is not necessary for the female advisers to go and sit next to the judge, since one of the gentlemen thought that such an action would be improper. A woman adviser could give her advice in writing and then the judge is free to use her advice.
>
> (*Zaneh Rouz*, 4 May 1994)

Nor would they be emotional or sentimental:

> Some imagine that if women wish to advise the Judge then the advice would be such as to prevent the judge from remaining impartial; whereas this is not the case. A woman lawyer who becomes an adviser to a judge would undoubtedly be a learned, wise and intelligent woman with deep social insight who would certainly offer

advice that is beneficial to humanity, male or female.

(*Zaneh Rouz*, 4 May 1994)

Eventually the women parliamentarians managed to fight a rearguard action and prevent the removal of Clause 5 from the Judicial Codes. It was only at this point that Behrouzi went on to blame some of her male colleagues and praise others:

> Unfortunately we still have views in the *Majlis* which encourages people not to vote for our cause. But this is a problem of views and not Islamic laws. It is not the laws that are biased against us, it is not Islamic rules that are biased against us. But there is such a bias which is rooted in the culture and perspectives of some people. But with the ratification of the laws concerning women's posts as advisors and the divorce laws it is obvious that such prejudices do not form the majority view of the *Majlis*.

(*Zaneh Rouz*, 4 May 1994)

However to placate the more traditionalist parliamentarians, the Head of the Judiciary, Ayatollah Mohamad Yazdi, set up the Judiciary's Women's Bureaux and appointed Malikeh Yazdi to head it. She had worked in the President's Women's Bureaux and in her new post was required to

> pay a deeper attention to affairs and prevent *tadakhol*, intervention and mix up, between the judiciary and the administrative branch.

(*Zaneh Rouz*, 17 September 1994)

DIVORCE AND OBEDIENCE

Women have become the standard bearers of the honour of the post-revolutionary state in Iran. The honour of the state is measured in terms of how well they wear the veil, in terms of how well they behave and, in particular, in terms of how obedient they are as wives and how dutiful they remain. This demand for obedience is at the core of the gendered politics of Islam. Disobedient women are seen as a potential source of rebellion and disorder and the destruction of the existing political order. As Fatima Mernissi explains:

> Arabic has a word, *al-nashir*, to define a woman who rebels against the will of her husband. The concept of *nushuz* is only applied to

women. It is a declaration by a woman of her decision not to follow
the will of her husband.... And *nushuz* is obviously synonymous
with *fitna*, disorder.

(Mernissi 1993: 177)

So that by default Islamist women must, in their negotiations with the
state, accept the centrality of obedience. This acceptance has been put
to some use. In 1993 Behrouzi piloted a bill which curtailed men's
automatic right of divorce, by stipulating that men who 'unjustly'
divorce their 'obedient' wives should do their Koranic duty and pay
'wages' for the wife's domestic services during their marriage:

The ones who fear us feel that giving women rights, for example
paying them for housework if they decide to divorce them, makes for
unruliness and disobedience amongst the women folk. They worry
about the prospect of marriage and feel that women may become
uppity once they have got a financial security of their own, they
might then go for divorce. But this is not so... If women are happy
and comfortable in their lives they would not seek to divorce a
husband.

(*Zaneh Rouz*, 4 May 1994)

She argued that far from it being the fault of unruly, disobedient
women, it was men who chose to break the family up. But if they
destroyed the domestic hearth, then they had to be made to pay for
their destruction of the home:

The law is about those women whose husbands' seek to divorce
them. Its for women who have done no wrong, who have been
obedient, who have not misbehaved and still the husband wants to
divorce them. Yet we still have people who think that if women have
such a right they would exercise it to gain grounds in the family and
are therefore against it.

(*Zaneh Rouz*, 4 May 1994)

Being an astute politician Behrouzi announced that the bill indicated
that the Islamic solution could be vastly preferable to the Western
alternative:

We have some of the most advanced laws concerning women, such
as the law for payment of wages for housework which is unique in

the world . . . In the West they require couples who divorce to halve their worldly goods, but that is because there women are obliged to work, so from the start they put in half each into their married life. So when they split they take half each. But here women are not obliged to work. Women don't even have to bring in a dowry – those who do so are offering a gift. But it is the duty of the men to provide housing to furnish and equip the house and to pay for the household. Even so those women who stipulate it in their marriage contract can get up to half of their husband's worldly goods, if they have stipulated it in their marriage contract. They can also claim for suckling the baby or they can claim wages for housework, if they have been dutiful and obedient.

(*Zaneh Rouz*, 28 June 1993 and 4 May 1994)

CURTAILED MOTHERHOOD

But the Islamist definition of women as belonging primarily in the domain of domesticity, and functioning as obedient wives and mothers poses serious problems not only for them as independent individuals, but also for their fulfilment of their maternal duties as they see fit.

They have not been given the entitlements that Islamist women claimed for their antecedents in the first centuries of Islam. After all, the women of the Prophet's entourage, his wives Khadijah and Ayishah, had both been acclaimed for their economic independence. But at the end of the twentieth century the Islamification process in Iran has defined women as second-class citizens and by doing so has prevented them from providing economic security for their own children.

This problem is rooted in the inability of Iranian women, at the end of the twentieth century, to have the automatic right of custody over the very children that they are supposed to mother, raise and protect. Even if the divorce proceedings are initiated by men against the most obedient of women, that wayward man has the uncontested right of custody over his children.

But Islamist women have been seeking to use *ijtehad*, interpretation, to alter this situation and have succeeded in convincing *Majlis* to offer an opportunity for children and mothers to avoid paternal custody. In an interview with the campaigning women's journal *Zaneh Rouz*, Khomeini's daughter, Farideh Mostafavi Khomeini argued that there was much room for negotiation:

The views about custody differ; the traditionalist, *motoghademin*, believe that mothers should have custody till puberty and then the children have the right to choose based on a *hadith* from Imam Sadegh who said that so long as the woman has not remarried she should have custody. But the modernists *motoakherin* have argued that sons till two and daughters till 7 can be kept by mothers and our laws have been passed accordingly. Article 1169 of the civil codes endorses this, but *Majlis* has decreed that at puberty the children can choose.

(*Zaneh Rouz*, 4 May 1994)

But although children now have a choice in the matter, mothers, who have been praised as the very bastions of the family, mothers who are seen as the very cornerstone of the revolution, remain powerless where their children and particularly their financial futures are concerned. In a hard-hitting public denunciation of this situation the veteran lawyer and author, Mehrangiz Kar, demanded to know 'Why women are barred from opening saving accounts for their children?' (*Zanan*, no. 22, February/March 1995).

Kar notes that the fact that women have been barred from having custody and guardianship of their children has resulted in the decision by banks not to allow them to open interest-bearing accounts for their children. Although in the early days of the revolution these were the only forms of account that were available, in subsequent years banks have been permitted to start interest bearing accounts for their customers. But, unlike their male counterparts, Iranian mothers are obliged to opt for the strictly Islamic, non-interest-paying kinds of account, whereas even the children themselves could open the interest-bearing accounts.

The banks have decided to follow the provisions of Article 1169 of the civil codes which essentially defines women as child carrying vessels, rather than responsible adults entitled to take charge of those children. Therefore mothers can only open the *hessabeh pasandazeh qarzeh hassaneh*, which does not pay any interest at all.

The pre-revolutionary banking laws of April 1978 allowed both mothers and children to open accounts:

children who have reached the age of twelve may open their own bank accounts. Only the person opening the account is entitled to withdraw any money from these accounts. These account holders will be entitled to withdraw money from their accounts when they reach the age of 15. Note: a mother may open an account in name of her minor child in which case until the child reaches the age of majority at 18 it is the mother who is entitled to withdraw monies from this account.

This note was added to ensure that fathers were not able to abuse their right of guardianship and withdraw the mother's hard-earned savings which were specifically earmarked for the child. But in September 1979 when fathers regained automatic custody and guardianship of their children, all laws relating to guardianship of mothers were revised and this article came under close scrutiny. Kar points out that initially mother's rights seemed to have been protected. In 1980 the legal section of the Ministry of Justice gave its opinion that:

Since according to this note, the right to take money out of the account is specifically given to the mother who is the person who has opened the account in the first place, this does not impute the right of custody or guardianship. Which means that fathers or paternal grandfathers are not entitled to withdraw sums from such accounts.

(8 March 1980)

But in 1994 the government issued a banking directive which stated categorically that:

Mothers are not, under any circumstances, entitled to open any saving accounts for their children other that the *hessabeh pasandazeh qarzeh hassaneh*. The only exception is mothers who have been given formal, legal custody over their children and have the appropriate legal documents.

(26 April 1994)

This means that mothers have been officially barred from opening fixed term saving accounts that carry between 8 and 15 per cent interest rates, for their children.

CONCLUSION

It would be a mistake to be unreservedly sanguine about the progress of women and their cause in Iran. As Kar's case of new retrograde directives about saving accounts clearly demonstrates, even in the mid-

1990s Iranian women are likely to lose some ground while gaining others. Iranian politics can now best be characterised by factionalism and unsteady alliances. In a process which demonstrates the use of power to generate resistance without domination (Rowlands, this volume) women have succeeded in positioning themselves at the centre of the political arena, not least because they are amongst the last remaining emblems of Islamification. But it is not always easy or possible to turn this situation to their advantage. It is therefore all the more remarkable to see how very far they have managed to come under such difficult circumstances.

NOTE

1. For a comparative study of the Syrian case, see this volume, chapter 6.
2. Quoted by Fatemeh Homayun Moadam, *Majlis* representative for Tabriz, at a press conference, 30 April 1994.

REFFERENCES

Afshar, H. (1985) 'Women, State and Ideology in Iran', *Third World Quarterly* 7(2), April, pp. 256–78.

Afshar, H (1989) 'Women in the Work and Poverty Trap in Iran', in H. Afshar and B. Agarwal (eds) *Women, Poverty and Ideology in Asia*, Basingstoke: Macmillan.

Afshar, H. (1992) 'Women and Work: Ideology not Adjustment at Work in Iran', in H. Afshar and C. Dennis (eds), *Women and Adjustment Policies in the Third World*, Basingstoke: Macmillan, Women's Studies at York Series.

Afshar, H. (1995) 'Women and the Politics of Fundamentalism in Iran', in H. Afshar (ed.), *Women and Politics in the Third World*, London: Routledge.

Afshar, H. (1996) 'Islam and Feminism: An Analysis of Political Stratigies', in M. Yamani (ed.), *Feminism and Islam, Legal and Literary Perspectives*, Reading: Ithaca Press.

Behdad, Sohrab (1995) *Iran dar bezangah bohran eqtesadi*, [Iran at the point of economic crisis], Paris.

Mernissi, Fatima (1993) *The Forgotten Queens of Islam*, Mineapolis: University of Minneapolis Press.

Mir-Hosseini, Ziba 1993 *Marriage on Trial, A Study of Islamic Family Law*, London: I. B. Tauris.

Moghissi, Haideh (1996) 'Factionalism and Muslim feminine elite in Iran' in Rahnema Saeed (ed.) *Post revolutionary Iran*, London: Zed Press.

Moghissi, Haideh (1994) *Populism and Feminism in Iran*, Basingstoke: Macmillan, Women's Studies at York.

Omid, H. (1994) *Islam and the Post revolutionary State in Iran*, Basingstoke: Macmillan.

Qahraman, S. (1989) *Siyasateh hokumateh Eslami piramuneh dastressi zanan beh amouzesheh ali va assarateh an bar moqeyiyateh ejtemayi va eqtessadi zanan* [the Islamic Republic's policies on women's access to higher education and its impact on the soci-economic position of women], *Nimeyeh Digar*, no. 7 summer.

Rahnavard, Zahra (1995) *Zan, Eslam va feminism* ['Women, Islam and Feminism'], *Majaleh Saisateh Khareji* [The Journal of Foreign Policy], vol. IX, no. 2, summer.

Rahnavard, Z. (n.d.) *Toloueh Zaneh Mosalman*, Tehran Mahboubeh Publication.

Rejali, D. M. (1993) *Torture and Modernity: Self, Society and State in Modern Iran*, Boulder: Westview Press.

Rezayi, M. (1979) *Horiat va Hoquqeh Zan dar Eslam*, Milad Publication, 3rd reprint, Shahrivar.

Journals and Newspapers

Cesmandaz, no. 15, autumn 1995.
Iran Bulletin, no. 3, second series, July–Sept 1993
Nimeyeh Digar.
Zanan, no. 22, February/March 1995
Zaneh Rouz, 4 May 1994, 31 August 1991.

8 Violence in Intimate Relationships: A Research Project in India
Purna Sen

INTRODUCTION

The Constitution of India declares equality for all citizens. Many laws and policies translate this statement of intent into measures which address gendered disadvantage. However, there is also a complex interrelationship of social, economic and legal practices and beliefs which oppresses women. The sex ratio has a masculine bias, female labour-force participation is low, female literacy and educational attainment are low, and women do not experience the property and inheritance rights which are theirs according to the law.

An insidious and horrific indication of the oppression which women (and girls) experience is that of male violence. At times cross-cutting issues of class, caste and ethnicity play a part in such violence which takes many forms, from caste-based rape, through wife-beating to female infanticide and foeticide. Unfortunately, there are many others too. This chapter reports on women's experiences of male violence at the hands of husbands and male partners, on which I conducted research in Calcutta. Information was collected on 52 relationships by interviewing women about their histories – educational experience, migration patterns, paid employment, physical and sexual violence. Women of different classes and ages were interviewed, living in slums, from women's shelters and elsewhere. A number of women had suffered extreme physical abuse, some abuse was repeated over many years, while other women said that violence stopped after a short time. Women suffered many injuries, and whether or not implements had been used, almost everyone spoke of the pain they had endured.

Many women said that the interview was the first time that they had spoken about some details of their abuse, particularly concerning sexual violence. Women also remarked that they felt much 'lighter', much easier, for having spoken in this way: speaking out serves to validate their experience and to end their isolation. It was clear that although many women had spoken about and sought help against physical violence, there remains a widespread silence on sexual abuse. Despite these personal histories of secrecy, many women did speak to me about forced and painful sex and of having their experiences of pain ignored by their husbands. The research sought to explore the ways in which women respond to violence, where they find support and the ways in which they deal with violence in intimate relationships. Women were asked about the people to whom they had spoken about the violence and what those different people had said or done to help. The stories of women who have moved from violent to violence-free lives provide important indications of what can be done to enable women to resist such violence.

INDIA: VIOLENCE AGAINST WOMEN

The constitution of India asserts that the state shall not discrimination on the grounds of religion, race, caste, sex or place of birth (e.g. Articles 15[1] and 15[3], Constitution of India). It allows for specific measures in favour of women towards the aim of social justice for all citizens. The population is diverse in terms of language, religion, ethnicity and culture. Disadvantage also exists in many forms. Here I am concerned with the experience of women.

The women's movement in India is well established, articulate and effective. The contemporary movement has agitated on a number of issues and has been particularly vocal on violence against women. The national Committee on the Status of Women reported in the mid-1970s providing a broad and detailed exposition of discrimination against women and girls across the country, which then formed the basis for lobbying for policy and legal changes, some of which have been very successful. For example, in politics there is now a quota of 33 per cent for women for both membership and leadership positions in the local elective bodies (Panchayat) and in Maharashtra state amniocentesis tests for sex determination have been banned, and a policy for women was announced in 1994 (*India Today*, 1995).

The effect of bias and discrimination against women and girls is manifest in the pattern of female mortality, morbidity and the sex ratio. Evidence has been provided to demonstrate that these are related to childhood resource allocation which favours males (Anker, Buvinic and Youssef 1982; Harriss and Watson 1987). Female infanticide has been investigated by the Adithi project in Bihar, which found that the bias against girls operates even in the practice of female infanticide at the time of birth, in the very rooms where the babies are born (Adithi project 1994). Additionally, for India as a whole,

> [d]eaths of young girls . . . exceed those of young boys by almost one third of a million every year. Every sixth infant death is specifically due to gender discrimination.
>
> (Bennett 1991: 123)

Male violence against women is an expression of the power which men have to control and punish women, unrestricted by adequate penalty or disincentives. The National Crime Bureau has calculated that there is one criminal offence against women every 7 minutes (1991 figures). Certain cases have highlighted legal shortcomings and male bias and the contemporary women's movement in India have been extremely vocal and effective around such issues as dowry death and rape. (There is a wide literature on this, examples include Radha Kumar 1993; Joseph and Sharma 1994; Sarkar 1994).

As in all countries there is a range of forms which this violence takes, including rape in public spaces as well as in the home, physical abuse and sexual harassment. As in various countries the recorded rape statistics show a rise in recent years – in India as a whole the increase was 26 per cent between 1987 and 1991 (National Crime Bureau). Increased awareness and agitation around rape followed the Mathura rape case, in which a young tribal girl was raped by two policemen in the police station. No visible evidence of harm was observed on the young girl while there was evidence of sexual intercourse. A previous sexual relationship of the victim was cited to discredit her and the policemen who had been charged were acquitted by the Supreme Court. Mathura 'was thus a loose woman who could not, by definition be raped' (Kumar 1993: 129). The outcry against this interpretation was broad; rape became a central and critical issue around which Indian feminists have since organised, particularly with the rise in reports of custodial rape. However, marital rape remains an act which escapes legal censure, although it is legally acknowledged if the wife is a minor. But even the rape of a young girl between the ages of 12 and 15 years[1] carries a lesser sentence if the rapist is married to the victim (Sarkar 1994: 83).

Other expressions of violence appear to be more specific to the Indian experience, such as dowry death, *sati* and female foeticide and infanticide, although it has been argued that they are spreading to neighbouring countries. 'Dowry death' is a term used to describe the death of a wife whose in-laws dispute the amount of dowry received at the time of marriage and pursue their demands for more by abusing the wife to the point of her death. This practice appears to be more common in north India than in the south, and increased rapidly during the early 1980s (Calman: 1992 127). Between 1987 and 1991 there was an increase of 170 per cent in the recorded incidence of dowry death in India as a whole (National Crime Bureau). A complicating factor common in such deaths is that they often involve burning beside a kerosene cooker, allowing the in-laws successfully to account for them as suicides, which is how they become reported in official statistics. Agitation by women in India in the 1980s succeeded in bringing an amendment to the law which recognised the phenomenon of 'dowry death', covering any death of a woman within seven years of her marriage where 'cruelty' and dowry demands can also be shown to have existed.

CALCUTTA

Calcutta is the capital city of the state of West Bengal. The population is over 68 million and population density is 788 inhabitants per sq km (1995 figures). The Left Front state government has been led by the Communist Party of India (Marxist) since 1977 and has enthusiastically embraced the economic liberalisation programme of the central government, particularly since the introduction of the national New Economic Policy in 1991. Foreign investors have increased their interest in West Bengal in the mid-1990s, with British interest being shown with the encouragement of the British government.

Poverty is widespread in Calcutta and is particularly visible in the dwellings occupied by the poor. Many eke out their existence by begging on the streets where some also sleep. Others have a home to which they return, which is likely to be in one of the many sprawling slums spread throughout the city. It is estimated that Calcutta has 3.02 million slum dwellers who live in 'stinkingly squalid conditions ... completely unaware of what is quality of life' (SLARTC 1994: 5). Any visit to a slum has a marked impact on a newcomer:

They are so congested that there is nowhere more than an arm's span in the dirt-track lanes that separate one row from another. And open drains run down the middle of each lane so that you tend to walk them at the straddle. People sit in these lanes chopping wood,

cooking at open fires, even buying and selling at open stalls. As
many as seven or eight sleep in one room of a shanty...

(Moorhouse 1983: 99)

Free education and the literacy campaigns have both raised the
levels of education and opened up the possibility of broader expectations and aspirations to these populations than previously existed.
Similarly, immunisation programmes and limited health services have
become more easily available in these places (SLARTC 1994).
Physical conditions are very hard in the slums, but not uniform.
There are *bustees* and *jhupris*: *bustees* have solid walls and a roof and
an arrangement between tenant and landlord which affords the dweller
some degree of security. Many also now have an electricity connection
so are able to run fans or televisions. *Jhupris* are altogether a more
insecure existence, often consisting of woven straw huts with no uti-
lities whatsoever. Water has to be fetched from nearby standpipes,
which operate at certain hours only. The people for whom these huts
are home have no certainty about their accommodation – they may
find that their homes have been cleared away without any notice at all.
In both varieties of slum the living arrangements ensure that most lives
are conducted almost in public, as the physical conditions make privacy an alien concept. This also means that there is great scope for
intervention by others into the affairs of any individual, family or
household and potential for social sanction.

It has been argued that the position of women in West Bengal
indicates less discrimination than elsewhere in the country. Female
labour force participation in India as a whole is comparatively low
(24 per cent in 1994, UNDP 1995), but in Calcutta it has been found
that 'in the urban areas women's employment is increasing at a significant rate in an otherwise stagnant labour market' (Banerjee 1985:
24). Although a general relationship exists between high labour force
participation rates among 15–34-year-old women and the survival of
young girls (Miller 1981) in West Bengal, it has been argued that
despite the low female labour force participation rate there is a cultural
climate in which females enjoy some degree of protection (Bennett
1991). This appears to be supported by a positive trend in the sex
ratio over the past 50 years. It remains to be seen how the new
economic policies in the country as whole and in West Bengal will
impact upon female labour force participation and the nature of that
participation in terms of pay, distribution between formal and informal sectors, management and promotion prospects.

Although research noted earlier indicates that the nature and degree of violence against women in West Bengal is not as severe as in other parts of the country, the figures remain alarming. It has been estimated that on average there are 2 rapes, 5 criminal offences against women and 33 female suicides each day (reported in West Bengal Assembly Debates, 10 February 1994).

THE STUDY

Most studies on violence against women in general and domestic violence in particular have been conducted in Europe, United States and Australia. My research was carried out in Calcutta between 1994 and 1995 and the main concern was to examine the conditions in which women are best able to resist and to end situations in which they are abused by their husbands or partners. There are several questions which this project seeks to address: Is it women's preferred response to leave a violent home? Does economic activity provide women with the means to live a financially independent life and therefore leave a violent relationship? If not, what is or are their preferred responses? How do women respond to domestic violence? Where do women find support in dealing with domestic violence? Is it the case that if women exercise control over other aspects of their lives, such as voting intentions, take-up of contraception, allocating income, choosing whether and when to seek medical help, they are more likely to offer resistance to violent partners? If women have contacts outside their natal and in-law families do they seek support there? For women who do leave men, or succeed in getting the men to leave them, what leads them to that decision? (These are not all reported in this chapter).

The project gathered data through semi-structured interviews in Calcutta, drawing on two broad groups of respondents: organisations, agencies and key individuals working on issues of violence against women; and individual women themselves. Forty-seven women were interviewed and information was gathered about the 52 relationships they had between them. The individual women were asked to talk about their family and educational background, their history of economic activity and a number of issues relating to their exercise of control over their activities: their autonomy. Lastly, they were asked about their marital lives, in particular their experiences of physical and sexual violence within intimate relationships. This chapter draws on their accounts.

Interviews were conducted wherever women were able to speak. Several were in slums, where a local researcher, Ratnabole Biswas, worked with me. It was extremely difficult to conduct interviews in private, particularly, although not exclusively, in the *jhupri* slums. The women interviewed range across age, religion and class. Eighty per cent of the women were in their twenties or thirties, the remainder were in their forties or in their teens. The majority of the sample were Hindu women with a few Islamic women (including one woman who converted from Hinduism) and a very small proportion was Christian. Almost three-quarters (73 per cent) were poor working-class women with 15 per cent lower middle class and 12 per cent upper middle-class. There was a range of educational backgrounds in the sample. Many women (43 per cent) had had no experience of formal education, 35 per cent have some schooling with a further 6 per cent completing the additional two years of available schooling. Another small group of women had experience of tertiary, adult or other non-formal education only.

The women interviewed were of childbearing age. Forty per cent of women said that they had at some time used contraception, of whom over half had taken oral contraceptive pills. But the women had experienced many problems when using different types of contraception – headaches, impaired vision, nausea, sickness and heavy menstrual bleeding. Few had sought medical advice concerning the problems they had, even though some had endured these effects for long periods, up to several years. There was a bimodal pattern of number of pregnancies with peaks (23 per cent) at 2 and 4 pregnancies. Forty-one women between them have 87 living children, giving a mean average of 2.12 children per woman. Many women began their first pregnancy within a couple of years of their marriage and had several children after that. Despite this the rate of contraceptive use was lower than might be expected and only 15 per cent had ever had an abortion. However, the sterilisation rate is high at 41 per cent: this intrusive act is a more commonly used method of birth control than are contraceptives. All the women who have been sterilised are low class, poor women. This method of birth control appears to be most widely taken up by the poorest, least powerful, politically articulate and mobilised women.

Despite the preponderance of poor women living in squalid conditions over 40 per cent of the women described their own health as being good or adequate. Such an assessment incorporates the normalisation of certain ailments even when they may involve regular fever or digestive tract problems. Such low-level or everyday disturbances are thus overlooked in reports of 'good' health. Amongst the health problems cited by the others were some major illnesses such as jaundice, typhoid and ulcers, but the majority complained of headaches, diarrhoea, indigestion and other less dramatic but persistent ailments. When asked about the use of medical services, a surprisingly high proportion said they had seen a doctor or visited a hospital for their own health needs. Over half said that they had the recommended treatment, although a few said that they took prescribed medicines only as long as they (or their husband) could afford to buy them.

The sample was divided almost evenly between those who were employed (55 per cent) and those who were not. Some of those not employed at the time had worked previously, leaving a quarter who have never had any paid employment. The employment histories are varied, with women working in many types of jobs, but with concentrations in domestic and other low-paid, insecure work, both amongst those in work now and those who had worked previously. A very small number of women were in home-based paid work. Education is an employment area in which women are concentrated in India generally, and in Calcutta also (see Standing 1991); in this sample only 4 per cent of those currently employed and 8 per cent of those previously employed were involved in teaching or tuition.

Although very few women spoke of having any income to spare, over a third said that they had a bank account in their own name. Some had saved money in other local informal savings schemes, but had lost their money without knowing the reason why. Several women had clearly been duped by others, who had successfully withdrawn the funds from the women's accounts and some women lost their money because the saving schemes in which they participated were unsuccessful. A larger proportion of women (44 per cent) had loans in their own names and used a number of methods, some quite creative and involving their husband's funds, to repay them.

Of the women who spoke about resources, one third said that they had assets of some kind. Most often this consisted of jewellery and a large proportion of those who previously had assets had their jewellery pawned or sold to pay for family expenses or for their husband to use. Sometimes this was unexplained expenditure and for others it related to their husbands' business ventures. Few women had access, therefore, to resources which could be used in meeting their living expenses; only two women referred to inherited property: one said she expected to receive her share of her father's property and another said that she had signed over what she had received to her brother, hoping that he would then take care of her if needed. Despite the Hindu woman's legal right to inherit from her parents no one in my sample currently owned property and only one had done so previously. Of course, for poor women there is unlikely to be any property to inherit but even the limited resources which they are customarily given (jewellery on marriage) are vulnerable to pawning, sale or use by their husbands. When this use is without the woman's permission it amounts to theft – and this was experienced by a number of women.

Just under half of the women said they had contacts with government or other organisations or agencies. This is influenced heavily by those women who had been contacted for interview through support organisations, so a large proportion of those who do have such contacts have them with women's organisations and development organisations. West Bengal has a reputation both for a highly politicised population and for the ruling political parties' claim to have reached the 'masses'. Of the women interviewed 18 per cent named political parties or their women's sections in the contacts they had. In another indication of female political participation rates almost 80 per cent of women said that they exercised their right to vote in elections. When asked who determined the party for which they cast their votes three out of four women claimed that they did so themselves. However, over 18 per cent referred to their husband or his family for this decision and one woman was honest enough to say that she casts her vote as she is requested to by the numerous visitors she has at election time. She called these people the 'party boys' who come and take her to the polling booth to vote for their party – but these 'boys' would come from several different parties so she dutifully voted for several parties in a single election!

VIOLENCE IN INTIMATE RELATIONSHIPS

In the interview guidelines the last section related to violence. This structure was followed where possible and in those interviews where the women were merely responding to questions. However, in many interviews the women themselves broached topics without being asked, including experiences of violence. In fact, in a number of interviews this is what women wanted to discuss at the very outset, having understood that the discussion was to be about their lives and problems. This willingness – keenness in some cases, to discuss their intimate lives and pain with a stranger suggests that they do not think of such violence as acceptable. It is this vocalisation of experience, pain and quest for support which are central to the process of empowerment. While it may be true that the absence of privacy in the slum settlements results in widespread knowledge of domestic violence, this cannot be equated with the significant act of discussion. Talking about violence remains important both in an individual journey towards resistance and in a broader struggle against violence against women. Talking can break the isolation of the experience of violence by inviting others into that intimate space, thereby validating the pain and the deeply felt sense of injustice.

Physical violence was reported in 64 per cent of relationships; sexual violence was reported in half of the relationships. In total, women experienced physical and/or sexual violence in 79 per cent of all relationships about which information was gathered. Some women were selected for interview through the organisations where they had gone for help and this group will necessarily have a higher reporting rate. If they are disregarded and we consider only those women of whom there was no prior knowledge, the level of violence remains very high at 77 per cent. There has been much concern in India about the role of dowry and on-going demands for dowry, especially in relation to the use of domestic violence as a tool to further dowry demands. Many of the marriages in this sample did not involve the payment of a dowry, particularly 'love marriages' – those that were not arranged by family – and the data show no clear link between the payment of dowry and the existence of male violence against wives or partners. This should not be interpreted as meaning that dowry plays no part in such violence but that violence in intimate relationships is a much wider issue than can be explained by dowry: it is more a 'normal' part of marriage than an exceptional experience.

If we wish to understand the experiences of the women and the problems they face it is important to look at the violence in some detail. I will go through a number of aspects here: the nature of the beatings as described by the women, the physical consequences of these beatings, the emotional and mental impact of violence on the women and the events which precede a bout of violence. Then I shall turn to the ways in which women respond to and resist everyday violence.

Women have their own understandings of what constitutes violence or abuse. I have adopted the women's own definition of physical abuse as this necessarily determines whether or not the women will choose to report violence. Where they were asked for, rather than volunteering, information the question (in Bengali) used the verb *'maar'*, which means to hit or to beat *Has your husband ever hit/beaten you?* Obviously women filtered any incidents or behaviour which they themselves did not consider to fall within this description. For all those who answered yes or who spoke of violence without prompting, I asked for information about the nature of the violence (see Table 8.1). All the descriptions listed fall within a definition of violence which fits a prescribed and consistently applied minimum level of force, as used by Russell[2] (Russell 1990: 48).

Table 8.1 Description of Physical Violence

Hit me with with his hand
Hit me with his hand, a shoe; pulled my hair
Kicked me
Hurt me with his hand, sticks and a poker
Hit me and punched me
Hit me, punched me, with a stick, pushed me to the floor
Hit me, used a stick
Hit me, punched me, kicked me
Kicked me, hit me with a rolling pin
Kicked me, pulled my hair, punched me, used many objects
Smacked my face, my back, pulled my hair
Hurt me with his hand or anything he could find
Slapped me, pulled my hair, pushed me onto the table, pushed my face into the food
Pulled my hair; squeezed my throat, punched my stomach, hit me with a shoe
Tried to strangle me, hit my head on the wall, twisted my wrist
Kicked my stomach, put his hands around my throat, pulled my hair
Hurt me with his hand, a stick, a towel
Slapped me, pulled my hair, twisted my arm, tore my clothes, tried to hang me
Beat me with his hands while I was pregnant, beat me with a stick

The severity of the beatings to which the women had been subjected is indicated effectively by the injuries of which they spoke. Husbands had attempted to strangle their wives and had pushed women hard against solid walls. Several women had fractured bones or dislocated joints and one was beaten so badly when nine months pregnant that the baby became dislodged. One woman had poker burn scars on her leg:

He hit me with his hands and often with a stick ... Once I got badly injured – when he burned me with a poker ... I didn't go to the doctor or hospital, I bought myself some ointment to put on the burn and cared for myself at home.

(Shyamoli)

Even those who said that no serious injury had been sustained said that they had felt pain for varying lengths of time. Almost one half of these women spoke of violence which had been carried out upon them with the use of some implement: these ranged from shoes and sticks to hot pokers. With or without implements the violence which women experienced is not insignificant in nature. While some women either did not suffer 'serious' violence or did not describe it as such, the vast majority (82 per cent) related the pain and injuries they had endured:

Q When did he last beat you?
A Fifteen days ago
Q How did he beat you?
A On my back, in my face, on my head...all over sometimes I get headaches, I have problems in my chest where he hit me...
(Pushpa)

Even though women often experience abuse, they are expected to continue with their duties within their in-laws' house. Maya was educated to degree level, comes from a middle class family and has work experience. She told me about how she had to cook for her in-laws and take care of them. Not only would her husband abuse her, but his parents were also violent towards her. After a particularly upsetting incident she gave up the symbols of Bengali wifehood:

I'll tell you about an incident. One day I was in the middle of cooking when my husband asked me to take some fish I had cooked over to his parents. I told him that I would take it over after I had cleaned up the kitchen and had a wash. I was running a bit late. I went into my bathroom for a wash when he started to bang on the door and demanded to know why I was so late in taking the fish over. I told him why. He dragged me out of the bathroom and pushed my face into the cooked fish. This was how he used to torture me. At that time I used to wear the red spot on my forehead which Bengali married women have to wear and I used to wear the conch bangles. The day he shoved my face in the food and kept saying 'you eat it, you eat it', that was when I stopped observing these traditions. I was so angry that I took a vow never to wear them again

It might be thought that specific incidents or calamities may trigger the start of violence in intimate relationships. But almost one third were initially abused within one year of the marriage or start of the relationship. In these cases it would seem to be marriage itself, or the start of sexual relations, which triggers the violence. Some women did, however, report that they perceived particular circumstances to have been the 'cause' of the violence – for example not being able to get pregnant or since giving birth to the first child. The majority of women have experienced either sex against their will or pre-pubescent sex. Women spoke of the pain and sometimes the injuries they had received as a result of such sexual relations and a small number detailed the nature of sexual violence perpetrated against them. Internal cuts and pain lasting several days were mentioned by most (83 per cent) women. Other injuries were also mentioned – one woman had had her breasts bitten and had been deliberately cut around the vagina. Other women hinted at abuse but did not speak about it in detail.

Precipitating events is a term which refers to the incidents which occur immediately prior to the onset of violence. It is carefully described and specifically used in order not to be confused with any connotation of blame; it is not synonymous with cause. Women were asked to relate examples of precipitating events from their own lives: almost one third said that their own actions had been disliked or disapproved of by their husbands, actions such as having been out when the husband had forbidden it, or asking the husband to take care of a young baby when the woman was trying to prepare food, or not preparing his food the 'correct' way or at the given time. Only 17 per cent of women said disagreements concerned money and the same proportion mentioned alcohol.

Understanding the women's experience of violence goes further than simply dealing with the physical facts of the case, as it were, and we need to understand the emotional and psychological impact of violence on the lives of the women. Table 8.2 shows the ways in which women described how they felt about being beaten.

Table 8.2 How Did/Do You Feel when He Beat(s) You?

This is what happens in marriages
This is what happens in poor families
I wanted to commit suicide
I cry inside because my life is so hard
I want to leave him – it will be better than being beaten
I feel pain, but if I leave leave him people will shun me – he is my husband
I think that I must have done something wrong. Sometimes I want to die
It is not right for a man to beat his wife. I had nowhere to go

I want to go to my parents but I can't because of the kids. I would like to
separate everything from him – my whole life
I think – why should I stay? I have an income, I can live with just my children
but other men will harass me.
I felt scared. I kept trying to make it work but left him eventually
I felt bad, I had nobody to talk to. I felt I had to make things work
We were mutually incompatible
I was so upset I wanted to get a divorce
I was so scared
I left him because he treated me so badly
I have nobody to help me – my family is in Bihar

These emotional and mental impacts can be grouped into four: being
upset and/or scared; wanting to leave the husband or separate from
him; having suicidal thoughts; and seeing the problem as a shared one
in which she must accommodate his behaviour. Interestingly, the last
category was one in which fewest women placed themselves. Very few
(17 per cent) made comments of this type – suggesting that fatalistic
acceptance or 'irrational' passivity is not the norm.

Responding to Violence

One of the questions in this project concerns women's responses to
domestic violence, in particular the type of resistance they offer. The
women had a range of responses – few claimed that they did 'nothing'
(11 per cent) and this comment was often coupled with a description of
the man as too big or too strong to tackle. Many cried or responded in
ways which I have interpreted as not challenging the man (29 per cent).
A third of the women resisted by challenging the violence in a number
of ways, such as grabbing the man's hands to stop him or tearing his
clothes. Those women who involved other people in their attempts to
deal with the violence were a small but not insignificant proportion of
the women who had been beaten. Retaliating with violence was a
rarely used strategy and when employed it was more out of frustration
or anger than a tactic to stop the initial violence. Uma was married at
the age of 13 and had her first child one year later. She started to hit
her husband in retaliation when her son was aged about 6 or 7 (he is
now 20) and reported that her husband has not hit her for the past 3
years. In this case it is not clear that her retaliation in itself was
successful, as a calculation shows that she retaliated for about 10
years before the violence stopped. However, Uma does say that
women must hit back and make their husbands understand that they

have to behave. One woman, Bula, who had hit back was somewhat embarrassed to mention it and more so when I interpreted her actions as a strategy, although everyone present laughed about it:

Q: You never hit him?
Bula: Me? Yes I hit him once... he came home drunk and started hitting me and smashing up our home. I couldn't stand it and I hit him... then someone hid me in their room. When he became sober again it was OK.
Q: When did he last hit you?
Bula: That time I told you about when I hit him? That was the last time. He hasn't hit me since then.
Q: How long ago was that?
Bula: That would be about three years ago.

Most of the women who spoke about sexual violence said they had communicated their unwillingness to have sex to their husband or partners in various ways – by telling them, by moving away or crying. However, only in 14 per cent of these cases did the women report that they had been taken notice of and the sex had not continued. The data suggest that rape in marriage is not uncommon, is seldom talked about and too often is suffered in silence. As noted earlier it is not recognised in law.

MOVING ON

This project is concerned with the ways in which women deal with violence in their home lives and how they can contribute to the ending of such violence. This does not absolve responsibility from the perpetrators of the violence – that is, the men. Rather, it is in recognition that women are not merely passive victims of circumstances that their role is examined here.

How do women move from lives that are marked by violence to lives that are free from violence? There are three routes through which domestic violence comes to an end: these are where the violence is stopped and the relationship continues; the violence stops when the relationship is ended by one or both people concerned; or one or other person dies.

What characteristics or conditions help women to move on from violent relationships? Does paid employment make a difference to those women who have moved from violence marked to violence-free lives? Taking the women who reported physical abuse, a simple check can be made of current employment status (whether or not women are currently employed) with whether or not the violence has stopped (see Table 8.3). This observation might be expected to indicate that a proportionately larger number of women in employment have been able to move on from violent relationships than those not employed.

Table 8.3 Employment and Resolution

Current status of physical violence	Current employment status		Total %
	Employed %	Not employed %	
Continuing	26	29	27
Stopped	74	71	73
Total (reporting physical violence)	100	100	100

In fact, the violence had stopped in 74 per cent of cases where women are currently employed and in 71 per cent of cases where women are not currently employed; that is, there is no significant difference. It appears not to be a sufficient condition for women to leave violent partners and the question remains as to whether or not it is necessary. Leaving a violent husband or partner is not the only option to consider – perhaps having an income allows women to leave home more quickly than being unemployed but if this is an option which she does not wish to take, then it becomes less critical a variable.

Much literature in the West proceeds on the assumption that the optimal outcome for women is to leave abusive men. It is indeed true that in half of the cases where the violence has successfully been resisted[3] women have left their husbands. Most of these women are currently employed, but it is noteworthy that all but one of them have contacts with organisations or agencies offering support. Although so many women talked to me about the abuse and the violence which marks their lives; less than 40 per cent of the women had spoken to anyone in their own social network about these experiences and very few had been to the police. All the women who had been to the police also had contact with support agencies. Contacts with government or other agencies seems to have a stronger relationship with the resolution of violence than does employment – 89 per cent of women who have contacts report that the violence has stopped, compared to 74 per cent of those who are currently employed. Supriya told me that since she joined the ruling political party she has found the strength to challenge her husband's violence and she now grabs hold of him when he comes to beat her. She says this strategy is effective and she is no longer being beaten.

Resolution is used here to refer to situations in which violence has stopped, where the transition from a violent relationship to a violence-free life has been made (at least at the time of interview). How do women move from lives which are marked by violence to lives which are free from violence? Just as the reporting rate was high so too is the resolution rate – over 70 per cent. Excluding the pre-selected group of women who were contacted through agencies, the resolution rate amongst women who were previously unknown to us is still high, 65 per cent. Of the women who have made the transition, two thirds have access to support networks. I have already noted the importance of formal organisations but informal networks have an impact on the day-to-day experience of violence. Rekha indicates the importance of seeking help from others:

What can be done? If there are five other people around they can stop him and make him understand. Women have to tell others for this sort of help. It isn't right for men to force women to have sex.

Women do make the transition from abusive relationships to lives free from violence. It appears that if women can gain immediate support from friends, family or neighbours, they may be able to get intervention which can stop a single incident of violence. In the longer term the formal agencies seem to be important in contributing to the resolution of violence. Contacts with such agencies have a stronger association with resolution than does having paid work.

CONCLUSIONS

There may be popularly held beliefs that physical violence is rare or unusual, a conception which the reporting rate here challenges. This finding is in the same range as those of small scale qualitative research (e.g. Kelly 1988) and larger sample surveys (e.g. Russell 1990) through which we are able to substantiate that *violence is endemic and not exceptional.* Nor is it the case, as has been shown by a number of studies, that the experience of violence is significantly mediated by class, or ethnicity. Unfortunately, one of the ways in which class is significant is that it constrains the behaviour of women and influences the expectations they have in ways which made it very difficult to interview middle class women.

Do women accept some degree of violence? Overall there were very few women who demonstrated neither regret, nor pain, anger nor sorrow at the way they had been treated by their husbands or male partners. They do not accept the violence they experience, nor do they really tolerate it – many express their disapproval directly to their husbands. They do not, by and large, think that it is acceptable for men to abuse women, nor do they think it is right for men to force their wives to have sexual relations. This disapproval does not always involve unequivocal condemnation of violence or approval of all attempts to resist male violence, but most women found ways of making known their own dissatisfaction to their husbands or to others. And in most cases where others knew what was going on the women were able to get some sort of support.

At this stage of analysis it appears that speaking out about violence helps most women to obtain support; in fact, in most of the cases where women spoke to their natal families they received some form of help or encouragement to confront the abuse. Contacts with agencies and organisations are key to seeking formal redress through the legal system and to securing short-term alternative shelter. Neither employment nor education alone appears to have a significant impact on the way in which women respond to violence in intimate relationships.

No matter whether women are employed, have their own income or have children there is a widespread felt obligation to exist as one of a pair which contributes to the ties women feel they have to violent homes. A number of the women who left violent husbands did so when they felt their lives were in danger or when their husband and/ or in-laws made them leave. The majority of the women in the sample are employed and therefore receiving some income. However, their income is neither regular nor large in many cases and is a precarious base on which to support a family in the absence of state welfare provisions or family or social support. Some women who are earning 'respectable' salaries told me, in personal conversations, that despite having the financial means to keep themselves and any children, it was extremely difficult to find any accommodation as single women. There is only one dedicated refuge for battered women in Calcutta, and the demand for places from destitute women is so great that they fill the available places. Where is a woman to go if she needs a place to stay, if her family cannot or will not support her? There are a number of government shelters, but again the places tend to be filled by women previously living on the streets, particularly young women, and those sent there by the police. In interviews with agencies a complaint was raised that development agencies and aid programmes do not fund shelters for such women, even where training and employment programmes had been written into such projects.

Quite apart from the social and economic conditions which constrain the options available to women, there is the emotional tie which keeps women in the home where their children have been born and where their father lives. Few of the women to whom we spoke talked of love, but they did rate the husband–wife bond very highly. Some remarked that the ideal response of women facing violence should be to reason with the man and to make the relationship work. It remains an exceptionally difficult task for any woman to separate from her husband when the strength of this ideology is so strong. Given the reluctance to break this bond, perhaps more attention needs to be given to the means by which violence against women in the home can be ended without terminating the relationship itself. This is an option which is often hard to understand or encourage. As outsiders we may prefer to see an abusive relationship come to an end. However, if the task is to enable women to take greater control of their own lives then it has to be considered carefully.

This book is concerned with empowerment as a process, which may be contradictory, at least in appearance. It may seem contradictory that the women to whom I spoke were dissatisfied with the violence which marked their lives but that they remain in abusive relationships. It may appear contradictory that women express a sense of powerlessness yet make decisions about birth control, sterilisation, voting and household economic management. However, reflection may show us how familiar such contradictions are in lives and relationships with which we may be familiar – in our research and personal lives. Contradictions may be the expression of conflicting dynamics – for example, while finding violence unacceptable women may not separate from their husbands because of the difficulties faced by single women and mothers. The women I spoke to in Calcutta operate within constraints which impede their capacity to make decisions over their own lives. An emerging message of this research is that networks and contacts play an important role in challenging those constraints. Women's groups, government agencies and development projects can all contribute to mounting such challenges.

NOTES

1 The Child Marriage Restraint Act 1978 raised the minimum age at marriage to 18 years, but there remain a number of inconsistencies in the law which continues in certain cases to recognise as legal marriages involving girls under this age.
2 In her study of abuse within marital relations Diana Russell devised a 'consistent definition of force, threat of force, and violence' with which to analyse the responses given by women interviewed: 'we determined a minimum level of physical force which included such acts as pushing, pinning, and being held down by a husband's weight so that the woman couldn't move' (Russell 1990: 48).
3 Successful resistance, or resolution, is used here to refer to the ending of violence where the well-being of the woman concerned is protected. This definition excludes suicide.

REFERENCES

Adithi Project (1994) *Female Infanticide in Bihar: An Interim Report*, report for Adithi by Parinita
Anker, R., Buvinic, M. and Youssef N. H. (eds). (1982) *Women's Roles and Population Trends in the Third World*. London: Croom Helm.
Banerjee, N. (1985) *Women Workers in the Unorganised Sector*. Hyderabad: Sanyan Books.
Bennett, L. (1991) *Gender and Poverty in India*, A World Bank Country Study. Washington: World Bank.
Bunch, C. and Carillo, R. (1991) *Gender Violence: A Development and Human Rights Issue*. New Brunswick: Center for Women's Global Leadership.
Calman, L. (1992), *Toward Empowerment: Women and Movement Politics in India*. Oxford: Westview Press.
Harriss, B. and Watson, E. (1987) 'The Sex Ratio in South Asia', in J. Townsend and J.H. Momsen, *Geography of Gender in the Third World*. London: Hutchinson.
Joseph A. and Sharma, K. (eds) (1994) *Whose News? The Media and Women's Issues*. New Delhi: Sage.
Kelly, L. (1988) *Surviving Sexual Violence*. Cambridge: Polity Press.
Kumar, R. (1993) *The History of Doing: An Illustrated Account of Movements for Women's Rights and Feminism in India, 1800–1990*, London: Verso.

Miller, B. (1981) *The Endangered Sex – Neglect of Female Children in Rural North India*. Ithaca, NY: Cornell University Press.
Moorhouse, G. (1983) *Calcutta: The City Revealed*. London: Penguin Books.
Russell, D. (1990) *Rape in Marriage*. New York: Collier.
Sarkar, L. (1994) 'Rape: A Human Rights versus a Patriarchal Interpretation', in *Indian Journal of Gender Studies*, vol. 1 no. 1, New Delhi: Sage.
SLARTC (Socio-Legal Training and Research Centre) (1994) *A Report on Socio-Legal Problems in Identified Slum Areas of Calcutta Slum Improvement Project*. Calcutta: SLARTC.
Standing, H. (1991) *Dependence and Autonomy: Women's Employment and the Family in Calcutta*. London: Routledge.
UNDP (1992, 1995) *Human Development Reports*. Oxford: Oxford University Press.

9 Engendering the Analysis of Conflict: A Southern Perspective
Donna Pankhurst and Jenny Pearce

INTRODUCTION

The study of women's empowerment, in all the meanings outlined in this volume by Rowlands, must rest on the conceptualisation and analysis of gender relations, as the other chapters in the volume amply demonstrate. Yet such a conceptualisation and analysis is still rarely located within other concerns of social science. The *engendering* of a discipline which is required by the effective integration of gender-aware analyses is all too slow and partial, albeit differentially so in different areas of study. In this chapter we explore the chances of this process occurring in the study of conflict, with a view to assessing the degree to which women's situations in the ending of conflict might lead to conditions which are conducive to their empowerment.

ENGENDERING A DISCIPLINE

With a background in Development Studies (DS), as a Latin Americanist and an Africanist, we were struck by the much slower process of engendering in International Relations (IR) which we noticed on taking up positions in a Department of Peace Studies. Taking the comparison further, to look at Conflict Analysis (CA), we have identified four levels of achievement in an engendering process, although unfortunately these do not seem to be inevitable or unilinear, and an area or discipline does not, of course, change uniformly across its range:

1. An initial level which begins to fill in the absences and 'make women visible' through work typically titled, 'Women and...', and 'Women in...' studies.
2. Widespread removal of *male bias* in data collection and analysis. *Male bias* was made prominent as a term in DS by Diane Elson

(1991) and is very useful as a means of emphasising the intellectual and academic inadequacy of a discipline which systematically distorts its area of study by looking at it through a male-only lens. This agenda was promoted in DS both on grounds of equity but also in order to obtain a more accurately focused picture of the world.

3. The study of gender relations becomes more predominant than the analysis of the situation of women and men separately.

4. A comprehensive rethinking of the discipline's theoretical constructs to take *gender* into account without privileging *women* as a social category. Although feminists have been engaging with this project for a long time in many areas, the key characteristic of this stage is that the activity becomes widespread and the outcome comprehensive.

5. A stage where it becomes part of the mainstream of the discipline (i.e. a normal, unexceptional activity) to ask: 'What difference does gender make here?'

There are some parts of DS which are not far off from the fourth level, but many which are barely at the first stage. In IR, postmodernist feminist theory is having a critical impact on some of the theoretical constructions, and the 'making women visible' stage is also making some inroads (Grant and Newland, 1991), albeit somewhat limited. There is little evidence of change at the other levels, and the discipline appears more like one where women are 'allowed' the space to engage with feminist critiques at the first level, whilst the men tend to get on with what they regard as the 'serious' work. Elsewhere we have argued that part of the distinctiveness of the engendering of DS was the great impetus given by efficiency concerns of the practitioners in development planning and policy-making who could no longer afford to ignore women or gender relations when striving to achieve the objectives of poverty alleviation and economic development (Pankhurst and Pearce 1993). IR has no policy arm which faces an equivalent challenge, and so the pressures for change seem to be limited to feminist critiques of the orthodoxies.

The relative slowness in engendering IR is an intriguing one in its own right, but also one which has parallels with Conflict Analysis (CA). CA increasingly overlaps with DS as an areas of study, as so many of the world's conflicts occur in the South, but the cross-over of individual academics does not seem to result in the good practice of gender-aware analysis being carried over to CA. Furthermore, CA is influential in the practical field of Conflict Resolution (CR) where there is little pressure to take gender seriously, but which is a field and profession having an increasingly significant role to play in 'adjudicating' the endings of conflicts in the South.

CONFLICT ANALYSIS

Conflict Analysis is sometimes used in quite a vague way and does not connote any particular methodology, and so perhaps should properly be regarded as an area of study which usually resembles a specific type of risk analysis. It monitors information through many sources, seeks patterns in outbreaks of violence and war, and engages in informed prediction. It embraces no particular methodology or analytical framework which is able to explain why two places with similar structural conditions rarely break out into violence at the same time, or at all, and so the 'trigger' is often imbued with great significance. Perhaps this analytical weakness is most striking where violence is linked with identity. As information about shifting identities do not appear on databases or other standard sources of evidence used in CA, the analysis of identity tends to remain at a very simplistic level. Where identity is recognised as an important factor (it always has been assumed to be by Africa-watchers in CA), this very often leads to a simplistic description of socially bounded groups of people with fixed and predictable political positions which can somehow be read off from their ascribed identity.

CA and CR tend to be primarily concerned with violence and its escalation and termination, rather than wider concepts of conflict and its endings. There is no consensus on conceptualising conflict in CA or CR, and both tend to underplay structural conflict and ignore the wider conceptualisations deriving from sociology and psychology. *International social conflict* is an increasingly popular categorisation within CA and CR of Europe and Africa's recent wars which does not engage with *class* as a concept or identify it as a possible identity group, even where the possibility that poverty and economic inequality could play a significant role amongst the causes of wars in these regions is considered. It does not engage with issues of gender at all. It also incorporates an essentialist use of the term *communal* violence, with no sensitivity as to its colonial origin and misleading connotations, and no engagement with its meanings.

CR is likely to be influenced by this categorisation of Africa's recent conflicts, particularly as this is closely associated with debates about humanitarian intervention as part of conflict resolution. A recent suggestion put forward distinguishes between the *deep intervention* required for a full resolution of conflict – something which is rarely, if ever, taken on – and the more common *shallow intervention,* which aims only to achieve the *settlement* of conflicts, in the sense of ending violence and war. The latter is the more common activity in the South and is also often misleadingly referred to as conflict *resolution* instead of the more precise conflict *settlement.*

THE PERTINENCE OF A GENDERED ANALYSIS OF CONFLICT

Apart from the usual pleas made for engendering an area of study, that is for the sake of justice and intellectual integrity, a gendered analysis of conflict would help to provide a more sophisticated understanding of conflict which could assist in conflict settlement and conflict resolution. In understanding the causes of conflict, there is a need even to reach the first level of engendering, i.e. making women visible amongst the male-dominated narratives of war which dominate those of conflict analysis. Interestingly, there is already a sophisticated *feminist* literature on the role of women in wars, although this is more limited with regard to wars in the South (Elshtain, 1987; Enloe, 1983; Roach-Pierson, 1987, etc.) and even of the role and implications of changing gender relations, but this is rarely, if ever, taken into account in analyses of the causes of war or violence in CA.

This literature demonstrates that women are not intrinsically more peaceful than men, and under some circumstances play key roles in motivating men to fight and be prepared to die in the build up to and duration of war, whilst at other times they act as peacemakers. In both they are key actors in shifting identities, and themselves become symbols of changing identities as definitions of *womanhood* are used to defend and define 'essential' group identities. This literature provides analytical and theoretical frameworks to explore these different roles which women take on in the context of shifting gender relations. Incorporating these analyses would help to shed light on the mechanisms of shifting identities and their connections with violence, as well as leading to a more sophisticated analysis of the more peaceful roles which women play at different times.

During wars (or the transition from violence to war), women and men normally have very different experiences, but it is almost always the male experience that dominates accounts, and to which outsiders relate, even where women effectively or obviously play 'combative' roles. Combative and non-combative roles are often indistinguishable in many areas of conflict in the South, and yet the male experience dominates outsiders' analyses and the mechanisms of intervention. An analysis of gender relations can help enormously in considering the chances of success of a community's survival strategies and of post-conflict recovery, not least because such a focus helps to reveal the links between the private and public spheres (El Bushra and Lopez 1994: 4).

TYPES OF CONFLICT IN THE SOUTH AND THEIR 'RESOLUTION'

It is a commonly made assertion in CA that during the Cold War, because of the risk that conflicts in the South would escalate into more global conflagrations, a set of rules about the conduct of wars were maintained by the superpowers in order to restrain fighting in some areas. Since the ending of the Cold War, a perception has grown in these areas of study that the nature of conflict itself has changed, to one in which the rules of the Geneva Convention have been abandoned, in the absence of their 'policing' by the superpowers. Whilst we certainly note the apparent absence of these rules in many recent conflicts, we do take exception to the rather racist view that this is due to the absence of interference from the superpowers. The superpowers often broke the rules, by using napalm in counter-insurgency, bombing civilians and by the use of torture, for example. However, now cast in a world without such rules of war, the South is often seen as riven with 'ethnic', 'tribal', messianic conflagrations, to a much greater extent than it was previously, even where there has not been that much of a change in the actual practice of warfare.

During the Cold War, the roots of conflicts in the South were obfuscated by an overlay of explanations derived from superpower rivalry. The new world order might have presented an opportunity for a more sensitive analysis of these, which would take into account the structural roots of conflict, as well as the construction of identity and their connections with a range of social relations which includes gender. Conflicts in Africa (as in Europe) are now increasingly cast as being fundamentally about identity or some other 'social' issue, as opposed to structural[1] issues. This produces a pessimistic view about the potential outcome from many observers who conclude that it is notoriously difficult to compromise on identity. CR theorists concerned with conflict settlement, on the other hand, see a window of opportunity in 'identity conflicts', as they can make use of the premises that improved communications can ease, if not remove, conflict and violence. Many practitioners in CR ignore or downplay structural factors which generate conflict (e.g. vast inequalities in wealth distribution) and concentrate on building up communication between opposing parties as a means of ending fighting, even where this does not in any way necessitate the ending of social violence or structural conflict. The common confusion, if not conflation, between conflict and violence means that the success of mediation and resolution tends to be measured merely by the absence of armed combat, and the overall picture is still dominated by a crudely essentialist set of ethnic stereotypes articulated predominantly through the voice of fighting men.

An acute example is to be found in El Salvador, where conflict had its roots in a range of oppressions, and the long civil war had a major impact on social relations of all kinds, including class and gender relations. Many small international and national NGOs laboured through these difficult years to support the popular movements, and gave solidarity and humanitarian assistance to movements like the relatives of the disappeared, organised mostly by women. The 'peace process' has ended the more extreme elements of violence, but the issues of land, poverty and human rights violations remain as persistent as ever, many exacerbated by the very conflict itself. Yet, this is widely regarded as a *successful* mediation; so much so that major multilateral agencies are now seeking to export it elsewhere in Latin America and Africa. The lesson is said to be: concentrate on the epiphenomena of the violent aspects of the war and its most visible causes, and the conflict will be settled.

THE 'GENDERED DEAL' IN THE ENDINGS OF WAR

Brokering or defining the ending of wars usually focuses on reducing death rates from direct armed combat. Particularly in externally brokered peace settlements there is sometimes a clearly identifiable gendered difference in the way peace is facilitated for women and men, and even where this is less deliberate, there are usually highly significant differences in the experiences for women and men in the post-conflict situation. This occurs even when women have taken an active part in direct combat and have taken on many responsibilities during wartime which were formerly confined to men.

Examples of explicit gender deals include the differential rights granted to men and women in new constitutions and states. For example, in the 'new' South Africa, where conceding the social control over women facilitated by the operation of Customary Law was seen as a trade-off to men for other aspects of the constitution. Similarly, in Nicaragua, deals between Sandinistas and Contras often specifically excluded women from owning land, even though the war left many women as widows and single mothers.

Sometimes the gendered deals are more subtle, and women are simply left to fend for themselves. This is most striking in the conflict regions of Colombia, where male social activists and militants are systematically gunned down, and their wives and children forced out of the family home in traumatic circumstances. Many peasant women have ended up in desperate situations in the most abandoned and squalid environments. The internally displaced of Colombia are mostly widows with five or six children, abandoned by the state and by the other parties in the war. By contrast, male guerrilla leaders have often been able to make political deals which allow them to reintegrate into public life, while the widows remain invisible and prey to all manner of exploitation.

In the post-conflict situation, other kinds of violence may not only persist, but actually increase – particularly that directed at women. On the streets women usually face particular kinds of danger after a conflict has ended, if there are many surviving young male ex-combatants, with their newly increased social status, who often turn to armed crime, having led a life dominated by war and violence. Domestic violence also often increases in post-war situations. It is fundamental that an engendered analysis of conflict settlement is used to review these experiences. At present, where these harsh aspects of the gendered nature of peace do not always or inevitably accompany the ending of war, they are not noticed by CA and – crucially – not affected by CR. At the same time, a polarised viewpoint which only looked at the experiences of women could obscure or eclipse the suffering and sacrifice of men during and sometimes after war.

PROSPECTS FOR ENGENDERING CA AND CR

By taking gender into account it would be possible to obtain a better understanding of the build-up to, and maintenance of, violence and war; to assess more fully the implications of conflict settlements; and perhaps be in a better position to assess the chances for positive peace. However, it seems to be left to feminists working outside the field of CA to raise these issues and undertake the relevant research. In seeking an explanation for the slow pace of CA and CR as compared with DS, or even IR, we have to take into account that not only is there relevant research already in existence, but also that there is an increasing overlap between DS and CA, with a good number of people with DS experience now working in CA who do not seem to have brought with them the good practice of DS. We reluctantly note the correlation between this slow pace and the predominance of men in CA.

However, perhaps it will not remain solely the work of feminists to engender CA, as there are some 'efficiency gains' to be made in CR by taking gender seriously, which might parallel the pressure from below which was so significant in the engendering of DS. As increasing disenchantment is voiced about the lack of meaningful conflict resolution underpinning many conflict settlements the apparent success of internationally brokered deals may crumble sufficiently for at least some of the practitioners to engage with solutions which embody greater degrees of justice. There is some suggestion that this pressure is emerging from the grassroots in Central America.

The use of women as peacemakers in a more gender-aware strategy is itself problematic, as is the parallel experience of using women as 'efficient and reliable development partners'. The push to focus on women, and even gender relations, in DS from the efficiency perspective led to the eclipsing of much of the liberatory project for feminists who had developed the analysis. Thus the empowerment of women as power to, with and from within, became marginalised in WID analyses and initiatives. So too might such marginalisation occur in CR as women's usefulness as peacemakers and the guardians of communities' livelihood systems are facilitated on terms which restrict their ability to challenge those gender relations which inhibit their empowerment.

A more positive scenario might result if CA and CR take on the significance of gender relations in the build up to conflict and their significance in maintaining peace. Then perhaps the empowerment of women itself might be seen as an essential component not only of the luxury of positive peace, but also as a useful mechanism for lessening and avoiding the escalation of violent conflict in the first place.

NOTE

1. 'Structural' is used in discussions of *international social conflict* to refer to the lack of fit between states and nations or other ethnic group, rather than anything relating to power or economics.

REFERENCES

El Bushra, J. and Lopez, E. (1994) *Development in Conflict: the Gender Dimension*, OXFAM Discussion Paper 3.

Elson, D. (1991) *Male Bias in the Development Process*, Manchester: Manchester University Press.

Elshtain, J.B. (1987) *Women and War*, New York: Basic Books.

Enloe, C. (1983)*Does Khaki Become You?*, London: Pluto Press.

Grant, R. and Newland, K. (eds) (1991) *Gender and International Relations*, Milton Keynes: Open University Press.

Gender and History (1989) Review article, 1.

Pankhurst, D. and Pearce, J. (1993) 'Gender and International Relations: Views from Development Studies', paper presented at the BISA Gender and International Relations Conference, May at LSE.

Peterson, V.S. (1992), *Gendered States: Feminist (Re)Visions of International Relations*, Boulder: Lynne Rienner.

Peterson, V.S. and Rungan, A.S. (1993) *Global Gender Issues*, Oxford: Westview Press.

Ramsbotham, O. and Woodhouse, T. (1995) 'Post-Cold War Conflict as International-Social Conflict: Implications for Third Party Intervention', paper presented at BISA conference, December, Southampton.

Roach-Pierson, R. (1987) *Women and Peace*, London: Croom Helm.

10 Women Dying, Women Working: Disempowerment in British India

Jocelyn Kynch and
Maureen Sibbons

Empowerment as a corollary of development is an attractive notion, but socioeconomic change has variable effects on women, which include the potential for disempowerment as well as empowerment. This is not a new phenomenon, for women's present subordination is part of the history of their negotiations and renegotiations of what they can do or be.

We shall consider disempowerment and empowerment potentials in the context of British Indian policy and its interactions with the lives of Indian men and women. Periods of socioeconomic transformations, such as the one that we study in this chapter, are of particular interest to gender studies because they contain moments when social and cultural rules and behaviours have to be questioned, for example, when traditional gender roles, forms of deference, or traditional forms of insurance fail to provide men and women with the expected protection within their societies that tradition embodied. From the period of transformation of British India, we shall look at evidence about 'windows of opportunity' which opened for women during crises, and the documented debates about how the social interactions of gender were addressed. We shall focus on two issues: how relief wage systems affected the right to work on public employment works during declared famines, and the reduction of epidemic deaths from cholera and plague.

The British Indian officials who implemented policy routinely reported data and activities by sex as required by the government. They therefore could claim to prioritise operations to reduce male or female vulnerability to famine mortality, or epidemic mortality, on the basis of facts. The main criterion for successful relief of famine, or control of an epidemic, was cost-effective reduction of deaths. It was

164

believed that during famine or epidemic cholera, women had a biological superiority in survival, but women were more vulnerable to die from plague. However, from analysis of the available information we have found that vulnerability or protection are the result of social rather than biological factors (Sibbons 1995; Kynch forthcoming). So, for example, higher male than female deaths from cholera are a result of gender roles and greater male activity in public space, not the result of superior male vulnerability to the cholera vibrio. The reduction of the initially very high mortality of young women from plague could not be explained by biology alone: knowledge was sometimes power.

This social and biological distinction is of relevance to the history of women's employment. Women's employment was perceived as culturally, economically and biologically proscribed, except when in their homes: the social and the biological were combined to determine acceptibility of place and nature of employment – loosely linked to the reproductive and productive roles ascribed to women and men. Women were dislocated from control over their own labour or its value. The factor of women's presence in public space links these two debates on relief employment and epidemic control, and includes two aspects of empowerment. First, that women's knowledge is generative power. Second, that access to paid employment increases women's bargaining position in the household: access to paid employment is therefore an empowering situation. We shall show that women's knowledge about health (often officially unacknowledged and unutilised) and their means of access to famine relief employment were systematically excluded from the public arena.

Indian women were disempowered in the longer run. Their role as biological reproducers was affirmed; low valuation of little girls became entrenched; the high risk to women's social and economic security in the absence of a working male remained unchallenged; their knowledge as health carers was unrecognised.

This chapter exemplifies that, in the process of reduction of mortality from epidemics or famine, external agents such as British Indian officials can unwittingly influence women's control of resources and control over their own labour ('power over') and abilities to use their knowledge ('generative power'). We offer examples of negative impact. The failure to recognise how gender roles, and not sex, pattern mortality, or consequently how changes in gender roles could affect future survival chances, has led to inadvertant but robust and enduring low well-being for Indian women.

In section 1, we critically evaluate some literature on women's empowerment in terms of their right to work and inclusion of their knowledge. We argue that experiences from the past have too often remained invisible or have been ignored when they suggest disempowerment. In section 2, this argument is taken further by considering selected debates on men and women with respect to public health through control of epidemics and famine relief operations. We then examine, in sections 3 and 4, how women experienced mortality crises (epidemics, often conflated with famine) and hunger crises (famine) as periods of disempowerment. In the final section we consider the longer-term effects of disempowerment.

THE CONTEXT: WOMEN'S EMPOWERMENT IN THE INDIAN SUBCONTINENT

Empowerment and disempowerment are both possible outcomes for the poor during transformations in society. As 'winners' or as 'equals' women have fared badly. Indeed, as Martha Nussbaum writes: 'no country treats its women as well as it treats its men, a disappointing result after so many years of debate on gender equality, so many struggles by women and so many changes in national laws' (Nussbaum 1995: 33). Aslanbeigui *et al.* (1994: 2) find that in recent economic transformations, 'whether per capita income has increased, stagnated or decreased, women have been over-represented among the losers or under-represented among the winners'. In the case of the Indian subcontinent, there are several reasons to be pessimistic that socioeconomic transformations – from the emergence of modern India under colonial rule (Sarkar 1983), through planned economic development (Kohli 1987) up to the recent liberalisation – have favoured women's empowerment. In recent decades, analyses have included women's voices (e.g Sharma 1980; Hartman and Boyce 1983; Jeffery, Jeffery and Lyon 1989), and there have been some remarkable achievements, often begun by exceptional individuals, such as SEWA or the Chipko movement. However, we cannot show that long-run trends in women's well-being relative to men's have been significantly improved. For example, the female:male ratio in India has continuously declined since the turn of the century (Kynch and Sen 1983), and, if we calculate the number of 'missing women' on the basis of the question 'How many more women than there are now would be alive if the sex ratio were the same as in Sub-Saharan Africa?', Dreze and Sen (1989: 52) suggest that the highest proportions 'missing' are in the Indian sub-continent (8.7 per cent in Bangladesh, 9.5 per cent in India, 12.9 per cent in Pakistan).

There are lessons from the experiences of women in the past, in particular from the famine period (1860–1920) and non-famine period (1920-40) in British India, which exemplify the problems of disempowerment and entrenchment of bias. In this section, we shall illustrate the importance of taking into account discourses over visibility of women in public space, critically examining recent studies of public employment schemes and projects which aim to raise women's participation.

Martha Chen's (1995) field study in rural Bangladesh (part of Bengal in British India) focuses on women's right to work, which Nussbaum (1995: 7) writes: 'plays such a pivotal role in relation to other "capabilities" of women: in relation to health and nutrition, to self-respect and autonomy, to full political functioning.' Chen emphasises that poor women in poor economies face a particular predicament when they must 'break with tradition and act independently because they lack the security the tradition is supposed to offer' (1995: 37). Chen considers the discourses over women's employment on food-for-work programmes in the famine of 1974–5. On these schemes, Chen found that women faced two main problems: first, they were denied work by local officials, and second, they were paid less than men. The argument over women's participation on the schemes involved UN formal committees, the Cabinet, local officials and donor representatives; research findings helped legitimise earlier recommendations. Chen points out that the direction of change for women depends on impoverishment and loss of men's earnings, which result in *forced entry* of women into labour markets, and on upward mobility, which results in *forced withdrawal* of women from labour markets (1995: 46). This forcing or control of women's labour is part of their subordination during rural transformation or crises. Chen also analyses the impact of seclusion of women, meaning occupational *purdah* (citing Pranab Bardhan), which is broader and more secular than the designation of what is proper demeanour or behaviour, or strict *purdah*. In seeking work, the women from poor and female- headed households of Bangladesh are defying occupational *purdah* (1995: 40).

Chen's work forms the centre-piece of Nussbaum and Glover's (1995) volume, which addresses issues of universal justice. Despite its many insights, Chen's paper nevertheless can be criticised for offering no evidence that 'the participation of women was *a new phenomenon.*

The government was simply not prepared to accept women into its rural works programme' (1995: 41, added emphasis). In fact, there have been, and indeed usually are, high proportions of women on the various employment schemes and relief works, and officials and administrators considered women's right to relief work throughout British India during the period of recurrent famine. Many of the arguments used then are identical to those seven decades later, although a crucial difference is the absence of women's voices from the earlier debates. A question about why there is no folk or memory trace is valid. We shall also, in our conclusion, suggest other differences, in particular that the earlier debate was conducted on the basis of biological or sexual rather than gender differences (on the latter, see Okin 1995: 281–3).

Women's wider participation in the development process is argued to be central to their empowerment: women have to be informed and consulted (Kate Young, cited in Karl 1995: 109). The widespread use of non-governmental or non-profit organisations as agents of change has been argued to increase grassroots participation in current debates about women's rights, including the right to work (Viswanath 1991). Nevertheless, these efforts are open to the criticism that they remain officialised paper exercises. For example, David Mosse (1995) has argued that projects need to diversify methods of articulation of local knowledge. He points out that 'participatory exercises [such as participatory rural appraisal] involve "public" social events which construct "local knowledge" in ways which are strongly influenced by existing social relationships.' Experiences in a project, in three tribal districts of western India, leads Mosse (1995: 19) to conclude, *inter alia*, that,

> In a society which ascribes to women a sphere characterised as private, domestic, manual, low status, informal and by implication socially less visible and valued, any event which creates processes which are perceived and understood as public and formal tends to exclude women.

Part of women's subordination is inarticulation of their concerns except in their reproductive roles, in other words, articulation is within a 'socially acceptable profile of women's activities' (1995: 21). The possibility exists for well-intentioned projects, which aim to empower women, actually repressing or muting certain kinds of knowledge and reinforcing women's invisibility.

While the dilemma of the role of the outsider is acute in projects, Chen rightly reminds us that legitimation and enforcement of women's right to work (or other rights) is of fundamental importance. However, many aspects of gender relations are quasi-legal, such as kinship support or systems of patronage, or common property rights (Agarwal 1991, 1992; Gasper 1993; Gore 1993). Agarwal (1994) drawing upon the works of Amartya Sen and James Scott, emphasises women as actors who resist gender inequalities. She contrasts two polar views of the oppressed: false consciousness, or covert and subtle forms of resistance. Agarwal argues that we should distinguish between *individual-covert* acts of resistance, and *group-overt* acts. It is only the latter that effectively empower women. She examines peasant movements in the period before Independence, and the maternity and child welfare movements. However, Agarwal does not explain why these movements failed to sustain a challenge to the dominant norms that men provision households and women monopolise reproduction, an arrangement that Kabeer (1991) finds as a common outcome of bargaining in South Asian households. Furthermore, Caplan (1978) puts a different interpretation on voluntarist women's organisations in Madras: 'women's organizations for social welfare help to support the norms regarding the 'proper' role of women.... If women's organizations tend to play an essentially conservative role *vis-à-vis* women, this is even more pronounced in regard to the working classes.'

These studies provide some key pointers to understanding the potentials for empowerment and disempowerment in transformations. We should investigate the historical context of social structuring of gender relations, and significant events that lever relations (Kynch forthcoming). The low valuation of women's work and of women's knowledge is strengthened through seclusion in its secular meaning (a theme in Chen and Agarwal's work). The right to work is linked to a challenge of women's 'traditional' behaviours, which is most likely to be coerced during individual or socioeconomic crises, when women, including women without husbands, sons or other male support, are present in the public arena.

DEBATES IN BRITISH INDIA ABOUT MEN AND WOMEN

The late nineteenth and early twentieth centuries were times of socioeconomic transformation in India (now India, Pakistan and Bangladesh). Such periods contain potential for social emancipation and added social value for women, but also changes in vulnerability. In this section we shall use the public health and famine relief debates about women as exemplars of a discourse which justified men's continuing prejudice against women's presence in public space. Our main sources of information, including data, are the annual provincial Sanitary Commissioners' Reports (after 1919 Directors of Public Health), and Famine Commissioners' and provincial Government Reports and Codes. Sanitary Commissioners' annual reports recorded data on and debates about male and female deaths and their causes. Famine relief organisation was a related activity. Following the recommendations of the Famine Commission of 1880, each province published a Famine Code and monitored the condition of the people, and reports following a famine complement the observations of the Sanitary Commissioners. The provincial Sanitary Commissioners' reports often contain vivid descriptions of people's activities and environment, as well as analyses of their observations. However, the Government of India and policy-makers did not always appreciate analyses (which vary from the astute to quite silly), or incorporate recommendations into policy.

We shall most frequently refer to four northern provinces (see Kynch and Sibbons 1993, on selected districts). Punjab (in north-west India) has been called the epicentre of bias against women; high-wage agricultural labouring developed there after 1900. Central Provinces (now mainly Madhya Pradesh) was traversed by trade which developed with railway links. Bombay (western India) included industrialising Gujarat and Konkan coastal strip and the declining Deccan and Karnatak. Bengal (eastern India) had endemic cholera; it included Orissa and Bihar – both poor and famine-prone divisions – as well as the jute cash-cropping divisions which are now West Bengal and Bangladesh.

We have divided the period 1870–1940 crudely into 'famine' up to 1920 and 'non-famine' from 1920 to 1940 (Kynch and Sibbons 1993, section 1.2 and Table 1.1). Lal (1988) estimates that rural real wages stagnated between 1873 and 1900 in the earlier period, and rose at 0.47 per cent per annum between 1919 and 1946, roughly the non-famine period. Cholera records show a peak of deaths in 1900, plague deaths peaked in 1907 and influenza in 1918, which were all major famine years. Mortality declined and became less variable in most districts in the 'non-famine' period, which Zurbrigg (1995) suggests was a consequence, and benefit, of famine prevention.

In examining epidemics, we need to take account of transformations. For example, movements of people and trade routes had existed for centuries, and cannot *per se* explain the increases in cholera in nineteenth-century India. Klein (1994) suggests that an ecological imbalance, overuse and abuse of some water supplies, was precipitated by the rapid mobility of resources and modernisation of the economy without a compensatory increase in 'assets for human survival'. A parallel argument has been used about famine: that the transition towards a wage-labour economy and increasing trade broke down traditional hunger insurance mechanisms without providing compensatory social security measures, and this exacerbated the collapses in food entitlement among landless labourers and rural artisans which characterised Indian famines of the transitional period.

In British India, higher mortality of men, such as in cholera epidemics or famine, was recognised and structured debates about public health and famine relief priorities. The interpretations were in terms of sexuality: the greater 'resistance' of women being understood to be due to biological factors or natural predispositions, and little attention was paid to women except in terms of their reproductive health. For example, in the distressed year of 1878 in United Provinces (then North-West Provinces), it was remarked that:

The high mortality of the year seems to have affected male life more than female. ... it would appear that this superior vitality of females is common to all periods of life [and] this excess [male mortality] becomes more marked in the successive periods of life. Under each special form of disease – cholera, fever, small-pox, &c. – the same excess of mortality among the males appears.

(No. 338 of 1879 to N-W Provinces & Oudh SCR)

and the Sanitary Commissioner's Report (1897), despite acknowledging the influence of region, occupation and habits, concluded that the excess of infant male mortality 'must depend on some constitutional difference' (Bengal SCR 1897, quoting Longstaff). Reviewing the evidence from other provinces, the Government of India pointed out that:

The statement that male children are more difficult to rear does not, however, explain this phenomenon [greater mortality of males in Bengal], and the questions arise, are adult males among the masses in Bengal, and in India generally, more exposed to vicissitudes of climate and accident than females? If they are, does this extra exposure compensate for the effects of premature marriage and maternity and primeval midwifery?

(GoI SCR 1897)

At the same time, women were expected to be predisposed to be sickly, and a health problem and strain on sanitation if they migrated with men (Kynch, 1987: 142–3). The seclusion of women in their homes was often cited as the reason: 'Women in this country lead an in-door life in houses which are generally small, dirty and ill-venti-lated . . . situated in the midst of insanitary conditions which exist to a greater or lesser extent everywhere' (Punjab SCR 1901). Again, biolo-gical reproduction and a predisposition to remain at home were blamed: 'Under ordinary circumstances, males die at a greater rate than females at all ages except those at which reproduction takes place' (GoI SCR 1901, para. 93).

The consensus of contemporary opinion at the end of the last century was that men suffered higher mortality then women in famines. For example, the increased number of females per male between the 1891 and 1901 Censuses (the sex ratio rose from 958 to 963) was attributed to the 'relatively high mortality among males in the tracts affected by the great famines of 1897 and 1900', and the Census of 1911 supported this view with extracts from the famine reports and other papers on famine mortality (Natarajan 1972: 5, 79–83). After the turn of the century, two factors changed: first, the greater impact of epidemics (plague, influenza and malaria) on famine deaths of females, and second, the reduced deaths of men which were attributed to the 'absence of wandering' achieved because 'the people . . . had learnt by experience that Govern-ment was anxious and willing to assist them' (extract from United Provinces Census Report 1911, in Natarajan 1972: 82–3).

There were two reasons why men's suffering received attention: a belief in men's predisposition to cause social disturbances, and the staff-ing of administration. The famine reports and sanitary establishment prioritised the problems resulting from men suffering and wandering – aimless wandering leading to social disorder, unlike regular and seasonal migration (Mohanty 1992), migrant agricultural labourers being perceived as a collective threat. The British administration and famine operations were, of course, entirely staffed by men – police, district officers, village headmen or landowners – British or Indian they were all men. Agricultural labourers had no voice, and women had no voice except through men. Advances for village works, revenue remissions, grants and loans under the land improvement acts or bounties, and even the monthly payments to village *chaukidars* (record-keepers), advan-taged the controllers of assets, and were man-to-man transactions.

In the evolution of the Indian famine relief policy and codes, famines were seen as crises of employment rather than of food, especially for the growing numbers of wage-labourers and declining occupational groups. The central policy was relief through public employment works for able-bodied men and women, including women without men.

However, in British Indian famines, this opportunity for women to earn wages and control their own labour was severely constrained by the turn of the century, as we shall show in section 4. The objective of relief was to save life, but lowering the cost of saving a life had become the priority (Kynch 1997; Bhatia 1967). Access to relief during famine may be especially crucial for young women. Kynch (forthcoming) remarks on evidence of the 22 Punjab, Central Provinces and Bombay districts, that proportions of male and female deaths remained remarkably constant. However, on disaggregating the data by age, Kynch finds first, that the proportion of young women's deaths was consistently higher than young men's, and second, that it increased over time, being significantly higher in the post-transition non-famine period. This suggests that gender vulnerabilities of young adults became entrenched.

WOMEN IN 'MORTALITY' CRISES AND PUBLIC HEALTH

While it is difficult to universalise across regions and across social classes, we find that the relative inaccessibility of women to public space, and the ascribing of certain roles which reinforced this social structuring of mobility, appears to have had contradictory results in terms of public health. On the one hand, men were reported to die in larger numbers than women during cholera epidemics; on the other hand, plague was recorded as producing excess female deaths (GoI SCR 1901).

The different experiences of plague epidemics compared to cholera are in part related to the biomedical attributes of the two diseases, which precipitated different responses from the authorities and, in reaction to these, from the population.

Famine drove large numbers to relief camps and raised the [death] rates in poor houses included in municipal limits; plague is said to have caused movements in the opposite direction, *vis.*, from the towns to the rural areas, to escape the sanitary regulations; cholera caused large numbers to fly panic-stricken from one place to another.
(GoI SCR, 1900)

A further comparison of the two diseases can be made in relation to knowledge and perceptions of the illnesses. In both, despite identification of their caring and home-based roles, women's understanding of the illnesses was overlooked by the policy-makers and, rather than being used for the common good, their knowledge was subsumed beneath that of the Government of India Sanitary Commissioners and their medical officers. Denial of women's knowledge is a means of disempowerment, and in these instances involved increased risks of illness. It is to these experiences of cholera and of plague that we now turn.

Famine periods in British India were closely associated with cholera, although cholera was not confined to famine, distress or scarcity years. Cholera was 'a disease which finds in famine its chief ally' (GoI SCR 1900). Cholera deaths declined together with the absence of widespread famine after 1920 (Sibbons 1995).

Cholera is a water-borne disease. The cholera vibrio, *Comma bacillus*, multiplies in the alimentary canal of an infected person or carrier and is excreted in stools. The vibrio survives in water, and is ingested through contaminated water or foodstuffs (WHO 1993; Sibbons 1995). However, ingestion in a healthy person rarely results in death: fatality is known to be associated with malnutrition (Morris 1976; Klein 1994). As Klein (1994: 497) notes:

> Decent nutrition sustained high resistance or slight susceptibility, normal among most Europeans in India (as was lesser exposure to befouled nalas and tanks), but Indians were often undernourished.

Sibbons' (1995) study of cholera emphasises this point: it was the poor who were most affected, especially at times of famine and in relation to migration; other groups affected were pilgrims travelling to and from festivals and fairs, trade fairs and other large social gatherings. The British troops played an important role in disseminating cholera from its endemic centre in Bengal (Arnold 1986: 127–8).

Sibbons sums up our approach:

> What is clear is the human agency involved in creating these patterns. The passivity which is inherent in many descriptions of cholera which comes to inflict death and suffering on vulnerable communities is clearly wrong. ... [I]t is the movement and actions of people (albeit unwittingly and without intent) which create the situation ripe for explosion into high mortality episodes.
>
> (Sibbons 1995: 3)

Cholera mortality in Punjab, Bombay and Central Provinces provide a variety of pattern. Differences in climate, with resulting changes in humidity and heat influence the multiplication of the *Comma bacillus*, and famine was associated with either drought or flood. Drought concentrates the cholera vibrio, and also results in exploration of deeper sources of water, some of which may be infected. Flood spreads the vibrio, but can also dilute and flush it away. The pattern of water use is gendered: everyone drinks water, but water-carrying is often a female task and irrigation a male task. In the 22 districts selected for intensive study from Punjab, Central Provinces and Bombay, men died in larger numbers than women from cholera. In a few years in some districts, this is reversed, but even in those years the numbers are small. The exceptional male bias of cholera deaths was noted even in Punjab, where the sex ratio of deaths was notoriously adverse to women (Kynch and Sibbons 1993).

Two examples of regular reversal of this characteristic higher male mortality are both declining, out-migrant districts: Ratnagiri in Bombay, and Puri in Orissa (Charlesworth 1985; Mohanty, 1992; Sibbons, 1995;). Regarding another reversal in the famine year of 1897, higher mortality of females from cholera was associated with 'bad cholera years' (GoI SCR 1897). The local employment search patterns, and population responses to economic changes, must be addressed in order to explain the reversals. We would therefore question McAlpin's (1983, 57–8, 67) argument that women have biologically superior resistance to cholera, and that this explained the lower famine mortality of women (considered below).

Cholera control violated Indian customs. Arnold (1986: 130–2) describes how a deeply entrenched set of local customs was regarded with suspicion by the British, who feared collective action – which, we noted above, was a perceived threat from men. Techniques to control cholera were imposed, and met considerable and understandable resistance where they rode roughshod over local or religious convictions about bathing in or drinking water. Nevertheless, the control of cholera through the incorporation of new ideas into existing explanatory models did progress (Kleinman 1980).

The public health administration was, as usual, quick to conclude that its own efforts and superior knowledge had overcome native prejudices and predispositions to die of cholera, and won people's confidence: 'Experience is a slow but sure teacher' (No. 33394 to Punjab SCR 1930). In a similar fashion, public health measures succeeded in preventing cholera deaths on famine relief works. By the time of the Hissar famine in 1938, it was reported that water-supply, spreading out of workers, provision of works close to villages to which workers returned overnight and provision of latrines helped prevent cholera (Punjab SCR 1938, Section XVI).

Plague, which arrived in 1896 and spread through north India, was termed a 'disease of the home', being associated with women's domestic tasks such as grain preparation. Bubonic plague is a vector-borne disease caused by bacteria, *Pasteurella pestis*, from infected rats by the bite of the rat flea. Other less common forms, such as pneumonic plague, are spread by droplet and there is no warning from dying rats. The high relative plague mortality of females was most pronounced in Punjab, the recorded excess female mortality being less in Bombay, United Provinces, Central Provinces and Bengal (GoI SCR 1904, para. 111). For example, the Punjab Sanitary Commissioner's Report of 1901 records 40–60 per cent excess female deaths over male deaths from plague, but only 1 per cent excess from all causes in the same districts. By 1907, this plague excess was reduced to 15 per cent. On the one hand, the Sanitary Commissioner in the Punjab emphasised the limits of compulsory measures and the need for measures to be acceptable to the people. Female mortality was cited because: 'female inmates [of houses], on account of their seclusion, are more liable to catch the disease. The fact that women die of plague in larger numbers than men furnishes a convincing argument regarding the immediate evacuation and disinfection of all plague-infected sites' (Punjab SCR 1901). In 1912 and 1913, the Lieutenant-Governor of Punjab remarked that the treatment of other sicknesses by plague staff was popular and 'bringing them in closer touch with the people'. This quickly changed in 1914 to 'the ultimate solution of the plague problem seems to be the education of women in domestic hygiene.' On the other hand, it was acknowledged that, even before being targeted with domestic hygiene education, women seemed to have learned 'by bitter experience to take better care in protecting themselves' in the first decade of plague in Punjab (Punjab SCR, 1905), and the fall in the preponderance of female mortality was not attributed to policy. Policy implementation acknowledged women's vulnerability but failed to take account of their knowledge or practices: this was disempowering.

Indeed, plague mortality is not necessarily best understood simply as a seclusion problem, for in Punjab, a high proportion was registered in the months of November and December – that is, associated with a peak of post-harvest land preparation and sowing operations. Rather than the seclusion of women making them more vulnerable to plague, it was their domestic productive activities which involved handling grain, that exposed them to the plague-carrying fleas. These were the experiences from which they learnt.

There were other examples of associations between plague deaths and occupational categories. For example,

> the comparative immunity of prostitutes who live in the upper storeys of well-built houses has been remarked in many towns. Weavers, whose occupation ties them to their houses, sometimes suffer exceptionally. There is one class who are nearly always among the first to be attacked, and among whom mortality is high – dealers in grain.
>
> (GoI SCR 1904: para. 117)

As with cholera, when reversals of the expected excess female mortality occurred in some districts, for example in Bombay or Berar, it was found that 'the proportion of female to male deaths is greatest when plague is most severe; when very few deaths are reported it frequently happens that the deaths of males are more numerous' (GoI SCR 1904: para. 111).

Some measures against villagers were extraordinarily harsh and harshly implemented: these included evacuation, exclusion and forced disinfection and decontamination. Overviewing plague in 1904, the Sanitary Commissioner remarked on Indians 'whose terror of such measures leads them to oppose them in every way ... It is not easy to deal with ... ignorance that is convinced plague is introduced and fostered by Government in order to reduce a redundant population ... or with a timidity that may be turned by an ill-considered action to fanatical frenzy' (GoI SCR 1904: para. 108). Nor were the measures demonstrably successful:

> the inconvenience which [disinfection] inevitably causes is so frequently followed by failure. The poorer classes have few possessions, but the fewer they are the greater the dread of their loss or injury, and the keener the anxiety to keep them in sight and avoid their being disinfected. ... in the begining of an outbreak of plague the people generally dread the preventive measures of the Government far more than the disease.
>
> (GoI SCR 1904, para. 108)

Disinfection and evacuation were deliberately and extremely invasive of the domestic space. Disinfection by desiccation – burning cow-dung cakes, the making of which is a female task – was 'said to be understood by all' and advocated in Punjab and Bengal (GoI SCR 1903, paras. 103,106). Evacuation, which is more domestically disruptive, was also said to be favoured: 'This is done spontaneously and generally fairly thoroughly by the people themselves without outside interference' (GoI SCR 1902: para. 113). Indeed, in Punjab:

> The Civil Surgeon of Ludhiana district gives instances of 22 villages in which the enormous death rates of 20 to 40 per cent. of the population were registered. ... those villagers who left their houses and did not visit them again mostly escaped.
>
> (GoI SCR 1902, para. 115)

This raises a question of whether there were more women outside houses, albeit constrained, than was acknowledged, and that public health measures systematically ignored these women and their understanding of protection from disease or of health care. We can infer that this was so from several sources, and we shall find support for this view when we look at the proportions of women on relief works.

First, the image of settled villagers is occasionally contradicted, especially during crises. There was a large, floating population 'of whom few have any tie to a particular dwelling' (GoI SCR 1904) who migrated by foot and rail. An indicator of famine was that migrating males were accompanied by women and children. Devotees at religious fairs in Puri included 'a large proportion of widows who left their homes surreptitiously' (GoI SCR 1899, para. 111). The female coolie was often invisible (Breman and Daniel 1992: 283–8; Kynch 1987: 145), and Breman and Daniel bring a moral dimension to their analysis, discussing her as 'incomplete' and immoral, or 'perennially on trial' – professional women labourers were not role models.

Public health control in new circumstances of epidemics and 'famines of employment' justified measures on men and women by the perception of biological vulnerability, but was also selective. Poor men who migrated were visible threats in public space, but women's caring or home-based productive roles were ignored. Women were disempowered through being made invisible in productive activities, and both muted and helpless in the respectable seclusion of the home.

WOMEN IN 'EMPLOYMENT' CRISES AND RELIEF EMPLOYMENT

We shall consider two aspects of relief employment: first the system of payment, and second, the introduction of piece-working in the home. Our exemplar will be the experience of famine relief operations during the massive 1896–7 famine which involved a debate about payment systems. The operations were judged to be successful, in particular being deemed 'efficient and economical' in saving life.

The arguments of the time are actually very persuasive in a limited way. For example, the Bengal Revenue Department, Agriculture (Famine) litter their Final Resolution (Government of Bengal, 1898) with phrases about communications (roads, rail, information), rights (knowing about, recording), power to resist (prosperity, physique, morale), local knowledge (facts, influences, detail). It sounds empowering as well as cheap.

In the Famine Codes adopted in each province after 1880, women's vulnerability was considered explicitly in two policy areas, which were both potentially socially innovative. The first was that relief was to individual sufferers, a potentially empowering situation which favoured equality of men and women even though it included a sex distinction of tasks and wages. The second was the introduction of homeworking for respectable *purdanishin* women on a piece-working contract basis.

Large proportions of women seeking famine relief were correctly forecast by the 1880 Famine Commission, which laid down the principles of relief:

An unusual proportion will certainly be women, and a large fraction will consist of children [and others] unfit for labour.... Any attempt, therefore, to make these classes earn their living by ordinary piece-work could not fail to result in great suffering and mortality.

(1880 Famine Commission, para. 133)

The Commission also predicted that, if piecework was the payment system, there would be increases in gratuitous relief, for which there was no test of need, although the recipients had to be selected as 'suitable objects for gratuitous relief'.

The Famine Codes opposed piecework in the 1890s. But in May 1897, the Government of India decided that, if distress was not so acute as to drive persons unaccustomed to labour onto relief works, payment by results was more economical than taskwork. When distress was acute, and many inefficient labourers had to be provided with employment, taskwork should be rigorously enforced.

Most women were employed as carriers, and the higher paid diggers, upon whom carriers depended, were usually men. Other classes were people unused to labouring, and the feeble. The task of the carriers was sometimes extremely hard, and a report pointing this out to the Government of Bengal was quoted with pride: 'there is no doubt that the carriers are more heavily tasked here than elsewhere, and that they have to work as hard as the diggers' (Govt of Bengal 1898: 41).

One attraction of relief works to women was the higher wage relative to men's wages which was available there, being 70–100 percent of the men's wage on famine relief works across India in the 1890's, compared to 50–75 on canal works (Kynch 1987). The same study emphasised the influence of biased perceptions of women on their access to relief work. On the one hand, professional labourers pushed women entrants off works, and the famine administrators discouraged women, arguing this was customary and that the men could earn enough to support women 'dependants'. On the other hand, reports are explicit that men (or older women) stayed in villages and sent women daily to nearby relief works (for example, Famine Reports from Mewar 1897; United Provinces 1913–14; see also Arnold 1988: 87–8; Kynch 1997). In each case, women became objects of social control, often with increased work burdens.

A dilemma was whether the system of relief payment should be based on individuals as economic actors with individual subsistence needs or as social beings whose activities were defined by custom. The debate was very pragmatic. The Codes stated that individual workers were to be assessed for tasks, but this was impossible in practice: work was done in gangs. An emphasis upon local responsibility and local factors ensured that social customs were taken into account (such as appropriate behaviour of respectable people with regard to working, or women's dependency on men), and there were major advantages to be gained from using family structure as a means to organise famine labour, such as cooperation, tolerance of short work and incentives to work harder. This was good practice in smoothing famine relief management, although the British administration remarked upon trade-offs between certain 'good management' practices and the effect on the availability of relief to women. The pursuit of good administration and cheap relief fashioned the government's response, which in the case of women happened to meet with Indian social approval.

For example, during the famine of 1896–7, the Government of Bengal was determined to keep an orderly relief operation, with enforcement of task and later 'piecework with a maximum wage'. The tasks to be done were drawn up by the Chief Engineer, who requested better staff after 'disciplinary failures' (that is, labourers demanding wages without work). In some districts, women were refused work. In June 1897, the touring officer found able-bodied women receiving gratuitous relief (charitable doles) in two districts in a relaxation of the Famine Code, which required the able-bodied to work. The need to keep a tight hold over local discretion was pointed out, and it was decided that lower-class females should be sent to the workhouse if able to work. From May onwards, numbers on relief works were less than numbers gratuitously relieved, despite this being a system based upon relief by employment.

Piecework was the solution to difficulties encountered in trying to run the works effectively and economically, and in preventing inconvenient floods of workers upsetting the administration:

the people understand it and prefer it; the necessity for large petty establishment is removed; the elaborate classifications of labour and of maximum, minimum and penal wages which lend themselves too readily to fraud on the part of the subordinate staff, are avoided; the relief worker is able to support his dependants, and the numbers on gratuitous relief are to that extent diminished; and lastly, the work is cheaper and more efficient. That the average daily wage was higher under the piece-work system was expected, and in fact intended; the wage or task work is calculated to support the worker only, but one of the objects of piece-work is that by hard work the labourer will earn sufficient to support his dependants.

(Govt of Bengal 1898: 45)

The advantages to professional labour are evident, while most disadvantages were detrimental to women workers: that it was difficult to set payments to maintain the weak or inexperienced without allowing professional labourers to profit; that it was difficult to stop small contractors from 'creeping in'; that it was difficult to prevent anyone without dependants from reaping a profit unnecessarily from the state. In particular, it was widely acknowledged that, there is a tendency for professional labour to drive others out of their gangs. That women and children on a piece-work will be less in proportion was anticipated, and the actual results exemplify this most clearly.

(Govt of Bengal 1898: 45)

The use of piecework allowed the relief employment to generate more outturn of work at lower cost. Piecework has remained a part of employment schemes to this day. Indeed the arguments remain similar: a study of the Employment Guarantee Scheme states:

EGS stipulates that men and women are to be paid equal wages. However, the actual system of payment mostly goes against women, since it is based on a 'piece rate' to the group which has completed the job, to be shared equally.

(World Bank 1991: 181)

In spite of hard work, low pay and barriers, women presented themselves in large numbers in Bengal, as elsewhere. In the districts which barred women from work, the highest relative numbers of women were found on gratuitous relief, and generally women dominated numbers on gratuitous relief. On the relief works, the proportion of women was high, usually between 30 and 45 per cent of all workers, and much higher on individual works or in some months. A later assessment of an average taskworking gang on works in Bengal in 1897 was that it would consist of '20 men capable of digging, 5 carrier men, 34 women, and 21 children between 10 and 14 years' (Bengal Famine Code 1913, Appendix II: 24).

The constraints on women undertaking piecework effectively denied them the right to earn higher wages on offer there: pieceworkers earned more than taskworkers, and village-based gratuitous relief was paid less in most districts, so that pressures on women not to do piecework dampened demand for costly relief. The alternative relief work was a piece-work system of homework for *purdanishin* women; otherwise, as we have seen, local discretion could be heavily criticised and lower-class women, not being proper *purdanishin*, could be sent to the workhouse or denied relief.

Purdah was a circumstance used to argue that some women refused help, and that respectable women needed special care (Kynch 1987). The Famine Codes laid down that 'Respectable women who are debarred by national custom from appearing in public shall always be relieved in their own homes', and suggested home-based tasks, like spinning, which 'is not repugnant to the feelings of any female' (Bombay Famine Code 1897: sections 43, 45). The disempowering nature of relief through homeworking for *purdanishin* is summed up by a modern study of Lahore by Shaheed, cited by Agarwal (1994: 113):

> the conflict between economic necessity and social disapproval is resolved by women taking up home-based piecework ... in effect rendering the fact of their working invisible to the outside world. ... [T]hey are vulnerable to economic exploitation and are not in a position to openly question the social mores that confine them.

Policy-makers believed that they recognised local customs in coping strategies – in families with benevolent male heads and male employment – and adopted piecework systems which reinforced this in the home (for *purdanishin*) or on relief works. This in itself ensured that there was to be no challenge to the prevailing system of rules, and limited negotiation of these rules. This was crucial for women because of the new and expanding opportunities during the socioeconomic transitions. Women's access to relief employment was conditional on consent in a way that men's access was not, and progressively became *forced entry* to labour under men's control (recalling Chen's terminology from section 1), undermining the potential to empower women.

Strict enforcement of a task or piece-rate satisfied the requirement of a test of need and reduced the demand for employment. The adoption of piecework encouraged relief of women as unpaid dependants, as secluded women, or on gratuitous relief, providing that local officials selected them. In effect, women's active agency was replaced by passive official protection. This bypassed the central tenet of Indian famine policy that employment should be available to those unused to labour such as needy women, which was the basis for rejection of piecework as unsuitable for famine relief. Relief works became as cheap as private commercial or ordinary public works, costs falling to the point where some works did not exceed contractors' rates in an ordinary year. It is questionable whether such economy is compatible with good relief policy. Having adopted a limited responsibility for relief, the Government of India permitted a payment system which it recognised was against the interests of women. However, the payment system adopted was part of a leaner, fitter, relief operation which released public funds for more infrastructural development – roads, railways, irrigation, conservancy (Bhatia 1967; McAlpin 1983). The question is, therefore, whether women's well-being gained more from the overall direction of policy than women lost from being discouraged from relief work. The system adopted for payment on famine relief or employment guarantee schemes remains problematic (Chen 1995; Kynch 1997).

CONCLUSIONS: THE LONGER-TERM EFFECTS

In British India, increasing emphasis on women's reproductive value within the family may well have reduced their relative mortality during crises because many were officially protected from situations outside the household which resulted in higher male mortality. Costs of these policies include the persistently low social value of little girls demonstrated by continuing excess female infant mortality in India and parts of South Asia, and poor fallback position of women in the absence of a working male (Cain 1986; Dreze 1990; Chen 1995).

The assertion that it is the biological difference of sex which leads to higher or lower relative deaths of males or females, or a particular relationship between women and work, has been challenged by social explanations of the same phenomena. An examination of aspects of mortality and employment using historical data of British India reinforces the view that socioeconomic relations of men with women rather than biological differences between them provide a more plausible and more robust explanation. Nevertheless, there were reductions in epidemic and famine mortality. On the one hand, women were protected from exposure to the life-threatening situations which resulted in higher male mortality. On the other hand, these policies had perverse results on women's social value, entrenching male prejudice against female employment.

There is an argument that the higher male mortality observed in famine and cholera is a longer-run recompense for the injustice men habitually inflict on their women, 'so much that they are forced to suffer higher mortality than men in normal times despite their superior biology of survival' (Osmani 1995). This is incorrect to the extent that we cannot confirm superior biology in women, and have noted that *bad cholera* and *severe plague* were arguably associated with excess female mortality. Osmani offers an alternative argument from a crucial, and perhaps realistic, premise: that women's well-being will be lower in the absence of working men. The higher widowhood of women is exacerbated by family breakdown during famine, resulting

in higher proportions of female-headed households which evidence
shows are the most disadvantaged in society. He goes on:

> The point is simply that in a society where women face constraints in
> their access to productive activity, any phenomenon which leaves
> more women to fend for themselves without at the same time remov-
> ing those constraints cannot be good for them.
>
> (Osmani 1995)

We have argued that the use of biological explanations of female
mortality or aptitude for work resulted in policies which allowed
famine to exert a leverage against women's access to public arenas.
Men's aptitude for mobility was taken for granted as policies to protect
water or provide employment met their social needs and countered a
perceived threat of collective action. When women sought work, their
presence was hidden; when women reduced mortality from plague,
their knowledge was ignored. Secular *purdah* was encouraged by
home-based pieceworking, and women's 'absence' from public space
helped to prioritise reproductive needs in public health. There was an
apparent incoherence in the policy responses to local customs and
knowledge. In the case of epidemics, these were rudely dismissed,
despite great opposition to imposed control measures. In the case of
relief working, social customs in employment were embraced and
upheld, to the benefit of professional labour and men, and with wide
consent and approval. Therefore, the exclusion or inclusion of local
knowledge in policy is not *per se* benevolent or empowering.

The longer-run implications of disempowerment such as we have
found in epidemic and famine mortality reduction are invidious. In
current debates about employment rights, articulation of knowledge,
and occupational *purdah* which we considered in section 1, we found a
lack of recollection of past challenges – the disempowerment agenda
was internalised by women and officially rearticulated against women.
If constraints on women's rights to work or participation are to
change, history teaches women to be wary of outside agents with good
intentions.

ACKNOWLEDGEMENT

The authors' research into British Indian data has been funded by
the Leverhulme Trust. Both authors are very grateful for the Trust's
support.

REFERENCES

Agarwal, Bina (1991) 'Social Security and the Family', in E Ahmad, J. Dreze, J. Hills and A. Sen (eds) (1991) *Social Security in Developing Countries*, WIDER Studies in Development Economics, Oxford: Clarendon Press.

Agarwal, Bina (1992) 'Gender Relations and Food Security: Coping with Seasonality, Drought and Famine in South Asia', in L. Beneria and S. Feldman (eds), *Unequal Burden: Economic Crises, Persistent Poverty and Women's Work*, Boulder: Westview Press.

Agarwal, Bina (1994) 'Gender, Resistance and Land: Interlinked Struggles over Resources and Meanings in South Asia', *Journal of Peasant Studies*, 22:1, 81–125.

Arnold, David (1986) 'Cholera and Colonialism in British India', *Past and Present*, 113: 118–51.

Arnold, David (1989) 'Cholera Mortality in British India, 1817–1947', in Tim Dyson (ed.), *India's Historical Demography*, London: Curzon Press.

Aslanbeigui, Nahid, Steven Pressman and Gale Summerfield (eds) (1994) *Women in the Age of Economic Transformation*, London: Routledge.

Bhatia, B.M. (1967) *Famines in India 1860–1965*, 2nd edition, Bombay: Asia Publishing House.

Breman, Jan and E. Valentine Daniel (1992) 'Conclusion: The Making of a Coolie', *Journal of Peasant Studies*, 19:3/4, 268–295.

Cain, Mead (1986) 'The Consequences of Reproductive Failure: Dependence, Mobility and Mortality among the Elderly of Rural South Asia', *Population Studies*, 40: 375–88.

Caplan, Patricia (1978) 'Women's Organisations in Madras City, India', in P. Caplan and J. Bujra (eds) *Women United, Women Divided: Cross-Cultural Perspectives on Female Solidarity*, London: Tavistock Publications.

Charlesworth, Neil (1985) *Peasants and Imperial Rule: Agriculture and Agrarian Society in the Bomaby Presidency 1850–1935*, Cambridge: Cambridge University Press.

Chen, Martha (1995) 'A Matter of Survival: Women's Right to Employment in India and Bangladesh', in M. Nussbaum and J. Glover (eds), *Women, Culture and Development*, Oxford: Clarendon Press.

Dreze, Jean (1990) 'Widows in Rural India', *Development Economics Research Programme DEP/26*, STICERD, London School of Economics.

Dreze, Jean and Amartya Sen (1989) *Hunger and Public Action*, Oxford: Clarendon Press.

Gasper, Des (1993) 'Entitlements Analysis: Relating Concepts and Contexts', *Development and Change*, 24: 679–718.

Gore, Charles (1993) 'Entitlement Relations and "Unruly" Social Practices: A Comment on the Work of Amartya Sen', *Journal of Development Studies*, 29(3): 429–60.

GoI SCR (various years) *Annual Report of the Sanitary Commissioner (later Public Health Commissioner) with the Government of India*, Government of India.

Government of Bengal (1898) *Final Resolution No. 385 on the Famine in Bengal of 1896–97*, Revenue Dept, Agriculture (Famine), Calcutta: Bengal Secretariat Press.

Hartman, Betty and James Boyce (1983) *A Quiet Violence: View from a Bangladesh Village*, London: Zed Press.

Jeffery, Patricia, Roger Jeffery and Andrew Lyon (1989) *Labour Pains and Labour Power: Women and Childbearing in India*, London: Zed Press.

Kabeer, Naila (1991) 'Gender, Production and Well-being: Rethinking the Household Economy', *Discussion Paper No. 288*, Institute of Development Studies, University of Sussex.

Karl, Marilee (1995) *Women and Empowerment: Participation and Decision Making*, London and New Jersey: Zed Books.

Klein, Ira (1994) 'Imperialism, Ecology and Disease: Cholera in India', *Indian Economic and Social History Review* 31:4, 491–518.

Kleinman, A. (1980) *Patients and Healers in the Context of Culture*, Berkeley: University of California Press.

Kohli, Atul (1987) *The State and Poverty in India: the Politics of Reform*, Cambridge: Cambridge University Press.

Kynch, Jocelyn (1987) 'Some State Responses to Male and Female Need in British India', in H. Afshar (ed.), *Women, State and Ideology*, London: Macmillan.

Kynch, Jocelyn (with Maureen Sibbons) (1997) 'Famine Relief, Piece-work and Women Workers: Experiences in British India', forthcoming in J. Toye and H. O'Neill (eds), *A World without Famine*, London: Macmillan.

Kynch, J. (forthcoming) 'Famine and Transformations in Gender Relations', in C. Jackson and R. Peason (eds), *Divided We Stand: Feminism Gender and Development*, London: Routledge.

Kynch, Jocelyn and Amartya Sen (1983) 'Indian Women: Well-being and Survival', *Cambridge Journal of Economics* 7.

Kynch, Jocelyn and Maureen Sibbons (1993) 'Famine in British India: Learning from Longitudinal Data', *Papers in International Development 9*, Centre for Development Studies, University of Wales, Swansea.

Lal, Deepak (1988) 'Trends in Real Wages in Rural India: 1880–1980', in T.N. Srinivasan and P.K. Bardhan (1988) *Rural Poverty in South Asia*, New York: Columbia University Press, 265–93.

McAlpin, Michelle B. (1983) *Subject to Famine: Food Crises and Economic Change in Western India 1860–1920*, Princeton, NJ: Princeton University Press.

Mohanty, Bidyut (1992) 'Migration, Famines and Sex Ratios in Orissa Division between 1881 and 1921', *Indian Economic and Social History Review*, Oct.–Dec. XXIX:4.

Morris, R. J. (1976) *Cholera 1832: The Responses to an Epidemic*, London: Croom Helm.

Mosse, David (1995) 'Authority, Gender and Knowledge: Theoretical Reflections on the Practice of Participatory Rural Appraisal', *KRIBP Working Paper No.2*, Centre for Development Studies, University of Wales, Swansea.

Natarajan, D. (1972) *The Changes in the Sex Ratio*, Census of India 1971, Centenary Monograph No. 6, New Delhi: Office of the Registrar General.

Nussbaum, Martha and Jonathan Glover (eds) (1995) *Women, Culture and Development: A Study of Human Capabilities*, Oxford: Clarendon Press.

Nussbaum, Martha C. (1995) 'Introduction', in Nussbaum and Glover (eds), op. cit.

Okin, Susan Moller (1995) 'Inequalities between the Sexes in Different Cultural Contexts', in Nussbaum and Glover (eds), op. cit.

Osmani, S.R. (1995) 'Famine, Demography and Endemic Poverty', mimeo, Development Studies Association Annual Conference, Dublin.

Sarkar, Sumit (1983) *Modern India 1885–1947*, Madras: Macmillan India.

SCR (various years) *Annual Report of the Sanitary Commissioner (later Public Health Report)*, published in each province.

Sharma, Ursula (1980) *Women, Work and Property in North-West India*, London: Tavistock.

Sibbons, Maureen (with Jocelyn Kynch) (1995) 'Cholera and Famine in British India 1870–1930', paper presented to the 18th International Congress of Historical Sciences, Montreal; *Papers in International Development 14*, Centre for Development Studies, University of Wales, Swansea.

Viswanath, Vanita (1991) *NGOs and Women's Development in Rural South India*, Boulder, CO and Oxford: Westview Press.

World Bank (1991) *Gender and Poverty in India: Issues and Opportunities Concerning Women in the Indian Economy*, Report No. 8072–In, World Bank.

Zurbrigg, Sheila (1995) 'Did Starvation Protect from Malaria? Distinguishing between Severity and Lethality of Infectious Disease in Colonial India', paper presented to the 18th International Congress of Historical Sciences, Montreal.

11 Assessing the Impact: NGOs and Empowerment
Elsa L. Dawson

INTRODUCTION

This volume has looked at many aspects of empowerment in different contexts of the globe. We now focus on some groups actively involved in bringing about empowerment, and in trying to measure their achievements. The chapter is based on work being carried out by Oxfam UK and Ireland and its Dutch sister agency, Novib.

Many development agencies see the main key to long-term poverty alleviation in developing countries as the empowerment, in its broadest sense of increasing self-reliance of poor people, and especially of poor women. The strategy documents of Oxfam UK/I and Novib talk of 'supporting the initiatives of poor people in the South' (Novib 1994b) and 'capacity-building' (Oxfam UK/I 1994), both agencies seeing these as ways of contributing to sustainable changes and improvements in their lives. They make explicit their particular concern for poor women and their position in low-income societies, their lack of autonomy and generally worse situation than that of men living in similar contexts. Experience has shown that providing health and education services, improved incomes and housing has not resolved deprivation in durable ways where it is not in conjunction with the empowerment of beneficiaries to use and sustain inputs in the most effective way from their own viewpoint.

They are, in fact, setting out either to be or to support *catalysts* in the empowerment processes of poor women in the countries where they administer aid programmes, as Jo Rowlands points out in her chapter.

A question such agencies are now urgently asking is whether such programmes aimed at local capacity-building and empowerment are actually producing measurable benefits for the poor women and girls concerned. Insistence on this point from their institutional donors, such as the ODA, and increased competition for public donations are behind the escalating pressure which agencies feel to come up with concrete evidence of their achievements.

However, can empowerment and such benefits be measured? Agency staff are hard at work on the task of developing systems and procedures to show to what extent the investment made has produced impact in terms both of empowerment of women and of real benefits to them. If they fail to show this, they stand to lose much support from donors who are increasingly querying the effectiveness of NGO projects.

For this reason Novib and Oxfam UK/I engaged in a research programme to identify methods and systems available and in use for the assessment of impact, particularly those which can be used to measure positive changes in the lives of women and girls. This chapter describes a range of tools and methods investigated and looks at whether they do indeed have the capacity in practice to measure such changes.

But first, we take a look at the constraints facing NGOs in measuring impact involving empowerment and benefits for women and girls (many of which apply equally to assessing change of benefit to men). They account for the limited NGO experience in applying impact assessment. We mention here only the most significant constraints in terms of developing new systems (there are of course many others).

Measuring the Intangible and the Abstract Nature of Empowerment

Whereas some benefits to women may be fairly easy to measure, such as improvements in health, increased childcare facilities, easier access to drinking water, other less tangible benefits, especially empowerment itself, are more involved.

First, there is the question of what 'empowerment' actually is. It is an abstract concept, capable of interpretation in many ways – (see Jo Rowlands' chapter for a full discussion). The word is difficult to translate satisfactorily into other languages, indicating the complex nature of the notion. For this chapter we have taken Rowlands' definitions as follows as a starting point:

> Bringing people who are outside the decision-making process, into it. This puts a strong emphasis on access to political structures and formal decision-making, on access to markets and incomes that enable people to participate in economic decision-making.

She also provides a definition with a more development focus:

> A process whereby women become able to organise themselves to increase their own self-reliance, to assert their independent right to make choices and to control resources which will assist in challenging and eliminating their own subordination.
>
> (Keller and Mbwewe, 1991 in Rowlands, 1995)

But what does all this mean in the infinite number of different contexts in which NGO empowerment initiatives are carried out, and particularly taking into account the women beneficiaries' own perspective? Haleh Afshar (1993) cites the example of how Western feminists frequently underestimate the achievements of women living under Islam, failing to recognise the progress towards empowerment achieved by such women *in their own view* despite wearing the veil, which Western women tend to see purely as an instrument of oppression.

Empowerment often seems to be taken to mean participation in communal activities, as so many interventions ostensibly aimed at assisting women seem to concentrate on, thereby merely increasing women's burden of work. It is only in fact where they are actually increasing women's *active participation in decision-making*, that empowerment could be occurring.

Finally, as Rowlands points out in this volume, the empowerment process is not necessarily linear, but more like a loop or a spiral. Furthermore, certain activities may be empowering in one way and disempowering in another, especially if the different kinds of power Rowlands mentions (power over, power to, power with, power within) are taken into account, and the two spheres of individual and collective power. There are many other arenas too in which women can become empowered – the political, the economic, health, education, the home. How can measurement of impact keep track of what is happening in all these different areas?

Time and Resources

The amount of time and resources available for carrying out impact assessment activities can be severely limited, especially if a project or organisation is small in terms of resources, human and others, or of short duration, or the organisation and its funders have other priorities. Both the Northern donor agencies themselves, and the small and

medium-sized NGOs which form the majority of their southern counterparts and are directly responsible for the implementation of projects
funded, largely lack effective impact assessment systems (Hopkins
1994). Development projects funded by Oxfam and Novib tend to
last typically between three and ten years, and have relatively low
budgets and numbers of immediate beneficiaries, apart from a few
large emergency-response programmes. Only systems which are easily
and rapidly applicable, and cheap in terms of the human and other
resources required, are likely to be taken up by such organisations and
projects.

Differences in Interests

What actually constitutes impact varies according to whom you are
talking. There are bound to be differences between what the Northern
aid agency, and even more so their supporting public, consider to be
impact and what the beneficiaries see as changes in their interest. There
will also be variations between the perspectives of beneficiaries themselves, between them and other sections of society in their countries,
between different classes, ethnic groups, castes, etc.

But whose opinion really matters? Obviously, it is the women beneficiaries of a particular project to whose views most significance must
be attached, since it is them the project is intended to assist. Many
agencies lack systems which are sufficiently participatory, so beneficiary views are inadequately recorded and outsiders' views often artifi-
cially imposed.

Other interests, such as those of the organisation implementing the
project, other NGOs working in the area, other communities not
directly targeted by the project, and those of local government
agencies, also have legitimate claims on their views being taken into
account. Systems frequently lack the ability to identify and recognise differing points of view, and assimilate them into the final assessment.

The Duration of Changes Achieved

How sustainable are the positive changes brought about by aid agency
projects? An important element of the word 'impact' is something that
is 'durable", and impact assessment includes the search for changes
sustainable over many years after the completion of an initiative. But
how can this be measured in the short term? If measurement takes

place during or immediately after completion of a project, the future of the process is uncertain. If it takes place after a certain number of years, much information may have been lost in the meantime, and the causal relationships will have become more complex and more difficult to identify. What can actually be attributed to the activities of the project, and what is rather due to other contextual factors becomes much harder to distinguish.

The Project Cycle

In a study carried out for Oxfam UK/I and Novib of a selected group of their counterpart organisations, Hopkins (1995) points out that a key problem for effective impact assessment is that many agencies fail to thoroughly carry out certain key tasks at each stage of the project cycle (see Table 11.1 and Appendix 11.1 for the basic stages he identifies in the implementation of a development project). This makes the possibilities of carrying out a thorough-going impact assessment even more limited.

For example, if a baseline study has not been carried out at the beginning of a project's life, changes occurring as a result of the project will be more difficult to identify. If no clear objectives have been set, or the ones set do not correlate with the problems identified, defining impact sought will be impossible. If information regarding indicators identified in accordance with the objectives set has not been gathered during the project's implementation, the job of impact assessment will again be more difficult, and have to rely on interviews of beneficiaries and staff after the activities have taken place.

The Nature of Development Agency Staff

A final constraint is that staff of development agencies tend to be driven by a moral commitment to help the less fortunate, and are highly committed to their activities aimed at the relief of poverty. They tend to see such routine tasks as measuring their work as less important administration, understandably when faced with situations of acute human suffering, and tasks related to project activities and funding administration are constantly given greater priority. They do nevertheless feel acutely the need to learn from experience, and seek methods that can efficiently provide them with greater possibilities of doing so.

INSTRUMENTS AND FRAMEWORKS FOR ASSESSING IMPACT OF INTEREST TO WOMEN AND GIRLS

So what are aid agencies doing to attempt to measure impact in relation to women's empowerment? And what do specialists in development have to offer them in carrying out this task? Hopkins (1994; and see Table 11.1) lists activities related to each stage of the project cycle which are important for impact assessment. Given the point he makes regarding the importance of certain tasks at each stage of the project cycle, we have used this scheme to identify and look at the instruments, methods and frameworks available to NGOs concerned about gender and women's interests when devising their impact assessment strategies. We have included both theoretical frameworks developed by academics as well as practical tools developed by aid agencies, since practitioners are exploiting the best of both worlds in this complex task. Where these activities have taken place, carrying out an impact assessment is likely to be more effective, as the evidence produced over the life of the project can be gathered and analysed.

Stage One: Identification/Analysis

Before a project is implemented, the main problems facing the population need to be identified and analysed, and if the situation of women, girls and gender relations is not analysed at this stage, it is harder to assess or even achieve impact in relation to these aspects. As Gianotten *et al.* (1994: 11) point out, 'when gender differences are overlooked in the planning phase, projects are unlikely to respond to women's needs and may even have negative consequences for women'. They continue: 'Development projects have been shown to have either positive or negative effects on the division of labour, access to and control over allocation of resources, benefits, and decision-making in a society'. Where these aspects are not included in the pre-project situation analysis, measuring impact in relation to the empowerment of women is much harder.

What methods are available to agencies tackling the task of adequately analysing the situation of beneficiaries before beginning a project?

Participatory Research Techniques
In order to achieve empowerment and improvements in the lives of women and girls from *their* perspective, participatory techniques are

applied to gather information regarding their lives, needs and potential. Many projects now go beyond seeing 'participation' as merely consulting women on their 'problems'. Ways are being found to ensure their 'full participation in the analysis' (Roche 1993), in order to record their problems from their perspective.

An example is the GRAAP technique (developed by the Groupe de Recherche et d'Appui pour l'Autopromotion Paysanne in Burkina Faso), used by many projects in Francophone West Africa. Its emphasis on the use of sub-group sessions for different groups within a community is particularly useful. A sub-group of women only has been found to be more likely to elicit active participation in giving opinions by women, and in certain contexts more so if the group is once again divided into older and younger women. The sub-groups are also used to avoid the domination of discussions by women elites. GRAAP's use of visual material (figures, symbols, etc.) to help participants express themselves, to make visual notes (analysis) and to rearrange those notes to show the results of the analysis (Roche 1993), make it easier for women and girls to participate, given the higher rates of illiteracy generally found amongst them. The use of visual representation in the Freirian *educación popular* tradition in Latin America and in PRA techniques has been found to be similarly useful.

Images are a particularly powerful means of transmitting ideas, in a culturally meaningful way. Women, because of ties to the home, tend to be more enveloped in local cultural domains than men, who are more likely to be those who leave home for markets and employment outside the household. However, sometimes women have been alienated by being asked to present visual images which they feel either incapable of or uncomfortable about producing, and project workers have reverted to dialogue, and, if culturally acceptable, role play.

Strategic versus Practical Needs
Moser (1993: 38–40) has pointed out that Molyneux's idea of identifying women's needs as either strategic or practical is a useful framework for planning with a gender perspective. Molyneux stressed the importance of recognising that women and girls have both *strategic gender needs*, which she saw as associated with their generally subordinated role in society, such as gender divisions of labour, power and control which adversely affect them, and the lack of legal rights, domestic violence, equal wages and women's control over their bodies;

and *practical gender needs* within those subordinated roles, which were generally concerned with inadequacies in living conditions, such as water provision, health care and employment. Moser shows that these different needs are frequently confused by planners, and that clarification helps to identify both what can actually be accomplished, and the limitations of interventions. The latter can be addressed in a way which also addresses the former. Moser (1993: 49) gives the following examples:

- Changing the gender division of labour, eg provision of masonry or carpentry skills for women and girls.
- Control over financial services, e.g. allocating credit to women.
- Overcoming discrimination against women owning land, by law or tradition, by means of settlement policies which put house owner-ship in the woman's name.
- Alleviation of the burden of domestic labour, eg by locating nurseries at father's workplace.

Kabeer (1994) gives more examples of ways in which both can be addressed, such as the provision of new economic resources, new analytical skills and awareness, and mobilisation around self-defined concerns and priorities.

The distinction between strategic and practical needs is useful for showing that where interventions are aimed at addressing both strategic and practical needs, empowerment in the long-term is more likely to be achieved, since to attend to welfare needs alone may not necessarily alter the power relationships between men and women, or challenge their overall role in society. As Wallace (1993) points out, however, it is important for the achievement of empowerment that women themselves define what their own strategic and practical needs are, given their own particular experience and understanding of their situation.

Moreover, the definition of what is a strategic and what is a practical need in a given context may not be easy, and may lead to confusion amongst funders, project staff and beneficiaries.

Social Relations Framework
Naila Kabeer (1994) emphasises that the impact of a given intervention on relations between genders can significantly affect women's living standards, and points to the importance of taking into account cultur-ally and contextually defined structures of gender relations when

analysing a population's problems prior to planning a project. By structures, she refers to the divisions between men and women of rules, resources, activities and power, within social organisations, such as the family, the market, the state and the community, and men and women's interests in the continuity of such relations. Inter-relations between class, caste, ethnicity and race, and all kinds of material inequalities, and gender, which determine the division of resources and responsibilities also require consideration. All these processes are *dynamic*, and *ongoing*. Finally, the state of *social resources* held by women needs to be analysed, such as women's organisation, as it is these which will allow them to take full advantage of economic development.

NGOs are therefore encouraged to use instruments to enable them to detect these ongoing processes. In order to reflect *dynamic* processes, these would need to be applied during various stages of a project. Kabeer suggests asking questions about institutions on the following:

• Rules, rights, customs, responsibilities, etc.
• Resources: who owns the inputs and who controls the outputs, the benefits.
• Division of labour within the institution – who does what.
• Hierarchies of command and control.

Empowerment is largely dependent on the state of women's relation-ships with men, and their gaining power in relation to them. Control over resources is also included in the definition quoted of empower-ment. Therefore, these questions are useful if applied to communities as part of a contextual analysis prior to planning an intervention, in order to determine where exactly efforts need to be made to achieve greater levels of women's empowerment.

Harvard Analytical Framework
The Harvard Framework for Gender Relations (Overholt *et al.* 1985) contains a checklist of questions regarding activities, access and con-trol, and influencing factors (see Table 11.1). Given the importance of seeing women's *control* over resources as just as important as access to them, the *access* and control questions are particularly relevant for detecting empowerment, as well as more tangible benefits accruing to women.

Table 11.1 Harvard Analytical Framework: Access and Control Profile

A. Resources	Access		Control	
	Women	*Men*	*Women*	*Men*
Land				
Equipment				
Work				
Money				
Education/ Training				
Others				

B. Benefits
External income
Property
Basic needs (food, clothes, shelter)
Education
Power/ political prestige
Others

Source: Overholt *et al.* (1985).

However, this table is complex and hard to use with a community. It is not easy to convey the ideas of access and control across different cultures and languages. NGOs have found that the table works well-only when used by people with detailed knowledge of the social group being analysed, and that it can be difficult to use across a region where social and economic circumstances differ widely (Oxfam 1994).

Gender Analysis Matrix
UNIFEM have developed a 'simple and systematic' instrument for determining the different impacts of development interventions on women and men, called the Gender Analysis Matrix. The matrix crosses the variables of women, men, household, and community, with labour, time, resources and culture. The variable 'culture' is not clearly defined, but can therefore be used for any other aspects of people's lives which appear important, such as social organisation, attitudes, etc. The matrix is a useful tool for identifying details regarding women's lives and problems, and has been especially developed for use with beneficiaries. (Both women *and* men are supposed to take part). The variables can easily be represented by visual images (except for 'culture'). The crossing of the variables men/women

with resources also provides useful information about who has access and control over resources.

Few Novib or Oxfam UK/I Southern counterparts have the resources to use all of the approaches described above for every project they implement. The Gender Analysis Matrix, however, combines simplicity, aptitude for being used participatively, with covering the main information required in order to detect impact of specific interest to women, including empowerment. It therefore constitutes a useful tool for projects and organisations with scarce time and resources.

Stage 2: Design/Planning

Once women's and girls' problems, needs and potentials have been adequately identified, aims, objectives and activities need to be planned which logically follow on from the precise situation detected, both in order to achieve impact and to measure it. How can this be done in ways which help ensure the benefit of women and girls?

Participatory Planning methods
In order to incorporate women's perspectives into the planning of a project, planning is carried out jointly with the women concerned. As Kabeer notes (1994), empowerment only occurs when a process is seen as the responsibility of those planned for.

However, the need to present a project proposal to a funding organisation before beginning to develop a relationship with a community, and consequent expectations of assistance, means that NGOs usually have to plan a project themselves before involving a community in the development of detailed planning. Few funding agencies allow counterparts to engage with a community in an open-ended fashion so that joint planning with beneficiaries can take place. Many NGOs are also afraid of raising expectations of assistance which they cannot fulfil. This is a real problem, although it can in some cases be addressed by putting communities in touch with organisations which do have the appropriate capacity and skills to respond.

As with Stage 1, participatory methods using visual images have been found useful for involving women in planning, eg those used in Freirian *educación popular* in Latin America, PRA approaches, and GRAAP techniques.

Some NGOs are also involving women in the identification of indicators, reflecting the issues raised during the analysis stage, and empowerment seen from their point of view.

Logical Frameworks: Gender Sensitivity Checklist
Logical frameworks for project planning are a systematic way of ensuring that project objectives, activities and indicators follow on consistently from problems identified. When they are developed in a participative manner together with women beneficiaries, this has the additional advantage of providing communities with a skill they can use to develop their own initiatives, an important contribution to the empowerment of women.

The EC Commission (1993) has produced a checklist for gender sensitivity in the logical framework, with questions to be addressed in relation to the wider objectives, specific objectives, outputs and inputs of a project (see Annexe 3). These cover such issues as: whether the choice of specific objectives influences relations between men and women, whether they distinguish between who is meant to benefit from the intervention, whether outputs are specified separately for men and women and are consistent with the needs of each, who will benefit in terms of gender division of labour and access to and control over resources, how the intervention will affect gender relations, the addressing of women's strategic needs, the inclusion of participant views on impact, and consistency with macro gender-specific policies. Many of the issues covered are significant for the achievement of long-term empowerment of women.

However, many NGOs have found the use of logical frameworks can lead to inflexibility. The rigid definition of objectives and indicators tends to hinder the ability of project staff and beneficiaries to learn from experience, take into account new events, unexpected consequences, and thereby maximise an intervention's impact. In the case of empowerment, this is particularly problematic, given the often contradictory nature of the process by which women become empowered.

For this reason, some projects now regularly revise their objectives in accordance with the information produced by monitoring indicators related to the gender issues analysed, especially empowerment as identified by the women beneficiaries (Wallace 1993). Where the Gender Analysis Matrix is regularly applied, this can be done in a participatory manner.

Stage 3: Appraisal

At this stage of the project cycle, the ability of those who are to carry out the intervention to do so in a way which is gender-aware is analysed. Do they listen to women beneficiaries? Are there women in the project team, and are their opinions accorded respect by male staff members? Are they experienced in the effective use of participatory methods for *all* stages of the project cycle? What do any previous impact assessment studies tell us about their achievements in relation to women's empowerment? What is their understanding of empowerment? For project-holders themselves, it is the moment when their project design is reviewed to ensure it has the potential to gain impact of interest to women beneficiaries.

A number of instruments, particularly checklists, have been developed for appraising projects from a gender perspective.

Gender Assessment Studies

These were developed by the Netherlands Directorate General for International Cooperation (DGIS) and are described in detail in Gianotten *et al.* (1994). They investigate a development project's expected impact on women as compared to men, and gender relations in a particular geographical region or specific cultural setting. They focus on gender roles and needs primarily in relation to the identified intervention sectors.

Their specific objectives are to:

- Gain insight into relevant gender relations in project areas and women's perception of proposed interventions.
- Gain insight into whether the institutions involved have the capacity to deal with gender issues in project planning and implementation.
- Assess from a gender perspective the possible impact of an intervention on different categories of women, and on the likely participation of women and men in various project phases.
- Formulate recommendations for further planning and monitoring of the project, so it will optimally strengthen women's position.

They contribute to the measurement of empowerment as the area of existing gender relations is examined so that changes brought about by the project can be monitored. Women's perceptions are examined, but not of expected *impact*, although impact is looked at from a gender perspective. They look at participation, but do not look specifically at the crucial aspect of participation *in decision-making*, rather than merely in activities. However, these aspects could feasibly be incorporated into the DGIS's design.

Gender Assessment Studies require considerable resources, since they take about 3 months to carry out, using rapid rural appraisal to produce mainly qualitative data, and extensive dialogue with men and women from beneficiary groups. Only funding agencies contemplating a substantial project in terms of budget and duration, or maybe a number of projects making up a strategy for a region, are able to consider carrying out such a detailed study.

Gender Audit
The ideas contained in Naila Kabeer's Gender Audit (1994: 302, 303) can be added to the Gender Assessment Study, to ensure social relations are taken into account in development planning. The Gender Audit consists of a checklist of questions for posing at the intervention planning stage, including issues such as the gender conceptualisation of the target group, assumptions made about the gender division of resources and responsibilities, access to and control over resources, and whether the intervention addresses women's strategic gender interests.

Appraisal Criteria
Sarah Llongwe has developed a check-list of criteria for how far a project promotes: (quoted in Wallace 1993: 6).

• women's welfare
• women's access
• women's conscientisation
• women's participation
• women's control

She relates progression down the list with increased impact on equality and empowerment, although NGOs have questioned the assumption that the different stages necessarily have to be worked through in this order (Oxfam 1994: 250). These criteria can also be used effectively at the Evaluation Stage.
Caroline Moser (also quoted by Wallace) has suggested criteria to see if a project can promote changes in gender relations and empowering them, rather than just trying to meet women's practical needs, such as

• welfare
• equity

- anti-poverty
- efficiency
- empowerment

To judge whether a project is designed to achieve women's empowerment in the long term, these two checklists can be combined and simplified as follows:
Women's empowerment, including

- women's welfare
- women's participation in decision-making
- women's access
- women's control

Gender Analysis Matrix
Since the Gender Analysis Matrix has been developed for looking at the potential impact of a project, it can be useful at the appraisal stage, especially for a small or recently formed NGO with insufficient resources to apply a full-scale study such as the DGIS have designed. Where it has been used at previous stages, project holders and their funding agencies merely have to review those already carried out.

Stage 4: Implementation

Many projects are now implemented as a joint effort between project staff and beneficiaries, the role of the former being that of facilitator and catalyst of the work determined and carried out by beneficiaries. Where this happens, women gain empowerment through the experience of being directly involved in managing their own projects.

Some NGOs collect information throughout implementation from monitoring the indicators set in the project design to enable impact to be judged. A small number establish new indicators together with women beneficiaries to reflect the empowerment process and positive changes being brought about from their point of view, as new elements are identified which need to be taken into account. Where this happens, both the women and the project implementors can effectively measure the contribution made to empowerment by the activities concerned.

However, the difficulty is the cumbersome nature of this task. Where NGOs have made efforts to carry it out conscientiously, the amount of information amassed has often been beyond their capacity to deal with and analyse.

Wallace (1993: 4) provides a valuable list of issues for monitoring the progress of projects during implementation, which can be adapted as follows:

- Are women able to participate in decision-making? How can participation be increased?
- Are women gaining or losing any of their rights of access, distribution, or production?
- What benefits are accruing to women?
- Is conflict between women and men diminishing or increasing?
- Are women's objectives being met?

The Gender Analysis Matrix is used during implementation to record changes and unexpected results emerging from the project's experience, providing information for assessing impact.

Stage 5: Evaluation

It is at this stage that the project's impact on the lives of women is actually analysed, either on completion or after a period, e.g. five years, ideally using the evidence documented during the first four stages.

NGO project evaluations tend to take one of three forms, or a combination of all three:

1. Self-evaluation, where a community evaluates the progress of its own intervention.
2. Participatory evaluation, where an external evaluator consults a community with regard to their opinions regarding the impact of an intervention.
3. External evaluation, where external evaluators conduct an audit of the methods and results of an intervention.

Where self-evaluations are carried out, this contributes to women's empowerment, since, by evaluating their own interventions, they will learn how to carry out development initiatives with improved impact in their own terms, and increase their levels of self-reliance. Indicators can be identified retrospectively too, using the experience of all those involved in the project.

Such informal participatory techniques as PIM (Participatory Impact Monitoring), GRAAP and PRA tools can be used for this purpose. For example, a matrix is sometimes drawn up with beneficiaries, with different criteria for what would constitute women's empowerment, using symbols to represent the criteria chosen, on which beneficiaries vote to show the degree of success they think has been achieved. GRAAP sub-groups are formed amongst women to allow them to develop their own criteria for success.

Chris Roche (1992) provides an interesting example of different criteria which men and women can come up with when evaluating the success of a project to increase fodder production for livestock along the Niger river, in accordance with their own priorities. Whereas men's interest in the activity consisted of whether they could offer visitors calabashes of milk at a later date in the year than usual, women considered whether they could give their children more Kundou (a sweet drink made from the same fodder crop) more important.

Where external evaluations are concerned, Wallace (1993) points out the relevance of including women on evaluation teams, and of including gender issues in their terms of reference. Also where they have appropriate language skills, they can communicate directly with women and interview them, since women frequently only speak local languages.

CONCLUSION

Do these instruments and theoretical frameworks overcome the constraints listed at the beginning of this chapter? The question is difficult to answer in that there is little written evidence of how they have been used and the results of the experience in practice. However, from the experience of the author and from what has been written up, the following points can be made.

As Jenny Pearce[1] points out, checklists are no substitute for thinking, and agencies need to train their field staff to think, but with the high staff turn-over of many agencies, organisations without some documented systems which can be easily passed on are at a disadvantage. However, even where such documents do exist there are difficulties in applying the kind of checklists and frameworks mentioned. Project staff are overwhelmed with manuals which they are given little time to read and assimilate.

The complex and contradictory nature of empowerment make it virtually impossible to say in absolute terms what a given intervention has achieved, especially in the long term. Nevertheless, this should not be an excuse for not trying to produce some evidence of progress.

However, how much time and resources an NGO can devote to doing this applying such instruments and frameworks as those described depends on the skills of its staff and the resources it has available for impact assessment and related activities. Those applying the Gender Analysis Matrix can improve their capacity, given its simplicity, that it is usable with beneficiaries, and that it has the potential to be adapted for most of the project cycle stages. If the Matrix is applied at different moments in the project's life, and also after completion, it can be used to identify changes over time and long-lasting changes. It lacks however the capacity to differentiate between the strategic gender needs of women and their practical needs, although this can be incorporated.

Where larger investments are being made, use of the other more complex tools and frameworks is possible. Oxfam UK/I is developing a programme approach to its country strategies, whereby a number of projects are grouped together to produce a synchronised effort contributing to the achievement of an overall strategic aim for a given country. It can therefore look at the collective impact of a whole programme, rather than at that of many small individual projects. Where this is done, methods like the Gender Assessment Studies, incorporating such theoretical frameworks as Molyneux's Strategic and Practical Gender Needs and Kabeer's Social Relations, can effectively be employed, as the cost involved is spread over a number of projects.

What NGOs have not found the answer to yet is how the views of other stakeholders, such as local government offices, other NGOs working in the area and communities not directly targeted by a project, can have their views represented, without an immense amount of documentation being amassed, which cannot be adequately assimilated by the agency concerned. Other methods need to be explored, such as workshops.

In summary, there are many ways in which NGOs are trying to measure the empowerment of women achieved by their work. However, whether they can ultimately be successful in doing so effectively is doubtful, given the problems cited, particularly the contradictory and complex nature of empowerment, and the fact that it must be about processes over long periods of time. What one activity of a project might achieve may be undone by another, let alone other factors in the local context.

It is, however, vital that they should continue to attempt to provide evidence of progress, given the urgent and ever-growing needs for the resources to which they have access. Twenty, thirty years of NGO activity in developing countries have gone by. What evidence do we have that their work is actually having a continuing beneficial effect on the women on whose behalf resources have been entrusted to them? A systematic explanation of the use of funds to these women is highly overdue, and also to those who generously give their support to organisations like Oxfam UK/I and Novib.

NOTES

1. Verbal communication, May 1995.

REFERENCES

Afshar, Haleh (1993) 'Development Studies and Women in the Middle East: The Dilemmas of Research and Development', in *Women in the Middle East: Perceptions, Realities and Struggles for Liberation*, ed. Haleh Afshar, London.

Commission of the European Communities 1993 *Women and Development: Gender Issues in Managing European Community Co-operation with Latin American, Asian and Mediterranean Countries*, Brussels.

Giannotten, Vera, Groverman, Verona, van Walsum, Edith and Zuidberg, Lida (1994) *Assessing the Gender Impact of Development Projects*, London.

Hopkins, Raul (1994) *Impact Assessment: Overview and Methods of Application*, Oxfam UK/I and Novib Research Programme on Impact Assessment.

Kabeer, Naila (n.d.) *Gender Planning: Some Key Issues* (unpublished).

Kabeer, Naila (1994) *Reversing Realities: Gender Hierarchies in Development Thought*, London: Verso.

Keller, B. and Mbwewe, B. C. (1991) 'Policy and Planning for the Empowerment of Zambia's Women Farmers', *Canadian Journal of Development Studies* 12/1: 75–88.

Moser, Caroline O. N. (1993) *Gender Planning and Development: Theory, Practice and Training*, London.

Novib (1994a) *Evaluation Policy Working Paper: Joint Project Evaluations*, The Hague.

Novib (1994b) *Multi-Year Plan 1995–1998*, The Hague.

Overholt, Catherine, Anderson, Mary B., Cloud, Kathleen and Austin, James B. (eds) (1985) *A Case Book: Gender Roles in Development Projects*, Connecticut: Kumarian Press.

Oxfam UK/I (1994) *The Oxfam Gender Training Manual*, Oxford.

Roche, Chris (1992) *A Case Study on an Evaluation Process in Mali*, Acord.

Roche, Chris (1993) *Some Ideas on PRA meets GRAAP: A Research-Action Proposal*, Acord, internal document.

Rowlands, Jo (1995) 'Empowerment Examined', in *Development in Practice*, vol. 5, no. 2, Oxfam UK/I.

UNIFEM, A. Rani Parker (1993) *Another Point of View: A Manual on Gender Analysis Training for Grassroots Workers*, New York.

Wallace, Tina (1993) *Gender and Evaluation*, Discussion Paper, NAWO.

SUGGESTED FURTHER READING

Giannotten, Vera, Groverman, Verona, van Walsum, Edith and Zuidberg, Lida (1994) *Assessing the Gender Impact of Development Projects*, London.

This book gives a detailed account of three case studies of the application of the gender assessment studies developed by the Dutch Government aid authority, DGIS. It provides valuable information on lessons learnt in the process of applying the model.

Moser, Caroline O. N. (1993) *Gender Planning and Development: Theory, Practice and Training*, London.

This volume explores the relationship between gender and development, and provides a comprehensive introduction to Third World gender policy and planning practice. It describes the conceptual rationale for a new planning tradition based on gender roles and needs, and identifies methodological procedures, tools and techniques to integrate gender into planning processes.

Oxfam UK/I, *The Oxfam Gender Training Manual*, Oxford, 1994.

The manual is a resource book for gender and development trainers, offering field-tested training activities and handouts, drawn from a wide range of sources and shaped into a coherent training programme. Activities are included which explore:

• gender-awareness and self-awareness for women and men
• gender roles and needs
• gender-sensitive appraisal and planning
• gender and major global issues
• working with counterparts on gender issues
• strategies for change.

UNIFEM, A. Rani Parker (1993) *Another Point of View: A Manual on Gender Analysis Training for Grassroots Workers*, New York.

UNIFEM's publication gives detailed assistance to those wishing to apply the Gender Analysis Matrix, with examples of completed tables.

APPENDIX 1 Impact Assessment in the Project Cycle and Gender

Stage	Task	Work related to impact assessment	Tools/frameworks for incorporating gender perspective
1. Identification / Analysis	Identify and analyse main problems facing women and men, and their needs and potentials.	Ensure problems, needs and potential of beneficiaries accurately identified and analyses.	Participatory research methods, e.g. PRA, GRAAP Social Relations Framework Strategic v practical gender needs Harvard F/W: Access/ Control Gender Analysis Matrix
2. Design/ Planning	Define aims and objectives and how to achieve them. Establish activities to be carried out. Compile baseline study in areas where activities to be carried out. Identify indicators to judge whether aims and objectives have been achieved.	Ensure aims, objectives and activities are coherent and follow logically from problems, needs and potentials identified, using logframes for example.	Participatory planning methods, e.g. *educación popular*, participatory log frames, PRA. Checklist for gender in log-frames.
3. Appraisal	Assess critically relevance, feasibility and potential effectiveness on the basis of financial, social, technical and environmental analysis.	Check design will produce anticipated impact.	Gender Assessment Studies Gender Audit Criteria sets Gender Analysis Matrix
4. Implementation	Set project in motion. Adapt project as necessary in light of learning, including objectives if required.	Collect and process impact indicators to assist project management decision-making. Identify new impact indicators as project develops.	Participatory implementation methods New indicators to reflect empowerment process Capacity-building of women team members. Gender Analysis Matrix
5. Evaluation	Analyse results of, and effects produced by the project.	Analyse project's impact on lives of beneficiaries, either on completion or after a period, e.g. five years.	Participatory evaluation methods Retrospective identification of indicators Women on evaluation teams Gender issues in TOR.

Source: Adapted from Hopkins (1994).

Index

Index